Introduction to
PHILOSOPHY

William James Earle, Ph.D.
The City University of New York
Baruch College and the Graduate Center

An American BookWorks Corporation Project

McGraw-Hill, Inc.

New York   St. Louis   San Francisco   Auckland   Bogotá   Caracas
Lisbon   London   Madrid   Mexico   Milan   Montreal   New Delhi   Paris
San Juan   Singapore   Sydney   Tokyo   Toronto

William James Earle is Associate Professor of Philosophy, The City University of New York, Baruch College and The Graduate Center. A former Woodrow Wilson and National Endowment for the Humanities Fellow, he has written many scholarly articles including the article on William James in the *Encyclopedia of Philosophy*. He is associate editor of the quarterly *The Philosophical Forum*.

Introduction to Philosophy

1 2 3 4 5 6 7 8 9 10 11 12 13 14 15 16 17 28 29 30 FGR FGR 9 2 1

ISBN 0-07-018783-5

Library of Congress Cataloging-in-Publication Data

Earle, William James,
    Introduction to philosophy / William James Earle.
       p.   cm.
    Includes index.
    ISBN 0-07-018783-5
    1. Philosophy—Introductions.   I. Title.
  BD21.E27   1992
  100—dc20   91-28891
                                      CIP

Preface

This book is designed to be used as a concise text or as a supplement for courses called Introduction to Philosophy, Philosophical Issues, Problems of Philosophy, or the like. For such courses, it will also function as an independent guide book. It is *not* suitable for courses tracing the history of philosophy or for logic courses. Logic—the systematic study of all types of arguments—is not covered in this book, since it is ordinarily taught as a separate course. However, certain terms and concepts from logic are introduced as needed to clarify the material presented. (Students who seek a concise survey of logic are directed to *Theory and Problems of Logic* by John Nolt and Dennis Rohatyn in Schaum's Outline Series published by McGraw-Hill.)

Each chapter in this book offers an up-to-date survey of a major field within philosophy. Each was prepared to be as self-contained as possible. This arrangement should provide instructors with a base around which a course can be organized, using a variety of approaches, learning sequences, primary material, and supplementary readings.

A number of special features have been included to enhance a student's comprehension and appreciation of philosophy. Particularly welcome should be the fully annotated bibliography at the end of each chapter. The glossary, which includes specialized terms drawn from all fields of philosophy, was designed not so much to give a dictionary-style definition of each term, but rather to say something helpful about how the term is used. In the text itself, a series of interlocking subheads break up the sometimes lengthy speculations, arguments, and explanations characteristic of philosophical discussion. Key terms and topics highlighted and interrelated in this way will help orient students in their initial study and make review much easier. Chapter overviews and summaries also provide guidance by introducing and reinforcing the main ideas of each chapter.

To the Student

The study of philosophy promises an adventure in thinking, a critical reflection on perplexing concepts and the provocative questions to which they give rise. What is reality? How is knowledge acquired? What is morality? These are but a few such questions.

Chapter 1, "The Nature of Philosophy," explains why philosophy is unlike physics, chemistry, or mathematics. In the physical sciences and mathematics, there is a high degree of consensus among experts as to what the facts or "right answers" are, and about what should be counted as the best theories. There is much less consensus in philosophy: its experts are so acknowledged because they are good at understanding philosophical questions and problems, because they are able to appreciate and criticize rival views, and because, finally, they can make clearer to us the concepts that underlie our deepest perplexities.

Successful students of philosophy are successful, ultimately, because they learn to participate in this activity. I hope this book will help make that happen for you. Keep in mind, though, that you cannot do well in—and probably not even pass—a philosophy course by memorizing a list of right answers. There is no such list.

Use this book, then, as a tool or resource in understanding the concerns and speculations of philosophers, and in thinking through whatever arguments and analyses you encounter in your readings and studies. Use this book as your guide to a new and exciting realm of thought about the basic questions of life.

William James Earle

Contents

CHAPTER 1

The Nature of Philosophy

Since its origin in ancient Greece, philosophy has had a complex history. However, characteristic of philosophy are its critical reflection on inherited cultural traditions and its pursuit of conceptual clarity through the analysis of conceptually perplexing questions, concepts, problems, and arguments. The first chapter introduces philosophy by considering its conceptual nature, explaining the methods it uses to analyze concepts, and describing the major areas of philosophical study.

Origins

Etymology

The word *philosophy* derives from two Greek words: *philia,* love or friendship, and *sophia,* wisdom. So philosophy, etymologically speaking, means "love of wisdom." Two major points should be made about this etymology. *First,* as many of the ancient philosophers pointed out, it is possible to love something without possessing it. Love should be thought of here, then, as involving "desiring" or "wanting to have."

To be a philosopher, accordingly, involves striving after wisdom, not necessarily possessing it. *Second, wisdom* is used inclusively to cover sustained intellectual inquiry in any area, the understanding and practice of morality, and the cultivation of such enlightened opinions and attitudes as lead to a life of happiness and contentment.

Thales and the Presocratics

A certain Thales is commonly said to be the father of Western philosophy. Thales was active around 585 B.C. (His exact dates are not known.) Indeed, little is known about Thales save that he was interested in astronomy, correctly predicted an eclipse, and held that everything that exists is made out of water. Obviously, then, he must have asked himself: What is everything made out of? Though his answer was wrong, his question was a very good one. Later on, questions like Thales' would be taken up by the natural sciences, but at the very beginning of our intellectual tradition philosophy included among its considerations questions about nature as well as questions about human life. (The various separate intellectual disciplines developed very gradually and at a much later date.)

Thales was one of a relatively small group of philosophers known collectively as the Presocratics. All the Presocratics were interested in aspects of the natural world, as is illustrated by a sampling of typical Presocratic questions: Why do the stars twinkle? Why does the moon wax and wane? Why does the sun make its daily journey across earth's sky? How did life begin? Is the universe eternal? It should be pointed out that the Presocratics did not answer these questions, but they nevertheless get credit for having asked them. Indeed, one important function of philosophy is and has always been *the invention of interesting, fruitful, thought-provoking questions.*

Although the questions asked by the Presocratics eventually got taken up by the natural sciences, there are three main reasons for regarding these questions as originally philosophical. (1) They call for inquiry or investigation, rather than acceptance of tradition. (2) They seek explanations framed in nonsupernatural (that is, nonmythical) terms. (3) The answers to these questions are expected to be supported by evidence and/or rational argument.

The Presocratics offered a sustained criticism of the mythological accounts of natural phenomena prevalent in the society of their day.

Rather than accept the idea that the earth, the sun, the stars, and other natural phenomena were gods and goddesses, they offered nonsupernatural accounts of nature, accounts that could be rationally argued for rather than dogmatically asserted.

It should be noted, finally, that the Presocratics, though curious about the natural world and capable of observing some of its more striking features, did not make systematic observations or perform any experiments.

Socrates

The same critical spirit and independence of mind that the Presocratics applied to natural phenomena Socrates (c. 470–399 B.C.) applied to human life. The following are typical Socratic questions: What is piety? What is human excellence? What kind of life is it worthwhile for a human to live? Can virtue be taught? Is there more than one virtue? What is justice? Socrates himself did not write anything, but rather devoted his life to discussing questions such as these with important people in his society. Thus, our conception of Socrates derives from *dialogues*—in effect, philosophical plays "starring" Socrates—written by his famous pupil, Plato (429–348 B.C.). Many of these dialogues focus on questions that have the form "What is *X*?" where *X* stands for some idea that is difficult to pin down let alone clearly explain.

Socrates is, accordingly, the first philosopher to focus on perplexing *concepts* (*concept* is the standard term in philosophy for *idea*), and to try to get clear about them. For example, the dialogue known as the *Symposium* focuses on the concept of love. Like us, the ancient Greeks could easily talk about love, but—again, like us—few Greeks were able to define it clearly and precisely. That takes sustained philosophical effort.

Facts and Concepts

Philosophy is a *conceptual*, rather than a *factual*, discipline. A fact is a truth about the world established through *observation*. There are everyday facts, historical facts, and scientific facts, but the crucial things to remember about facts of every kind are that they must be true and they must be established by observation. (*Observing* means checking to see whether something is indeed so.) Note also that what we take to be a fact at one time we may later discover to be not a fact at all; however, this fact about facts is not relevant to our present focus on the rough-and-ready distinction between facts and concepts.

The only close synonyms of concept in English are *idea* and *notion*. It is, however, easy to illustrate what philosophers have in mind when they talk about concepts. It is a fact that Columbus discovered America. (Or Leif Ericsson—if, in fact, he got there first!) In either case, that fact involves the concept of discovery. Facts are *known*; concepts are *understood.* You cannot understand the fact about Columbus (or Ericsson) unless you understand the concept of discovery. (As we get more clear about the concept of discovery, we may want to deny that either Ericsson or Columbus or any other foreigner "discovered" America: after all, huge numbers of native Americans knew about America ages before the first European arrived there.)

If you speak English and have the word *discovery* in your vocabulary, understanding the concept of discovery will, in practice, amount to the same thing as understanding the word *discovery*. However, it is not necessary to understand that particular *word*. A French speaker has exactly the same concept of discovery as we do, except that in the case of the French speaker it is associated with the word *découverte*.

Most concepts do not reward philosophical examination; for example, any problems we have with the word *table* or *chair* a decent dictionary will take care of. Nevertheless, there are many words that we use—and they happen to be among the most important—that can continue to puzzle us even after we have looked them up in a dictionary—words like *freedom, democracy, love,* and *morality,* for example. These are, of course, words that most people are able to use in the course of ordinary life. For this to be possible, then, it would seem that the users would have to have at least a partial mastery of the concepts the words express.

Suppose we ask: What exactly do we mean by freedom? In other words, in exactly what circumstances is it appropriate to say that someone is free? We may find that we cannot answer the question satisfactorily—that we cannot give a clear and consistent account of freedom. This is a sign that our mastery of the concept of freedom is partial rather than complete. Philosophy attempts to replace partial with complete conceptual mastery, using as its major tool the *analysis of concepts*.

Conceptual Analysis

Analysis in Terms of Necessary and Sufficient Conditions

When philosophers speak of analyzing concepts, they are actually using a metaphor borrowed from chemistry. Like chemical compounds, the more complex concepts can be broken down into the simpler ideas that compose them. This is precisely what conceptual analysis does. Of course, we cannot analyze all our concepts at once: the best we can do is use the better understood concepts to help us understand those we find more perplexing.

We will illustrate the machinery of analysis in terms of *necessary* and *sufficient conditions*—to begin with, on a concept that is not philosophically puzzling. Consider the ordinary concept of a *bachelor*. Analysis of this concept tells us exactly what makes someone a bachelor. This is accomplished by stating the exact circumstances in which it would be true to say of someone that he is a bachelor. The standard way of doing this looks like the following:

X is a bachelor IFF

   (i) X is a human;

  (ii) X is unmarried;

 (iii) X is male;

 (iv) X is an adult; and

  (v) X is not a priest or otherwise ineligible.

Explanatory comments follow:

X is what is called a variable—more specifically, a *name-variable*, and *any* name can be substituted for it. It allows us to talk of any and all bachelors. If you happen to be thinking of Smith and want to test out the hypothesis that *he* is a bachelor, you would substitute *Smith* for X in (i) through (v).

IFF is a standard abbreviation for "if and only if." It means *just when* or *just in case*.

Points (i), (ii), (iii), (iv), and (v) are all necessary conditions for being a bachelor. A *necessary condition* for anything is a condition that must be satisfied to have the thing for which it is a necessary condition. (Conditions are also sometimes said to be "met" or "fulfilled.") Thus, oxygen is a necessary condition for fire, meaning that where there is no oxygen, there can be no fire. In terms of the present example, anything failing to satisfy condition (i), whether or not it satisfies some or all of the other conditions (the subject could, for example, be a male gorilla), is automatically excluded from the class of bachelors. And exactly the same thing is true of each of the other conditions.

Not only are the five conditions listed individually *necessary*: the analysis is claiming that they are jointly, or as a sort of package, if you will, *sufficient*. Together, they constitute a complex *sufficient condition* for being a bachelor. This means that anything that satisfies all five conditions is automatically in the class of bachelors. There is nothing else that has to be done: if the analysis of being a bachelor is correct, there is no other condition that must be met or fulfilled.

Of course, one could argue about the necessity for any one of the conditions, as well as about their joint sufficiency. If you believe that priests fall under the concept *bachelor*, for example, you would want to get rid of condition (v). Similarly, if you do not think divorced men or widowers are bachelors, you might want to replace condition (ii) with something stronger, such as "X has never been married." What matters here—and this is *not* a philosophical question—is how the word *bachelor* is used in contemporary American English.

There are several things to bear in mind as one gets accustomed to thinking in terms of necessary and sufficient conditions. *First*, a necessary condition need not be a sufficient condition. Oxygen is a necessary condition for fire, but it is *not* a sufficient condition for fire (since other things are also needed). *Second*, a sufficient condition for something need not be a necessary condition. Imagine a class in which the results of three exams are averaged to produce a student's final grade. Getting a C on all three tests is a sufficient condition for getting a final grade of C, but getting one D, one C, and one B will do just as well—that is, it will constitute another sufficient (*but not necessary*) condition for getting a final grade of C.

Definition of Analysis by Necessary and Sufficient Conditions

Analysis can now be defined as follows: to give an analysis of a statement is to make as explicit and as clear as possible the necessary and sufficient conditions for the truth of the statement being analyzed. Notice that we speak of an analysis of a statement rather than a concept; this is because analysis gets clear about a concept by getting clear about key statements involving the concept. For example, instead of filling in the blank in "Freedom is _____," the analysis approach to understanding concepts tries to complete "X is free IFF _____." Philosophers also speak of the necessary and sufficient conditions for the *application* of a concept, so we can go on to ask, for example, what conditions have to be met in order for the concept of freedom to apply to X. If a certain concept applies to X, X can also be said to *fall under* that concept.

Each analysis is divided into two parts: *analysandum*, or what is to be analyzed, and *analysans*, or what does the analyzing. In our example, the *analysandum* is "X is a bachelor"; the *analysans* is the list of necessary—and jointly sufficient—conditions, (i) through (v).

Requirements for a Successful Analysis

There are three main requirements that any successful analysis must fulfill: (1) its *analysandum* and its *analysans* must mean the same thing; (2) its *analysandum* and *analysans* must be alike in truth-value; and (3) the *analysans* must be more clear (or less misleading) than the *analysandum*. If condition (3) is not met, the analyis may be correct so far as it goes but it is said to be "unenlightening" or "unilluminating."

Since analyses are ordinarily given in schematic form with appropriate variables, as in "X is a bachelor," the second success condition applies only when the same *value*—Jones, Smith, Brown, etc.—replaces the variable in each of its occurrences. "X is a bachelor" is not really a statement, so it lacks a truth-value. ("Truth-value" is a technical term used to refer to the two values, *true* and *false*.) Whereas "Jones is a bachelor"—formed by replacing the variable X with the value "Jones"—is a statement and possesses a truth-value—in other words, is either true or false.

Note that conditions (1) and (2) for a successful analysis are not entirely separate, since if two statements mean exactly the same thing

(1), they must have the same truth-value (2)—that is, either both must be true or both false. You may know nothing about my sister, but you *do* know that if the sentence "My sister is stingy" is true, the sentence "My female sibling is stingy" is also true. By the same token, you know also that if either of these sentences is false, both are false. (This is, of course, totally obvious.)

Counterexamples

Philosophy is a relentlessly critical activity, and when philosophers offer analyses, those analyses—if they are at all promising—are subject to the most rigorous scrutiny. This scrutiny can produce two main results: someone may be able to think of a *counterexample* to the necessity of one or more of the conditions listed in the *analysans*; or, someone may be able to think of a counterexample to the sufficiency of the package of conditions that make up the *analysans*. (*Counterexample* is a technical term meaning an example that shows that a certain claim is false.)

Counterexamples to Necessity

An analysis claims that each of the conditions listed in the *analysans* is a necessary condition. This claim is defeated (that is, shown to be false) by producing an example that doesn't satisfy one or more of the necessary conditions given in the *analysans*, but which is nevertheless a genuine instance of the *analysandum*. Since the analysis of being a bachelor is correct, there are no counterexamples to the necessity of each of its five conditions. (Remember that the concept *bachelor* is not really perplexing, but was used only to illustrate the nuts and bolts of analysis.)

Counterexamples to Sufficiency

An analysis claims that the package of conditions constituting the *analysans* is a sufficient condition. This claim is defeated by producing an example that satisfies *all* the conditions given in the *analysans*, but which is nevertheless not a genuine instance of the *analysandum*. Our analysis of being a bachelor can be used to illustrate the idea of a counterexample to the sufficiency of a certain set of conditions. In actual classroom discussions of what is involved in being a bachelor, students usually stop after listing the first four conditions. The claim is made that they are enough—that anyone who satisfies them is automatically a bachelor.

Eventually, however, someone almost always thinks of a Catholic priest—the perfect counterexample to the sufficiency of the first four conditions. Catholic priests satisfy the first four conditions, but it is incorrect to classify them as bachelors. (Again, this is only an example: if speakers of English now count priests as bachelors—which is possible but doubtful—then another example can be substituted to make the same point.)

Analysis in Terms of Criteria

At one time, it was widely thought that every concept that could be analyzed at all had to be analyzable in terms of necessary and sufficient conditions. This is no longer the standard view, however. Although there is something both very tidy and genuinely enlightening about analyses via necessary and sufficient conditions, there are some philosophically interesting concepts that simply do not yield to this kind of analysis. Many of these concepts can be successfully elucidated using *criteria*.

Definition of Criterion

We can define a *criterion* (plural: *criteria*) as any meaning-relevant factor that is not a necessary or a sufficient condition. Suppose, for example, that we are attempting to get clear about the concept of a "happy life." (This is not an artificial example: philosophers from Socrates to our own time have been interested in this concept, and people who are not professional philosophers also have a stake in getting clear about what kinds of lives would count as genuinely happy.) For example, does having nice children have anything to do with having a happy life? We certainly feel that there is some connection, yet we realize that having nice children is neither a necessary nor a sufficient condition for having a happy life. The connection in question is now commonly said to be *criterial*.

In our analysis of the concept of a happy life, then, we come up with a number of criteria rather than with a set of necessary and sufficient conditions. Each criterion for X, to put it abstractly, gives us a *strong reason* for thinking that X obtains. "Strong reason" must, however, be qualified by a phrase such as "other things being equal."

A person who has nice children, but whose life has otherwise been a torment of pain and disease, is not a very likely candidate for the application of the concept under analysis.

Criterial Connection

Like necessary and sufficient conditions, criterial connections are established by analytical thinking about concepts, not by factual surveys or observational data. Suppose it has been found, for example, that people with a certain level of blood sugar are, in 99 out of 100 cases, happy. This does not make having a certain level of blood sugar a criterion relative to having a happy life, however. It is not a part of what we mean or understand by a happy life. It is not built into the concept of happiness.

Criterial connections are best seen as part of an overall classification of connections. Connections among the properties of objects, whether encountered or thought about, can be classified as follows:

CONCEPTUAL CONNECTIONS, which are

—studied by philosophy;

—elucidated by analysis;

—built into our language.

Conceptual connections are either

necessary connections

that cannot not hold
(such as the connection between
being a bachelor
and being male)

or

criterial connections

which can fail to hold
(such as the connection between
having a happy life and having nice children).

CONTINGENT CONNECTIONS, which are

—*not* studied by philosophy;

—*not* elucidated by analyis;

—*not* built into our language.

Here, *contingent* simply means nonconceptual. Since contingent connections are nonconceptual, no amount of thinking about concepts will tell us anything about them; they have to be discovered by observing the world.

Other Philosophical Methods

Most of what philosophers have done and continue to do can be regarded as a form of analysis, either via necessary and sufficient conditions or via criteria. However, two other methods, both of which are historically important and of continuing interest to many philosophers, are worthy of brief discussion: the method of doubt and the phenomenological method.

Method of Doubt

Cartesian Doubt

The *method of doubt* is associated with the French philosopher René Descartes (1596–1650). Indeed, the "methodological doubt" Descartes advocated is often referred to as Cartesian doubt. Descartes said that when we begin to think philosophically—that is, to *philosophize*—the first thing we should do is to doubt everything of which we cannot be absolutely certain. We will then find that most of our beliefs, which we have acquired casually (if not carelessly) from parents and teachers, are not beliefs of which we can be absolutely certain. This is not really surprising, the reasoning continues, since so many of these beliefs were acquired before we had become capable of subjecting them to rational scrutiny.

Indubitable Belief

As adults, we find ourselves laden with a mixture of true and false beliefs. Through the practice of systematic doubt, we can distance ourselves from the whole mixture and make a fresh start, intellectually, based on a more solid foundation. That solid foundation, according to Descartes, consists of the small number of beliefs that we cannot doubt—beliefs that may be said to be "indubitable."

Evaluation of Cartesian Doubt

The practice of Cartesian doubt is certainly an effective way of addressing and perhaps overcoming an unreflective adherence, or commitment, to a body of traditional beliefs. However, two objections are commonly raised against the method of doubt:

Objection 1. It is not obvious that we can simply make up our minds to stop believing. In answer to this objection, it might be said that Descartes provides doubt-generating arguments, arguments that will really make us give up our usual beliefs. The three main arguments are:

(a) *The argument from sensory deception.* Since our senses sometimes deceive us, we can never trust them completely.

(b) *The argument from dreams.* There is no conclusive proof that we are not dreaming now.

(c) *The evil-demon argument.* There is no way we can rule out the possibility that our minds are being manipulated by an evil demon.

Objection 2. It is not obvious that there are any nonrelationally indubitable beliefs that can be used as a foundation for absolutely certain knowledge. There are certainly things that I cannot doubt (and the same would be true of anyone), but this is probably best explained relationally *in terms of other beliefs I (or someone) has.* If this is a fair criticism and Cartesian doubt does not lead to indubitable (and foundational) beliefs it remains a useful way of shaking ourselves free of our ordinary "naive" (or "pre-philosophical") confidence.

Phenomenological Method

Phenomenology

Although the term *phenomenology* has been used in a number of distinct senses, it is most commonly used to describe a philosophical movement associated with Edmund Husserl (1859–1938). Instead of describing the world around us, in terms of either common sense or science, phenomenology tries to describe our inner life—our subjective experience, or as phenomenologists often refer to it, our "lived experience." This is accomplished by using the phenomenological method.

Presuppositionless Observation of Consciousness

The phenomenological method consists in a careful, presuppositionless scrutiny of one's consciousness. The key term in this definition is "presuppositionless." In general, our observations (whether of ourselves or of the world around us) are the result of the interplay of two factors: (1) that which is there to be observed, and (2) the categories in terms of which we organize and describe our observations. Normally, our observation is shaped by our theories. We can sum this up by saying that, ordinarily, our observations *presuppose* our categories and theories. In employing the phenomenological method, we are supposed to suspend our categorical and theoretical commitments and describe what *appears*. (The word *phenomenon* derives from the Greek *phainesthai*, "to appear.")

Evaluation of the Phenomenological Method

Although the ideal of "pure" or "presuppositionless" observation and description has interested many twentieth-century philosophers, it remains unclear whether it is really possible to practice it. There is also the following additional difficulty: phenomenological observation of consciousness seems to be very much like the psychological self-observation known as *introspection*. Through introspection, we become aware of the particular contents of our minds, contents that "got there" because, as a matter of individual autobiography, we were exposed to a particular cultural tradition, education, and so forth. But phenomenological observation is supposed to reveal *necessary structures* of consciousness, or *essences*. It remains unclear whether, in addition to the contents of our minds that depend on historical contingencies, there are any necessary structures that can be captured through presuppositionless description. Perhaps certain very general structures having to do with the temporal character of our experience—regret and anticipation, for example—are necessary features of consciousness.

Methods and Algorithms. A general comment should be made here, one that applies to all philosophical methods but which is especially helpful in evaluating the phenomenological method. Most people first encounter methods (or "ways of doing something") which, in fact, belong to a very special subclass of methods known as algorithms. An *algorithm* is a set of step-by-step instructions which, if correctly followed, will lead always to a definite answer or solution. Algorithms are, in other words, foolproof methods. The basic arithmetical operations— addition, subtraction, multiplication, division—are *algorithmic*. Since the application of algorithmic methods does not require creativity or judgment, these are, not surprisingly, precisely the methods that computers can be programmed to employ.

On the other hand, no philosophical method is algorithmic. Methods of analysis, whether in terms of necessary and sufficient conditions or in terms of criteria, require judgments about what is and what is not conceptually crucial at every step in their application. The phenomenological method, for its part, requires something like the art of a great novelist—a Proust or a Joyce—to yield interesting results. It was once thought that the nonalgorithmic character of philosophy was the critical way in which philosophy differed from the natural sciences. However, we now know that even in the natural sciences, no significant discovery or theory results from the application of an algorithmic method. (See the discussion of science in chapter 3.)

Major Areas of Philosophy

Philosophy can be divided into a number of subfields, each of which can be defined in terms of the key questions it tries to answer. The major subfields, with the exception of logic, will be described briefly in this section. Logic—the systematic study of all types of arguments—is not included, since it is ordinarily taught in a separate course. Throughout this book, however, terms and concepts from logic will be introduced wherever they are needed to understand the material presented.

It should be pointed out that any human activity that involves perplexing concepts can generate philosophical reflection. For any conceptually interesting activity, X, there is room for a "philosophy of X"; for example, there is now a subfield of philosophy known as philosophy of law. Philosophy of X subfields can be viewed as extensions of the traditional major fields of philosophy. Philosophy of law, for example, fits into the field of social and political philosophy.

Epistemology

Epistemology, also known as theory of knowledge, is defined in terms of two key questions: (1) What is knowledge? and (2) How do human beings acquire knowledge? Dealing with these questions involves analyses of such concepts as belief, truth, and justification. How can I be sure that my beliefs are true? I know that people sometimes believe things without good reasons, without real evidence. What, then, should count as good reasons, or real evidence, for various kinds of beliefs? How do I know I have good reasons, or evidence, for my beliefs? Since all practical activity relies on knowledge—or, more precisely, on what we believe to be knowledge—the questions raised in epistemology have more than academic interest.

Philosophy of Science

Philosophy of science is defined in terms of the key question: What explains the extraordinary success of science? Physics, chemistry, and biology have made—and continue to make—steady progress in producing a more and more accurate picture of the world. Not only do these sciences provide us with accurate information (information that, among other things, provides the basis for modern technology), they also provide intellectually satisfying explanations of a broad range of natural phenomena.

The word *science*, unqualified, usually refers to the *natural sciences*—those that deal with physical, objectively measurable phenomena, as do physics, chemistry, and biology. However, there are also "human" or "social" sciences, such as psychology, sociology, economics, and anthropology. Up to the present, none of the latter has achieved the success of the natural sciences. Philosophy of science considers the question of why this is so. Perhaps there is something about human beings that makes their behavior, in principle, unpredictable. In chapter 3, two possible responses to unpredictability are considered: *First*, the human sciences may help us to understand human behavior, even though any detailed prediction of the course of individual behavior is impossible. *Second*, statistical prediction of aggregate human behavior is possible (as well as both enlightening and practically useful), even if individual behavior is unpredictable.

Metaphysics

Metaphysics, also known as ontology,* is defined in terms of the key question: What is there? This is a deceptively simple question, since it involves the most basic and pervasive contrast in human thinking: the contrast between *appearance* and *reality*. Our picture of reality is largely derived from the sciences. Were it not for the natural sciences, we would know nothing of electrons, black holes, quarks, and so forth. Why then do we need metaphysics? The answer, very simply, is that we have no guarantee that everything real ends up on the inventory of one of the sciences. Does God exist? Do I have a soul? Are angels real? These are questions that thoughtful people have asked (and continue to ask), and which are not settled by science.

Another important metaphysical topic is the question of whether there are *abstract objects*: numbers, sets, concepts, and propositions, for example. The question to be considered here is whether these "objects" have an existence independent of human thinking. Suppose there were no human beings to think about them: would numbers, sets, concepts, and propositions still exist? The nature of mathematical reality is one of the major topics in the subfield known as philosophy of mathematics.

Philosophy of Mind

Philosophy of mind, sometimes also called philosophical psychology, is defined in terms of the following key questions: (1) What is the nature of the mental? (2) How should we understand such terms as *intention, desire, belief, emotion, pleasure,* and *pain*? (3) How do the items that figure in the description of our mental life enter into the explanation of human action? (Note that some aspects of these questions also belong to metaphysics.) There is also a "philosophy of psychology" that reflects on the actual theories and research efforts of contemporary psychologists. This discipline may also throw light on questions which traditionally belong to philosophy of mind.

---

* Ontology is sometimes considered one of the two branches of metaphysics (*cosmology* being the other).

Philosophy of Language

Philosophy of language considers the following key questions: (1) How are thought and language related? (2) What makes the sentences we use meaningful? (3) How many kinds of meanings are there? (4) How do we manage to use bits of reality to refer to the extralinguistic world? (5) How much, if any, of our ability to use language is innate?

Ethics

Ethics, also known as moral philosophy, is defined in terms of the following key questions: (1) What is morality? (2) What is the basis of our classification of actions into the categories of morally permissible, impermissible, and obligatory? (3) How does morality relate to religion? (4) How does morality relate to legality?

Moral or ethical questions arise either as direct and more or less pressing practical questions about what is to be done or avoided, here and now, or as more reflective questions about the meaning, point, and defensibility of our moral classifications. Practical questions are sometimes referred to as *first-order questions*, while more reflective questions are sometimes referred to as *second-order questions*, or *meta-questions*.

Social and Political Philosophy

Social and political philosophy, treated as a unit (and as such sometimes called sociopolitical philosophy), is defined in terms of the following key questions: (1) How are questions about personal morality tied to our existence as members of such larger collectivities as families and countries? (2) What difference does it make that I am the citizen of a state? (3) Where do states come from, and where do they get their authority? (4) Do we—and, if so, *why* do we—have to obey the laws of the land? (5) When should the laws of the land be changed? Social and political philosophy provides the natural context for ethics, in which we consider the question of what should be counted as a desirable life. Here we ask: What is the relationship—competition? cooperation? indifference?—between a desirable life for an individual and desirable lives for those around that person?

Philosophy of Religion

Philosophy of religion is defined in terms of the following key questions: (1) Is religious language meaningful? (2) How do we decide between theism, atheism, and agnosticism? (3) Can God's existence be proven or disproven? (4) Is religious faith unreasonable? Clearly, questions touching upon the existence of God also belong to metaphysics. But the question of God's existence comes up in a somewhat different way in philosophy of religion. God's existence is part of what might be called "the religious picture of the world." Does this religious picture, as a whole, then, make sense? Can we, for example, provide a coherent analysis of the concept of God? Is there any reason to think that the religious picture is correct?

Two important topics belonging to the philosophy of religion should be mentioned here. *First*, the religious picture of the world is closely related, historically, to the question of the meaning of human life. If the religious picture should turn out to be false, is there some other basis for finding human life meaningful? *Second*, it has often been maintained that there is tension, if not outright incompatibility, between the correctness of the religious picture and the existence of evil. This is usually called "the problem of evil." This tension—or perhaps incompatibility—arises because most religious people believe in a God who is both omnipotent (all-powerful) and omnibenevolent (all-good). A God so conceived could eradicate all evil—and, presumably, would want to.

Aesthetics

Aesthetics, which includes the philosophy of art, is defined in terms of the following key questions: (1) What is beauty? (2) What makes an object a work of art? (3) Why are works of art so important? (4) Are judgments concerning what is to count as a work of art and about the relative worth of various works of art objective or subjective?

In our cultural tradition, works of art have generally been valued as more than sources of pleasure. For one thing, it is claimed that we learn something about ourselves and about the world from works of art. How is this possible? For example, Tolstoy's *War and Peace* is classified as a novel, a kind of fiction, rather than a work of history, sociology, or psychology. How can a fiction teach us something about the world?

Philosophy is the only academic subject that focuses on conceptual clarity. For example, the most common model of education pictures it as the progress from ignorance to knowledge. Progress in philosophy, however, cannot be thought of in this way. Progress in philosophy is progress from partial mastery of concepts to complete mastery of concepts, from confusion to clarity, from conceptual perplexity to full understanding. For the really important concepts, however, complete mastery/full understanding is an ideal toward which we can, at best, hope to make some degree of progress—and such progress is made as an individual journey. Although there are many ways in which philosophy, like science, can be a collaborative, many-person undertaking, each person must finally understand for him- or herself. "You understand it for me!" is an impossible request.

In philosophy, the clarification, or elucidation, of concepts is achieved through two kinds of conceptual analysis: (1) analysis via necessary and sufficient conditions, and (2) analysis via criteria. Other methods, such as the method of doubt and the phenomenological method, may also be helpful.

Each of the major areas of philosophy can be characterized in terms of a few key questions. These questions are conceptual rather than factual. Alternatively, we can define the basic areas of philosophy in terms of the perplexing concepts they seek to clarify—and these are precisely the concepts that give rise to the questions. Although it is useful to define the subfields of philosophy in this way, the lines drawn between the various areas should not be thought of as absolutely rigid. A single conceptual investigation may, for example, cut across the boundaries of metaphysics, philosophy of mind, and philosophy of language. Indeed, much of the most interesting contemporary work being done in philosophy is boundary-crossing in this sense.

Recommended Reading

Still the most useful research tool, for student and professional alike, is *The Encyclopedia of Philosophy* (1967). This eight-volume work includes articles on most of the topics mentioned in chapter 1. The last volume contains a detailed index. The articles on the Presocratics, Socrates, and each of the major areas of philosophy would probably be most useful. (Most libraries, academic and public, carry this work.)

F. M. Cornford's *Before and After Socrates* (1950) is in a class by itself—an extremely concise and clear introduction to Greek philosophy, and so to philosophy itself. The best comprehensive survey of the Presocratics is Jonathan Barnes's *The Presocratic Philosophers* (1979). On Socrates, see Gerasimos Xenophon Santas's *Socrates: Philosophy in Plato's Early Dialogues* (1979). A good contemporary general history of philosophy from the Greeks to the present day is D. W. Hamlyn's *A History of Western Philosophy* (1987).

Many of Plato's dialogues are themselves accessible to the beginning student. Three early dialogues that provide a vivid picture of Socrates (and which are often reprinted together) are the *Apology, Euthyphro,* and *Crito.*

Literally dozens of introductory textbooks exist. A sample of the best includes Bertrand Russell's *The Problems of Philosophy* (1912, and many reprintings); E. R. Emmet's *Learning to Philosophize* (1964); Robert G. Olson's *A Short Introduction to Philosophy* (1967); Ian Hacking's *Why Does Language Matter to Philosophy?* (1975); Thomas Nagel's *What Does It All Mean? A Very Short Introduction to Philosophy* (1987); Jonathan Rée's *Philosophical Tales* (1987); Arthur C. Danto's *Connections to the World: The Basic Concepts of Philosophy* (1989); and Douglas P. Lackey's *God, Immortality, Ethics: A Concise Introduction to Philosophy* (1990). All of the books mentioned have a certain style and flair; none is a chore to read, and Rée's book is actually a lot of fun.

Although some of its articles are quite technical, students should be aware of *The Handbook of Western Philosophy* under the general editorship of G. H. R. Parkinson (1988). This is a "state of the art" compendium with articles on all applicable topics of current interest.

An introduction to philosophy with special emphasis on the explanation of technical terms is A.W. Sparkes's *Talking Philosophy: A Wordbook* (1991).

One more introductory text, which approaches philosophy from a unique angle, is R. M. Saintsbury's *Paradoxes* (1988). A *paradox* arises when several seemingly acceptable premises lead to an unacceptable conclusion. Many of the basic problems of philosophy have the form of a paradox.

CHAPTER 2

Epistemology

This chapter provides a philosophically illuminating analysis of the concept of knowledge. Knowledge, it is shown, can be understood in terms of belief, truth, and justification. Each of the ideas in the analysans of "X knows that p" *needs to be analyzed in its turn. Accordingly, we discuss the nature of belief, the nature of truth, and the nature of justification.*

Knowledge is a good example of a concept that we all possess and use, but which few nonphilosophers could clearly explain. Furthermore, since knowledge is used as a basis for planning and action, being as clear as we can about what should count as knowledge is of great practical importance.

Etymology

The word *epistemology* derives from two Greek words: *epistēmē*, meaning "knowledge," and *logos*, meaning "study of" (or "theory of"). In English, *theory of knowledge* is used interchangeably with *epistemology*. In the ancient world, *epistēmē* was contrasted with *doxa*, meaning "belief," but belief in the sense of *mere opinion*—that is, something that falls short of genuine knowledge. In terms of the ancient contrast, we can state the fundamental question of epistemology as follows: How can *doxa* be transformed into *epistēmē*?

Knowledge

The Standard Analysis of Knowledge

The concept of knowledge is a perfect candidate for philosophical analysis. In the first place, it is not a strange or technical term: all of us can, and do, use the noun *knowledge* and various forms of the verb *to know* quite frequently and quite correctly. In the course of ordinary life, we often reject—often with good reasons—various people's claims to know this and that. (Admittedly, almost everybody has a certain tendency, which it takes a lot of philosophical therapy to overcome, to overestimate how much *he* or *she* knows.) In any case, it is not immediately obvious how we should spell out exactly what is involved in the concept of knowledge.

Fortunately, philosophers have developed a now widely accepted analysis of the concept of knowledge. According to this standard account, knowledge is *justified true belief*. This can be expressed, in explicit analytical form, as follows:

X knows that p IFF

(i) X believes that p ;

(ii) it is true that p ; and

(iii) X is justified in believing that p (if X does).

I know that $2 + 2 = 4$, for example, just in case (or just when) I believe that $2 + 2 = 4$; it is true that $2 + 2 = 4$; and I am justified in believing that $2 + 2 = 4$. Similarly, you know that the dog is in the backyard just in case you believe that the dog is in the backyard, that's where the dog is, and you are justified in your belief.

Acccording to the standard analysis, then, there are three necessary conditions for knowledge: (i) the belief condition, (ii) the truth condition, and (iii) the justification condition. No one who fails to satisfy one or more of these conditions can possibly know that p. The standard analysis of knowledge also claims that these three conditions are together sufficient—that is, there is no other requirement that needs to be met in order to have knowledge.

The "Knowing That"/"Knowing How" Distinction

The standard analysis of knowledge is an analysis of "knowing that." However, "knowing that" must be carefully distinguished from "knowing how." We know *how* to ride a bicycle, bake a pineapple upside-down cake, or do a handstand. This is common *know-how*, or knowledge-as-ability. Ordinarily, we cannot fully verbalize knowledge-as-ability: such knowledge is taught more by showing than by saying.

Knowledge in the "knowing that" sense is called *propositional knowledge*. Indeed, the "*p*" in both "believing that *p*" and "knowing that *p*" is called a *propositional variable*. It is generally assumed that propositional knowledge, unlike know-how, can be fully verbalized.

Before going on with the analysis of knowledge, though, we need to say something about propositions.

Declarative Sentences, Statements, Propositions

We have to build up to the idea of a proposition in several stages. As a start, we should note that all the sentences we use can be divided into those that possess truth-values and those that do not possess truth-values. In this connection, consider the following sentences:

How old are you?

Oh, to be young!

Shut the door!

Mt. Rainier is 3,852 feet high.

The first three—respectively, interrogative, exclamative, and imperative sentences—are neither true nor false; it does not make sense, immediately after any one of the first three is uttered, to ask "Is that true?" (You can establish this yourself by a simple mental experiment.) It is worth noticing that the interrogative, exclamative, and imperative each supposes that *something* is true, or has true/false presuppositions.

For example, the question presupposes that the person addressed has an age, which would be true of all humans but perhaps not of God.

It does, of course, make perfectly good sense to ask "Is that true?" after an utterance of the declarative sentence, "Mt. Rainier is 3,852 feet high." This sentence is obviously either true or false, and we can appreciate that even if we don't happen to know whether it is indeed true or false.

Sentences such as "Mt. Rainier is 3,852 feet high" that possess truth-values are generally called *statements*. The concept of a statement is important in logic, because the components of arguments *must* be statements. The question may arise, however, whether *statement*, as a technical term in logic, is really needed, since we already have "declarative sentence" from grammar. In point of fact, though, we do need *statement*, because not all grammatically declarative sentences are statements. "Some green numbers are lazy," though a declarative sentence, is neither true nor false, and therefore not a statement. To think it is true would involve—crazy idea!—not only believing that there are green numbers, but also that some of them are lazy. (Remember that a number is not the same as a numeral or inscription of a number name.) To think it is false would involve—also crazy!—thinking that no green numbers are lazy—that is, thinking that there are some green numbers, but that it's mistaken to say any of them are lazy! In fact, "Some green numbers are lazy" is a good example of a *pseudo-statement*—something that looks like a statement (just because it's grammatically declarative), but turns out not to be a statement (because it lacks a truth-value).

Although statements are just what we do substitute for p in the "believing that p" and "knowing that p" expressions, statements and propositions are not the same thing. A statement stands to the proposition it expresses in exactly the same way that the word *discovery* stands to the concept of discovery. We should remember that there are other words besides "discovery" that express the concept of discovery—for example, *découverte* and *Entdeckung*. Exactly the same point can be made about statements. The English sentence "It is raining" expresses the proposition that it is raining, but so do the French sentence "*Il fait pluie*" and the German sentence "*Es regnet*."

To believe that it is raining is not the same thing, then, as believing that the English sentence "It is raining" is true—although if you do speak English you probably have a belief about the sentence's being true along with your belief about the weather. A French or German speaker could have the same belief about the weather as an English speaker, but with no idea at all (assuming he or she to be monolingual) about which English sentences are supposed to be true. Beliefs about the weather are not beliefs about words, which is why people using different words can believe exactly the same thing.

These remarks are probably sufficient to show that propositions cannot be identified with statements. Statements are always statements in a particular language. Occasionally, particularly in older books, students will encounter *statement* used as a synonym for *proposition*, so perhaps we should say that statements, in the modern sense, are language-specific. This should be obvious, though, since a statement is defined as a *kind of sentence* (the kind with a truth-value), and sentences are always sentences of a particular language. A proposition is defined more abstractly, and in complete independence of particular languages. *A proposition is what a statement states.* "It is raining" states that it is raining; "*Il fait pluie*" states that it is raining; "*Es regnet*" states that it is raining. We need statements that belong to particular languages in order to express (or state) propositions, but what is expressed (or stated) does not belong to a particular language.

Propositional Attitudes

Many verbs in English (and an equivalent point could be made about other languages) take as objects expressions of the form "that *p*." Such verbs are said to express "propositional attitudes." When people believe that *p*, doubt that *p*, suspect that *p*, deny that *p*, fear that *p*, wish that *p*, and so forth, we credit them with a propositional attitude. A complete discussion of propositional attitudes belongs to the philosophy of mind. Here, however, we need only concern ourselves with "believing that *p*," since this is the propositional attitude that is part of the analysis of knowledge.

Belief

Belief as a Necessary Condition for Knowledge

Condition (i) in the standard analysis of knowledge tells us that we cannot know that which we do not believe. In other words, we cannot have knowledge without belief (although we can certainly have beliefs that do not amount to knowledge). It is precisely that *subset* of our beliefs that are both true and justified that constitute knowledge. Although this is a quite natural way of looking at knowledge, it has sometimes been challenged.

Alleged Counterexamples to the Necessity of Condition (i)

The claim that condition (i) is a necessary condition for knowledge has inspired attempts at counterexemplification (that is, attempts to produce counterexamples) along the following lines:

I know that smoking causes cancer, but I don't believe it;

I know that I am going to die someday, but I don't believe it;

I know that my parents had sex at least once, but I don't believe it.

There is no doubt that people say things like this; the question is whether they mean (or could mean) that they literally don't believe something that they know. What we are really asking is whether (to put it schematically) "knowing that p, but not believing that p" is logically possible. (Something is logically possible just in case it does not involve a contradiction.) So far as the three alleged counterexamples are concerned, people probably mean by "I don't believe it" something more like "I'm not capable of vividly imagining it, facing it, or doing anything about it." This is all perfectly compatible with their believing it. In making this point, we are using our concept of belief. But how should belief be analyzed?

The Analysis of Belief

Although everyone—we are, of course, generalizing about adult speakers of English—has the word *belief* in his or her vocabulary, the associated concept is very difficult to analyze. One initial clarification is easy to make: we should distinguish belief as a propositional attitude—that is, "believing *that*"—from belief as confidence—that is, "believing *in*". In the present discussion, we are not concerned with the concept involved in believing *in*, such as believing in democracy, the American way of life, votes for seventeen-year-olds, Senator X, or whatever.

One analysis of *belief that* reads as follows:

X believes that *p* IFF

X thinks that *p* is true.

This analysis certainly satisfies the first two requirements for a successful analysis: *analysandum* and *analysans* mean the same thing, and their truth-values are alike. But the third requirement that must be met by any analysis is that the *analysans* must be more clear (or less misleading) than the *analysandum*—and this requirement is, it is fair to say, only marginally satisfied by the present analysis of belief. It is a correct analysis, as far as it goes, but it is not very illuminating. A full analysis would have to explain how belief is connected to desire and action. Such an explanatory project is a central concern in the philosophy of mind, where claims about what a person believes are regarded as part of a coherent explanation of that person's actions. However, even our preliminary analysis helps us see why alleged counterexamples to the necessity of condition (i) are unsuccessful.

Any counterexample to the necessity of condition (i) for knowledge would require us to accept a situation in which a person could consistently say "I know that *p*, but I don't think it is true that *p*." If someone were to say something like "I know that I went to the movies last night, but I don't think I did," we would not, I think, credit that person with an unusual—but possible—state of mind; we would, instead, suppose that the person was using the word *know* or the word *think* (or maybe both words) incorrectly. It is the job of psychology to describe peculiar, including very confused, states of mind; philosophy, based on its analyses of concepts, can say that no state of mind, or psychological condition, could possibly be correctly described as a state, or condition, of "beliefless knowledge." "Beliefless knowledge" is a phrase that has as much chance of describing anything as "four-sided triangle" or "square circle."

Truth

Truth as a Necessary Condition for Knowledge

Condition (ii) in the standard analysis of knowledge tells us that we cannot know that which is not true—though certainly many things may be true that we don't know. (There may indeed be things that are true that no one knows!) Our first task, here, is to explain why condition (ii) is a necessary condition for knowledge.

Condition (ii) is a necessary condition for knowledge because a commitment to its necessity is built into our use of the term *knowledge* (and related terms), as well as into our thinking about knowledge. The necessity of condition (ii) regulates our use of *knowledge* (and related terms), even if we are not fully aware of this. Once again, conceptual analysis makes explicit something implicit in our actual, often quite unreflective, practice.

Suppose you are set the task of writing an essay on the Middle Ages. You might write "In the Middle Ages people believed the earth was flat," but you would never write "In the Middle Ages people knew the earth was flat." Suppose a certain person, X, goes around saying you cheat at cards, and even says he *knows* that you cheat at cards. If you were to react by saying "X knows that I cheat at cards," you would not be *neutrally describing* what X is going around saying; on the contrary, you would be *endorsing* X's view—in other words, admitting that you cheat.

The same principle is at work in both these examples: it is impossible to say that someone knows that *p* without implying that *p* is true. In saying "X knows that *p*," we are, in effect, saying that X believes something that is true. If you write "In the Middle Ages people knew the earth was flat," the reader will assume that you also believe (that is, think that it is true) that the earth is flat. (Similarly for the cheating example.)

In making the case that truth is built into the concept of knowledge, we can appeal to *ordinary usage*—that is, what ordinary speakers of English will or will not feel comfortable saying. However, we are not relying on ordinary usage alone. The account of knowledge provided here does square with ordinary usage (and that is a plus), but it also coheres with—and helps us make intellectual sense of—many things that have nothing to do with the correct use of expressions in English. In particular, the present account of knowledge helps us to understand the development of science.

That truth really is built into the concept of knowledge shows itself in the fact that you cannot say "X knows, falsely, that p" and make a sensible point. You can, though, say "X believes, falsely, that p," and in saying this, say something sensible and possibly true. Although we cannot guarantee that someone will not say "X knows, falsely, that p," it sounds odd, because it embodies a contradiction and that is enough, almost always, to stop people from saying it.

People, of course, quite often think they know something they don't know. But the correct way of describing this is never to say they know various things falsely. About the people in the Middle Ages who said "We know the earth is flat," the correct thing to say is that they were making two *necessarily interlocking* mistakes. Their first mistake was about the shape of the earth: they thought it was flat, but it wasn't and isn't. Their second mistake was about their inventory of knowledge: they thought it contained an item about the shape of the earth, but it didn't.

This is always the situation when people think they know what they cannot know because it is false. If X says "I know that p," but p is in fact false, necessarily X makes two mistakes: *first*, about himself and what he knows (he overestimates his supply of knowledge by one unit), and *second*, about p. Imagine a not very clever child, just learning arithmetic, who is delighted that he now "knows" that $2 + 2 = 5$. Necessarily, the child makes two mistakes: a mistake about what he knows (less than he thinks) and a mistake about what $2 + 2$ equals.

No Magic Connection Between Knowledge and Truth

When people first hear the principle, *If you know something, it has to be true*, they sometimes imagine they are being given a magical guarantee that reliably connects their saying "I know that p" (or their sincerely believing that they know that p) with p's being true. This gets the real connection between knowledge and truth backward, however: it works only the other way around. If p turns out to be false, you turn out not to know that p, whatever you may say or believe.

Alleged Counterexamples to the Necesssity of Condition (ii)

Proposed counterexamples to the necessity of condition (ii) for knowledge (the truth condition) all turn out to be counterexamples to such principles as "If X says he knows that p, then p" or "If X believes he knows that p, then p." These are false principles, and are of course open to counterexemplification.

There are no genuine counterexamples to "If X knows that p, then p." This should not be puzzling. We simply refuse to count anything as knowledge that is not true. This is why it is so often difficult to acquire knowledge, and why its acquisition counts as an accomplishment. It also explains why claims to know can be—and often are—incorrect. (We should add that, in refusing to count anything as knowledge that is not true, we are not following an arbitrary policy, but remaining faithful to a conception of knowledge which can play a central role in our intellectual life.)

It is sometimes maintained, despite the considerations above, that people in the Middle Ages really did know the earth was flat: it seemed flat to ordinary people, respected experts held that it was flat, belief in the earth's flatness was traditional. All of this may be true, but it is irrelevant. It may have been *reasonable* for people, in the Middle Ages, to believe that the earth was flat, but reasonable belief is not the same as knowledge.

Theories of Truth

In the discussion of the necessity of condition (ii) for knowledge, we have relied on the fact that everyone has some idea of what is meant by *true* and related terms. All of us have had a lot of practice in evaluating statements on the basis of their truth or falsity. Nevertheless, the question "What is truth?" has been proverbially puzzling to philosophers, and there is still no absolute agreement among them as to the correct account of the concept of truth. One obvious point (and one that is universally agreed on) is that *true* as it applies to statements or propositions should be distinguished from the *true* in expressions such as "true friend." In the present discussion, we are not concerned with cases where *true* is the synonym of *genuine* and the antonym of *fake* or *pseudo-*. We are concerned only with *propositional truth*. We turn, then, to the most important theories of propositional truth.

The No-Theory Theory of Truth

This odd-sounding, or paradoxical, label is appropriate for those philosophical views that deny we need any theory of truth at all. These should not be confused with the view (external to philosophy) that we do not need to bother analyzing the concept of truth because our ordinary ability to use *true* (and related terms) is good enough. The "no-theory theory of truth" is meant as a philosophical theory of truth. Its basic claim is that

"p" is true just means that *p*.

So *"It is raining" is true* just means that *It is raining*. We understand *"It is raining" is true* just in case (or just when) we understand *It is raining*. The "no-theory theory of truth" is also sometimes called the *disappearance theory* of truth. It is also called, somewhat misleadingly, the *disquotational view* of truth. The idea behind the latter label is that a quoted statement followed by "is true" is precisely equivalent to the original statement without the quotation marks, or, in other words, to the original statement "disquoted." For example,

"It is snowing" is true

is equivalent to

It is snowing.

Semantic Ascent. Associated with the "no-theory" (or *disappearance* or *disquotational*) view of truth is the idea that truth is a *device of semantic ascent.* The adjective *semantic* means "concerning the relation between words and the world" or, alternatively, between *our talk* and *what our talk is about*. There is a semantic relationship between "It is raining" and the weather by virtue of which "It is raining" is either true or false. The concept of truth simply allows us to talk about our talk about the world—in this case, the weather. *Ascent* (= "going up") is the appropriate term if we picture the situation as follows:

LEVEL 3	talk about our talk	
	about the weather	SEMANTIC
LEVEL 2	our talk about the	ASCENT
	weather	
LEVEL 1	the weather	

The Correspondence Theory of Truth

The corrrespondence theory of truth is the oldest, best known, and perhaps most natural theory of truth. Its basic claim is that

A statement is true IFF it corresponds with reality.

The statement "It is raining" is true just in case it corresponds with (the relevant portion of) reality. (It should be noted that even the no-theory theory of truth can be regarded as implicitly "correspondential," since the claim that a quoted statement is true amounts to the claim that what the [disquoted] statement says is so.) Of all the possible theories of truth, the correspondence theory connects most directly with the idea that truth is an *objective* property of statements. (*Objective* here means "mind-independent.") A speaker may utter a statement such as "It is raining" for all sorts of complicated psychological reasons. He may wish to mislead, tease, or disappoint; alternatively, he may have very good reasons for thinking that it is raining, or no reason at all. But, given the semantic meaning of "It is raining," his statement will be either true or false.

What determines this has nothing to do with the speaker, his psychology, motivation, or evidence. What determines the truth-value of "It is raining" is simply local weather—something that is "out there" and entirely mind-independent. What the sentence "It is raining" means may be up to humans, language being as it is a cumulative human invention that involves history, tradition, convention—which could, after all, have come out differently. But once a definite semantic meaning is given to "It is raining," it is not up to humans whether that sentence is true.

Trivial Semantic Conventionality. Trivial semantic conventionality—or the fact that the words we use could have meant (or could come to mean) something different—should not be confused with the nonobjectivity (or subjectivity) of truth. "Subjective truth" is, in fact, a contradiction in terms. Although people often say "It is true for me that *p*," truth—unlike, for example, belief, pain, and desire—is not really person-relative. "It is true for me that *p*" must mean either "I believe that *p*" or "It is true *of* me that *p*." (It is not true for me that blackberries taste better than strawberries, although it is *true of me*—that is, a truth *about me*—that I prefer blackberries to strawberries.) It is an advantage of the correspondence theory that it helps us avoid these confusions.

Difficulties with the Correspondence Theory. Two main difficulties have been raised against the correspondence theory. *First*, the correspondence theory, it has been claimed, presents a misleading and overly simple picture of how we determine the truth or falsity of statements. We do not, and really could not, check our statements one by one against reality. Even the decision to reject a simple statement like "It is raining" as false is made against a complicated background of belief. I jettison "It is raining" because it does not fit in with a number of other statements that I believe to be true—for example, that if it is raining and I am outside, I would get wet; that I am outside; that I am not getting wet; etc.

Second, the correspondence theory, it has been claimed, operates with the purely formal, or nonoperational, idea of "checking to see whether *p* corresponds with reality." Checking to see whether *p* corresponds with reality, however, is not something that can actually be done—is not a procedure, that is, that can be taught and learned and put into practice. What we do learn is an enormous plurality of procedures that, in various very complicated ways, guide us in our acceptance or rejection of statements.

Criticism of the correspondence theory has given rise to two other theories of truth, the *coherence theory* and the *pragmatic theory*. There are in fact a number of *versions* of each of these theories (as there are of the correspondence theory itself), so that it would be more correct to speak of two additional *families* of theories of truth. Sometimes, the other theories are regarded as *rivals* of the correspondence theory: this is the view that, if any one of them is correct, it follows that the correspondence theory must be incorrect. Sometimes, the other theories are regarded as *supplements* to the correspondence theory. This is the (theoretically pluralistic) view that the various theories of truth can be added together to produce an appropriately complex, rich, and "lifelike" picture of truth.

The Coherence Theory of Truth

The coherence theory of truth, though not without distinguished proponents, has always been much less widely accepted than the correspondence theory. According to the coherence theory,

A statement is true IFF it coheres with all true statements.

"To cohere with" means to be consistent with. Two statements are consistent just in case they can both be true at the same time. And they can both be true at the same time just in case their both being true does not involve a contradiction.

It should be obvious that consistency plays a major role in the acceptance or rejection of statements. If someone suggests that my study has been disarranged by poltergeists ("ghosts capable of moving things"), I summarily dismiss the suggestion just because it doesn't fit in with—or cohere with—the bulk of what I believe. So the coherence theory does capture something important in our cognitive ("cognitive" = concerning knowledge) practice. This does not mean, however, that the coherence theory is the overall best theory of truth. There are indeed two interrelated difficulties with the theory that need to be mentioned.

Difficulties with the Coherence Theory of Truth. First, it is more plausible to regard coherence as a necessary condition than it is to regard it as a sufficient condition for truth. In other words, statements that do not cohere are automatically excluded from the class of truths, but statements that do cohere are not automatically included in the class of truths. As the poltergeist example shows, we use coherence-failure to weed out candidate truths. There may still be several candidate truths ("My son messed up my study," "My dog messed up my study") among which we cannot choose based on coherence considerations alone.

Second, in using coherence in the screening-out process, we do not—and could not—test for coherence with all true statements. No one (with the possible exception of an all-knowing deity) is in possession of all true statements. "Checking to see whether p coheres with all true statements" is as totally nonoperational as "checking to see whether p corresponds with reality." Our actual practice is to check candidate truths for consistency with the set of statements we accept as true, or—put more simply—with our beliefs. It seems perfectly sensible to check candidate beliefs for consistency with our stock of beliefs if our confidence in those beliefs has some justification. It seems highly unlikely, however, that our justified confidence in our accumulated supply of beliefs could derive from coherence considerations alone.

The Pragmatic Theory of Truth

According to the pragmatic theory of truth,

A statement, p, is true IFF

believing that p is pragmatic.

It is easy enough to say that *pragmatic* means "useful," but this simply leads to the question: What does it mean to say that a belief is useful? Although some popular expositions have identified "useful" with whatever works for a given individual—that is, whatever makes him or her successful or happy—this has not been the idea put forward by serious pragmatists interested in pursuing a theory of truth.

Beliefs as Maps. Serious pragmatism starts with the idea that a belief should be regarded—in Frank Ramsey's words—as "a map by which we steer." A map is a good map if it helps us get where we want to go in a reasonably efficient manner. Although this doesn't sound all that different from the good-if-it-works view, there is nothing whimsical, arbitrary, willful, or subjective in our evaluation of maps. This is also the case for beliefs. Part of the point of comparing beliefs to maps is to emphasize that beliefs have practical functions, and—according to pragmatists—it is just these practical functions that the correspondence theory fails to take into account. The correspondence theory is essentially a *spectator theory* of truth, whereas pragmatism is an *actor* or *participant theory* of truth. (*Pragmatic* derives from the Greek *pragmatikos*, "versed in affairs" or "practical," and ultimately from *pragma*, "deed" or "act.")

Pragmatism and the Truth and Falsity of Statements. Common to the many interpretations of the term *pragmatic* is the assumption that "being pragmatic" is a property of beliefs and not directly of statements themselves. We do, however, want statements themselves to be true or false. This can be achieved as follows: We say that a statement is true just in case believing it *would be* pragmatic. This allows a statement to be true which no one happens to believe.

This does not by itself guarantee that truth is an objective property of statements; indeed, it is often claimed that—since it might turn out to be pragmatic for X to believe that p, but unpragmatic for another person, Y, to believe that p—the pragmatic theory of truth necessarily undercuts the objectivity of truth. Someone committed to a pragmatist account of truth may deny this. He admits that it may be pragmatic for

X but unpragmatic for Y to believe that p. But that it is pragmatic for X to believe that p has nothing to do with the contents of X's mind, with what X thinks: that it is pragmatic for X to believe that p is entirely mind-independent, or objective. Similarly for Y. It is, objectively speaking, unpragmatic for Y to believe that p. However, it is hard to see how, on this account, a single statement will not end up being true and false.

Evaluation of Pragmatism. Pragmatists are certainly right to emphasize the practical character of truth, of knowledge, and of human cognitive capacities. But this does not, by itself, mean that pragmatism is the best all-round theory of truth. For while the pragmatist says that a statement is true because believing it is pragmatic, it is open to the correspondence theorist—while accepting the pragmatic character of true beliefs—to claim that believing a statement is pragmatic because the statement is true. The pragmatist says the map is an accurate representation of reality because we can use it to steer; the correspondence theorist says we can use the map to steer because it is an accurate representation of reality. The pragmatist thinks that the only way of checking to see whether a belief corresponds to reality is by trying to steer with it, and seeing how one makes out; the correspondence theorist thinks that "seeing how one makes out" must involve producing a true representation of reality.

Here, as in many situations where philosophers attempt to explain our most fundamental concepts, arguments and counterarguments proliferate in complex *dialectical* patterns (*dialectical* = "concerning a series of opposing arguments"). At the very least, this shows how difficult it is to understand even a familiar concept like truth. We learn, in reviewing the mass of argumentation, that there is indeed no short and sweet answer to the question "What is truth?"

The Assertibility Theory of Truth

A more recent view of truth—one in the spirit of pragmatism, though not closely related historically—attempts to explain our basic cognitive practice in terms of *assertibility* (or *warranted assertibility*, or *justifiability of assertion*). According to this view,

A statement, S, is true IFF S is assertible.

First, a note on terminology. *Assertion* means the same as *statement*; *assertible* means worthy of being asserted. A statement is worthy of being asserted (or assertible) just in case its assertion is, or would be, justified or warranted. Following is an explanation, from the point of view of the assertibility theory of truth, of what goes on when someone decides to make an assertion.

Most people most of the time do not want to utter the statement "It is raining" unless it is true that it is raining. Typically, we assert (or say) that it is raining only after checking to see whether our statement corresponds with reality. For our example statement, this would involve such things as looking out the window to see whether it is raining. The assertibility theorist will grant that this is a correct account of what is going on, described at a certain level of abstractness (just the level of abstractness where the correspondence theory is obviously correct). In more concrete terms, however, all that we have done prior to our assertion that it is raining is gather evidence that is normally sufficient for our assertion.

Operationality. What crucially distinguishes the assertibility theory from the correspondence theory is the further claim that gathering evidence and the like is all that we can ever do. For every statement, there is an appropriate *test* (or *set of tests*) that we can actually perform. If these tests come out positive, we are justified in making the assertion. An equivalent way of putting this is to say that if the tests come out positive, our assertion cannot be criticized. The supposed advantage of the assertibility theory over the correspondence theory is its *fully operational* character: assertibility, relative to a given statement, is always defined in terms of tests that we can actually carry out or put into operation. In contrast, the correspondence theory, which tells us that we should make sure that our assertions are true, is *nonoperational.* "Making sure our assertions are true" is not a followable recipe, since it does not specify procedures.

It is open to the correspondence theorist to reply that his theory is not designed to provide followable recipes for determining truth, but it is precisely this that, in the eyes of the assertibility theorist, renders the correspondence theory a formally correct but *limited* theory of truth.

A Difficulty with the Assertibility Theory of Truth. A major difficulty with the assertibility theory is simply that *true* does not mean *assertible*. This can be shown by what is called the "open-question argument." We can sensibly ask: "*S* is assertible, but is *S* true?" In other words, even granting that *S* is assertible, it is still an open question (that is, not settled) whether S is true. And this would not be an open question if *assertible* and *true* were exact synonyms.

The open-question argument, which also works against pragmatic theories, is compelling. The assertibility theorist should not identify truth with assertibility. This does not mean that the assertibility theory should be flatly rejected: it makes an important contribution to our understanding of truth so long as we interpret it as claiming that "assertible" is the *operational counterpart* of "true." (What is really illuminating about the assertibility theory is that it shows *why* "true" needs an operational counterpart.)

Two Alleged Difficulties with the Assertibility Theory of Truth. First, it is sometimes claimed that the assertibility theory is a *social-consensus* theory of truth; in other words, our social group simply specifies which tests have to come out positive in order for our assertions to be exempt from criticism. Whatever tests are agreed upon are the tests that count. This argument reveals a misunderstanding of the assertibility theory, however: the appropriateness of tests is not based on the consensus of the social group, but on their relevance to the content of assertions. It is not the group, but the content of what is asserted, that determines which tests count. The relevance of a given test to a given assertion is supposed to be something that can be explained and demonstrated.

Second, it might be claimed that the assertibility theory makes it impossible to justifiably assert a falsehood, whereas common sense tells us that people are at least occasionally justified in asserting what is in fact false. The people in the Middle Ages asserting that the earth is flat might again provide an example. Once again, the open-question argument has force: that the earth was flat was justifiably assertible, but was it true? If *true* is defined as "justifiably assertible," the justified assertion of a falsehood will be ruled out by definition. We rely on the tests the passing of which makes us justified in our assertions, but we know that no tests are perfect. S can have passed all the tests we have at our disposal—tests it is reasonable to regard as settling the truth status of S—and still be false.

Justification

Justification as a Necessary Condition for Knowledge

Condition (iii) in the standard analysis of knowledge tells us that we cannot know what we believe without justification. The first thing that has to be made clear is that the justification condition is separate from the truth condition. You can satisfy condition (ii) and not satisfy condition (iii); in other words, you can believe something that is true and still not be justified in your belief. Similarly, you can satisfy condition (iii) and not satisfy condition (ii); in other words, you can be justified in believing something which is false. Of course it very often happens that you believe something that is true, and are justified in your belief (or believe something that is false, and fail to be justified in your belief). These are the most obvious possibilities, but instances where truth and justification go their separate ways are also possible.

Why Justification Is Necessary for Knowledge

Why isn't true belief enough for knowledge? The simplest answer is that justification is built into the concept of knowledge that we, as a matter of fact, employ. This is a correct answer as far as it goes. But there is an explanation of why we have the concept we have with just those necessary conditions we take to define it. The point of calling something knowledge is to indicate that we can rely on it, that we can be very—if not perfectly—certain that it is correct. Once something is classified as knowledge, we want to be able to use it, with as much security as possible, as the basis for plans and actions.

Although beliefs that are the products of lucky guesses or prejudices, or are otherwise arrived at irrationally, and which fail to be supported by relevant evidence, may occasionally be true, we can never be confident that they will be true. True beliefs that are true "by chance" do not provide the *maximal certainty* that it is the point of knowledge to provide. Hunches, guesses, "gut feelings," and the like, though we may on occasion be forced to fall back on them, are simply too risky. Using them is like gambling. By contrast, the employment of knowledge involves *minimal risk*.

The Nature of Justification

We are here talking about justification only in connection with beliefs—what is often called *doxastic* justification (*doxastic* simply meaning "concerning belief"). Decisions, actions, plans, rules, and possibly feelings can also be justified (or fail to be justified), but what it means to speak of *justification* in each of these cases is not the same as what it means to speak of the justification of belief. An analysis of belief, or doxastic, justification builds on the ordinary idea that a person is justified in believing something just in case he has "good reasons" for his belief. Although the word *reason* sometimes means *cause* (as in the sentence, "The reason my car didn't start was that it was out of gas"), *reason* here does not mean *cause*. A hypnotist might cause me to believe that Mickey Mouse is president of the United States but, although the causal story provides me with an excuse for believing something so absurd, it does not give me good reasons for my belief. Reasons that have justificatory force are, at least for most beliefs, to be understood in terms of the possession of adequate evidence.

Analyses of Doxastic Justification

Building on the idea that justification consists in having "good reasons," we offer the following analysis of doxastic justification:

X is justified in believing that *p* IFF

an ideally rational human, undistracted by passion or interest, would, given the evidence that *X* has, acquire the belief that *p*.

This is an analysis of justification based on human practice at its best. Actual human beings, when they are forming beliefs, are often not at their best: they may be careless, rushed, distracted, drunk, drugged, overtired, and so forth. Humans may also be under the sway of such passions as jealousy or anger, which distort their awareness and diminish their ability to process evidence. Again, when we have a strong interest in a certain statement's truth or falsity, we may be inclined to willful misinterpretation, wishful thinking, self-deception, and the like. There may also be purely intellectual deficiencies in our handling of evidence. We are justified in believing only if none of these negative factors are operating. This may sound like a very unusual state of affairs, but probably most belief formation—our coming to believe that it is raining when we look out the window and observe the weather, our coming to believe that the dog is in the backyard when we hear its characteristic bark coming from the right place—manages to avoid all these negative factors and is, consequently, justified.

Relativity to Evidence

X's being justified in the analysis above is to be understood relative to the evidence X has. So, there is nothing surprising that X, who has a lot of evidence for p, can be justified in believing that p; whereas Y, who has no evidence for p, fails to be justified in believing that p. There is one rather subtle complication here that should be mentioned. We judge X to be justified or not based on the evidence that X has. But there would certainly seem to be cases where X himself is responsible for how much (or how little) evidence he has: can X be rational in basing his beliefs on evidence if it is his fault that he has so little?

Cases of *self-deception* are like this—cases where there is a lot of evidence around, evidence a person could easily have if he wanted it, but which he deliberately looks away from or disguises. Such cases of self-deceptive belief formation should certainly not be counted as cases of justified belief formation. The question remains as to how much positive effort a person is required to make to acquire appropriate evidence before the beliefs formed on the basis of that evidence qualify as justified.

Nonevidentiary Justification

Although for most beliefs it makes sense to evaluate justification in relation to evidence, certain very important beliefs do not fit this pattern. What, for example, is my evidence for believing that triangles are three-sided, that $2 + 2 = 4$, or that I am in pain? I am certainly sometimes justified in believing each of these things, but my belief does not seem to be based on evidence. This suggests that there is such a thing as *nonevidentiary* (that is, not based on evidence) justification. The essence of this kind of justification is captured in the following analysis:

X is justified in believing that p IFF

there is no room for criticizing X for acquiring the belief that p.

This analysis provides a comprehensive account of justification. Like the first analysis, it covers cases where justification is relevant to belief formation—cases where a person is open to criticism if he does not have enough evidence, or the right kind of evidence, or his handling of evidence has been faulty. But the present analysis also covers cases of nonevidentiary justification, cases where evidence is not relevant. A person may have "good reasons" for believing that triangles are three-sided, that $2 + 2 = 4$, or that he is in pain; and if those good reasons are of the appropriate kind, he is not open to criticism.

"Being open to criticism," incidentally, has nothing to do with whether someone actually offers criticism. In the process of belief formation, people sometimes make mistakes that go undetected by themselves or others. It can also happen that people offer criticisms where criticism is not appropriate—that is, where no mistake of any type has been made. "Being open to criticism," then, is an objective matter that is determined by the content of what is believed and the reasons for believing it; it is not a matter of "social consensus." Still, if we are interested in whether, for example, a mathematician is justified in a certain mathematical belief, we will have to ask other mathematicians what they think, because they are most skilled in detecting the sorts of mistakes someone might make in the course of arriving at a mathematical belief.

Knowledge and Its Conditions

We have seen that conditions (i), (ii), and (iii) in the standard analysis of knowledge all have to be satisfied for a person to have knowledge. This happens only when a person believes something that is true and is also justified in his or her belief. When a person believes something that is false and also lacks justification, that person (very obviously) does not have knowledge. When a person believes something that is true but lacks justification, that person also does not have knowledge. (There are cases like this, where a person makes a lucky guess, or believes something based on superstition or prejudice, but happens—in the rare case—to believe something that is true.)

Finally, when a person believes something that is false, but nevertheless has justification, he still fails to have knowledge. And there are cases like this too, cases where there are "good reasons" for believing something that is in fact false. So we might judge that people in the Middle Ages, given the evidence then available, were justified in believing that the earth is flat.

Gettier Counterexamples

There is general agreement that each of the three conditions for knowledge discussed in this chapter is necessary. This leaves open the question of whether the three conditions are jointly sufficient, or sufficient as a "package." Could someone satisfy the three conditions and still not know? Recently, the American philosopher Edmund Gettier (b. 1927) has proposed counterexamples to the joint sufficiency of the three conditions constituting the standard analysis of knowledge. His counterexamples (and similar examples) have come to be known as *Gettier counterexamples*.

Let us consider one such example. Suppose I look out the window of my apartment, see what any reasonable person would take to be rain falling, and come to believe that it is indeed raining. In fact, though, what I am seeing is not real rain, but the special-effects rain produced by a movie crew. The "fake rain" is coming from sprinklers below a temporary roof. However, at the same time, it really is raining, and—if the temporary roof were not in place—real rain would be falling in place of the movie rain that I see. I believe that it is raining, it is true that it is raining, and I am justified; yet it seems odd to say that I know that it is raining. That my belief is true in the special circumstances of the Gettier counterexample seems a matter of pure coincidence. In any case, my evidence seems somehow defective: I have come to believe that it is raining via the false belief that the stuff falling outside my window is real rain.

There is no general agreement, among philosophers, on just how to handle Gettier counterexamples. Does the possibility of constructing such examples mean that the standard analysis is incomplete? Not necessarily. We might take Gettier counterexamples to show that judgments about justification are, like most other judgments, *fallible (fallible* = "possibly mistaken") or *corrigible (corrigible* = "subject to correction"). In the circumstances just described, a person who judges that it is raining arrives at that belief by a reasonable route. If it turns out that his actual process of belief formation, though of a generally reliable sort, relies on a false assumption ("That's real rain out there"), then it turns out that he is not justified. He does, after all, fail to satisfy condition (iii), so it is not surprising that he does not know that it is raining.

Considerations in the Concept of Knowledge

A final remark about knowledge. The single concept of knowledge fuses together three quite different considerations. One consideration concerns the knower and what he believes. Another consideration concerns what is actually true, which has absolutely nothing to do with what the knower (or would-be knower) believes to be true. And the last consideration concerns the knower (or would-be knower) and his reasons—good or bad, adequate or inadequate—for belief, but has nothing to do with his views about the quality of his reasons for belief.

We have seen that the concept of knowledge can be analyzed in terms of belief, truth, and justification. Each of these is a necessary condition for knowledge, and—despite Gettier counterexamples— should probably be regarded as jointly sufficient.

The kind of belief that is involved in the analysis of knowledge is "belief that" (belief as a propositional attitude) rather than "belief in" (belief as confidence). Believing that p involves "thinking that p is true." This leads us to an account of the concept of truth.

The relevant sense of "truth" is that of propositional truth. Each of the main theories of truth—the no-theory theory, the correspondence theory, the coherence theory, the pragmatic theory, and the assertibility theory—adds something to our understanding of the concept of truth.

Finally, to be justified in believing something is to have good reasons for one's belief. For most beliefs, this means having enough of the right kind of evidence. For all beliefs, it means arriving at one's belief (referred to as the process of belief formation) in a way that is not open to criticism.

Recommended Reading

The Encyclopedia of Philosophy referred to earlier has entries for all the major terms discussed in this chapter—for example, epistemology, knowledge, correspondence theory of truth, coherence theory of truth, and pragmatic theory of truth. In addition, each of the introductory textbooks listed in the recommended reading for chapter 1 has a useful section on epistemology.

Of the vast numbers of books on epistemology, the following are especially recommended: Robert J. Ackermann's *Belief and Knowledge* (1972); Roderick Chisholm's *Theory of Knowledge* (3rd. ed. 1988); Jaakko Hintikka's *Knowledge and Belief* (1962); Arthur C. Danto's *Analytical Philosophy of Knowledge* (1968) (this book contains a good discussion of Gettier counterexamples); Keith Lehrer's *Knowledge* (1974); Robert Nozick's *Philosophical Explanations* (1981); *Epistemology: New Essays in the Theory of Knowledge* (ed. Avrum Stroll, 1967); and Alan R. White's *Truth* (1970).

The single best book on the coherence theory of truth is Nicholas Rescher's *The Coherence Theory of Truth* (1973). Also recommended for its discussion of coherence theories is Laurence BonJour's *The Structure of Empirical Knowledge* (1985). On the pragmatic theory of truth, see William James's classic *Pragmatism* (1907, and many reprintings); Clarence Irving Lewis's *An Analysis of Knowledge and Valuation* (1946); and *Prospects for Pragmatism: Essays in Memory of F. P. Ramsey* (ed. D. H. Mellor, 1980).

A specialized volume on the origins of epistemology in ancient Greek thought that a serious beginner will find helpful is *Epistemology: Companion to Ancient Thought* (vol. 1, ed. Stephen Everson, 1990).

Finally, the phrase "a belief is a map by which we steer" derives from F. P. Ramsey's work collected in *The Foundations of Mathematics* (ed. D. H. Mellor, 1978). The term "semantic ascent" derives from the work of Willard Van Orman Quine; see his *Word and Object* (1960).

CHAPTER 3

Philosophy of Science

This chapter begins with a consideration of philosophical skepticism, or the view that human beings, even in the best of circumstances, cannot possess knowledge. Although most people today, including most philosophers, take it for granted that skepticism is a false view, it is worthwhile to examine this view if only to learn why some philosophers of the past were skeptics.

The two major philosophical positions concerning the sources of knowledge are rationalism, which holds that reason or intellect is the main source of knowledge, and empiricism, which holds that experience is the main source of knowledge.

From the seventeenth century to our own time, science has been the main source of new knowledge. Most of this chapter is devoted to philosophy's attempt to understand science, and to some of the more significant problems to which that attempt has given rise. (Among other things, our attempt to understand science should help us answer the question: Why has science been so successful?) We will also look at the difference between the physical sciences (such as physics and chemistry) and the social sciences (such as sociology and economics). Finally, we will consider the question of whether there are important kinds of knowledge that have nothing to do with science.

Skepticism

Etymology

The modern words *skepticism, skeptic, and skeptical* all derive from the ancient Greek *skeptikos*, which can be translated as "inquiring." Originally, a skeptic was simply someone who was still inquiring, still seeking answers, not yet having arrived at settled beliefs. Ancient skeptics distinguished themselves from *dogmatists*—people who have arrived at fixed views or dogmas. In modern English, a dogma usually means a mandatory belief relative to some—in most cases religious—system, and dogmatists are commonly thought of as people whose adherence to some belief is stubborn or irrational. However, this is not part of the ancient contrast between the skeptic's *suspension of judgment* and the dogmatist's *commitment to belief*.

Definition of Skepticism

Given its etymology, we might expect that skepticism would be the label for a temporary phase or provisional position, to be abandoned when the answers to certain pivotal questions were finally found. In fact, though, skepticism hardened into a permanent philosophical position. Skepticism holds that *humans lack knowledge*. The most consistent skeptics do not go beyond this bare assertion. In practice, however, most skeptics seem to regard knowledge as impossible.

Global Skepticism/Local Skepticism

A *global*, or complete, skeptic holds that humans lack all knowledge—in other words, that every claim to know something is, without exception, incorrect. A *local*, or partial, skeptic holds only that humans lack knowledge in particular areas or about particular topics. Some people claim knowledge of the future; others are skeptical. Some people claim knowledge of God and the afterlife; others are skeptical. Some people claim knowledge of morality; others are skeptical. And so on. Local (or partial, or area-specific) skepticism has to be supported by arguments relating to the possibility of knowledge in that area. Some area-specific skepticisms may be supported by good arguments, even if there is no good argument for global skepticism.

Arguments for Global Skepticism

A great many arguments have been advanced by skeptics, ancient and modern, to crush ordinary cognitive confidence. These arguments usually operate overlappingly and cumulatively. Following are three of the more important skepticism-generating arguments.

The Criterion Argument. We cannot distinguish truth from falsity without a criterion or rule. Of course, that criterion has to be true. Either we have no reason to think that it is true or we must introduce a second criterion that guarantees *its* truth. We then have our problem all over again, this time relative to the second criterion. Very little reflection is needed to see that we have entered on an *infinite regress*—that is, a series of steps, each of which logically requires a next step, and so on without end.

The Evidence Argument. Regardless of the evidence we have for a statement, we still cannot be absolutely certain that the statement is true. This is because it is possible, given that evidence, for the statement to be false. Evidence—or what we take to be evidence—can be entirely misleading.

The Equilibrium Argument. Whatever arguments can be advanced in favor of a statement, it is always possible to find (or for a clever person to construct) arguments that cut the other way. Arguments *pro* and *contra* are thus in equilibrium, so that the rational person suspends judgment, having no more reason to think the statement true than to think its opposite true.

Evaluation of Skepticism-Generating Arguments

Each of the arguments for skepticism shows us something about the concept of knowledge, but none should persuade us that knowledge is impossible. We will examine each argument in turn.

Evaluation of the Criterion Argument. It is not true, as the criterion argument alleges, that we rely on a single criterion when we decide what statements to accept. In making judgments about the truth or falsity of individual statements, we rely on a great many other statements that we take for granted. These taken-for-granted statements constitute our *background assumptions* on each occasion of judgment. As our cognitive life goes on, we may have occasion to modify or reject an item that was, until then, a background assumption; however, this is not a reason for global loss of cognitive confidence. Modesty, tentativeness, and a realistic recognition that there is often—indeed, almost always—room for cognitive improvement should not lead to defeatism.

Evaluation of the Evidence Argument. All of the premises of the evidence argument are correct, but they do not support the claim that we have no knowledge. No matter how much evidence we have supporting a statement, it is *logically possible* that the statement is false. This just means that it would involve no contradiction if it turned out that, even given very strong evidence in its support, a given statement turned out to be false. To make us see this, philosophers have often raised rather far-fetched possibilities. One famous example is The Brain in the Vat case. If I were a brain in a vat (let us say I'm being kept alive after an accident that destroyed the rest of my body), and it were so arranged that my nervous system received the right impulses, I could have experiences of any kind whatsoever. All of the experience-based judgments I am now making—for example, that I am sitting in my study; that I am pressing the keys of a word-processor; and so forth—could be false.

Two things should be said about this example and similar examples. What they say is logically possible is indeed logically possible. But what is *merely* logically possible, but which we have no reason to think is actually the case, should not undercut our cognitive confidence.

What the second argument for skepticism really does is introduce a new and unrealistically high standard for "being justified." X is justified in believing that p (according to the second argument) IFF it is logically impossible (given the evidence X has) for p to be false. Our actual concept of knowledge allows us to *discriminate* between situations in which someone knows something, and situations in which—whatever may be claimed—there is no knowledge. This ability to discriminate, which is what makes our actual concept of knowledge so useful, is lost if we accept standards for knowledge that are never met.

In the best of circumstances, we come to believe various things with the sort of evidence that would lead any rational person to embrace those same beliefs. In such circumstances, we are entitled to say that we know the things that we believe. We are also entitled, in the best of circumstances, to say that we are "certain." Are we entitled to say that we are "absolutely certain"? Not quite. For even in the best of circumstances, we could turn out to be wrong.

Once again, this realization should not provoke a crisis of cognitive confidence. Knowledge claims are *fallible* (that is, possibly mistaken), and accordingly—and fortunately!—*corrigible* (that is, subject to correction). Again, we have knowledge when we are as certain as it is *humanly possible* to be.

Evaluation of the Equilibrium Argument. The equilibrium argument might be thought of as a philosophical version of the platitude to the effect that "there are two sides to every story." Both the equilibrium argument and the related platitude capture something that is correct. It is almost always the case, especially regarding complicated or controversial or not entirely obvious matters, that there are arguments *pro* and *contra*. The equilibrium argument reminds us (very usefully) that we should not make up our minds until we have heard the arguments on both sides. That said, it remains the case that the equilibrium argument finally rests on something that is not correct: it is *not* true that the arguments on both sides have to be equally good, persuasive, or worthwhile. Though there may indeed be two sides to every story, one side often—for good, logical reasons—deserves to win.

The Paradox of Skepticism

A paradox arises when we feel we are forced to say something, on the basis of argument or common-sense obviousness, which we nevertheless feel cannot be correct. For the global skeptic (though not for the local skeptic), a paradox arises in the following way: when the global skeptic asserts that humans know nothing, he seems to be claiming to know that humans know nothing. But this can't be right: if humans really do know nothing, then the skeptic can't know that humans know nothing.

One famous ancient skeptic, Diogenes (*c*.412–324 B.C.), tried to evade the paradox of skepticism in a unique way. Having spent years of his life saying that humans know nothing, and that there is really nothing worth saying, Diogenes finally realized that he was indeed claiming himself to know at least one thing, and—by his actions—showing that he thought it was worth saying at least that nothing is worth saying! He finally adopted a policy of total silence, and lived the rest of his life on top of a pillar in the public square of a town, whose citizens would point out Diogenes as the only consistent skeptic. Diogenes could show what he couldn't assert or claim to know: skepticism might be true (Diogenes thought it was), but, if it is true, it can't be *known* to be true.

Rationalism

Etymology

The word *rationalism* derives from the Latin, *ratio*, meaning "reason." *Reason*, a word which has a number of loosely connected meanings in English, must be understood, in the present context, as referring to a faculty or power of the human mind. Reason, in this sense, is also called *intellect*. As is true of many crucial philosophical terms, the word *reason* is almost always used *contrastively*, the operative contrast being between reason and sense perception (or sense experience). A rough idea of what is meant by the faculty of reason can proceed from considering the following examples:

(1) We may take in the words of a joke (that is, hear it or read it) with our senses, but we "*get it*," or grasp its point, with our reason.

(2) We may become familiar with triangles by looking at pictures of triangles drawn on blackboards or printed in books, but the realization that triangles *must* have three sides is something we grasp with our reason.

(3) We may read the definition of a prime number in a dictionary, or a teacher may tell us what a prime number is (*prime number* = an integer that can be evenly divided by no other whole number save itself and 1), but it is by using our reason that we see that 2 is—and must be—the only even prime number.

Definition of Rationalism

A rationalist holds that reason is the source of all human knowledge. (There is also a less extreme form of rationalism that holds that reason is the *main* source of knowledge, or that reason is the source of the most important kind of knowledge.)

Rationalism and Mathematics

Most of the important rationalists, including Plato (*c*.428–347 B.C.) and Descartes (1596–1650), were also mathematicians. This is not just an accident, since rationalism views mathematics as the *model*, or *paradigm* (or *best example*), of human knowledge. Although there are many kinds of mathematical truths, they all have one very important feature in common: they are *necessary truths*. Necessary truths don't just happen to be true: they must be true; they have to be true; they cannot not be true; there are no circumstances which would or could make them false.

2 + 2 = 4 as an Example of a Necessary Truth

Consider the very elementary arithmetical equation, $2 + 2 = 4$. Although you and I may have been taught this by being shown such things as the aggregation of two blocks with two other blocks, rationalists correctly argue that $2 + 2 = 4$ does not depend on such experiences. It is not a generalization from our experiences of aggregation, or bringing things together. If it were a generalization from experience, it would be subject to correction based on further experience. (Thus, someone might reasonably make the generalization "All metals are solid at room temperature" before encountering mercury.) It would, in other words, be *corrigible*. But we do not regard $2 + 2 = 4$ as corrigible.

An example should make this clear. Not all aggregations are, in fact, additive. Two quarts of pure alcohol mixed with two quarts of water do not yield four quarts of liquid, but slightly less. (There is a perfectly good explanation of why this happens: molecules of different sizes slip between each other, much as—on a macroscopic level—do marbles and sand.) But we do not regard the alcohol/water case (or the marbles/sand case, for that matter) as showing that there is something wrong with arithmetic. $2 + 2 = 4$ is not a prediction about what you get when various things are brought together, mixed, or what have you; $2 + 2 = 4$ is about numbers, and what it says about numbers is necessarily true.

Evaluation of Rationalism

The rationalist's account of mathematical truths is much better than that provided by competitive accounts based on experience, since it can make sense of their necessity and incorrigibility. This does not mean, however, that rationalism is the best all-round view of our cognitive life. For it is not true, as rationalism claims, that all truths either are like or should be like the necessary truths of mathematics. What rationalism does, in effect, is to replace the second condition in the standard analysis of knowledge ("It is true that p") with the unrealistically strong condition, "It is *necessarily* true that p." In contemporary discussions of necessary truth, "necessarily" is often symbolized by "□." (□ is one of a small number of what are called *modal operators*.) Making the modal status of $2 + 2 = 4$ explicit, we would write "□ $2 + 2 = 4$."

Some of the things that we know do have the modal status indicated by "□." But there are many other things that we know that do not have the modal status indicated by the *necessity operator*. Suppose the dog is in the backyard. If I believe that the dog is in the backyard and have the right kind of reasons for my belief, then I know the dog is in the backyard. But the following is a false statement: □ the dog is in the backyard. It is not true, even when the dog is in the backyard, that the dog *has to be* in the backyard. Even if it is highly probable that the dog is in the backyard (because the dog always is; because the dog is fenced in; etc.), still something might have happened—for example, an earthquake—that would have resulted in the dog's being someplace else. In any case, it can't be a necessary truth that the dog is in the backyard because it is not a necessary truth that the particular dog we are talking about came into existence in the first place.

"A Priori," "Analytic," and "Synthetic"

Three widely used terms will help explain the difference between rationalists and nonrationalists.

1. *A Priori.* The Latin phrase "*a priori*" means, literally, first or prior, but in discussions of rationalism it has come to mean prior to, or independent of, experience. Rationalists certainly hold that there is such a thing as *a priori* knowledge. But so do many nonrationalists. To distinguish rationalists from nonrationalists requires the concept of an *analytic truth* or an *analytic statement.*

2. *Analytic.* A statement is *analytic* (and the truth it expresses is an analytic truth) IFF it is true by definition. "Bachelors are unmarried" and "Triangles have three sides" are examples of analytic statements.

3. *Synthetic.* Any truth that is not a truth by definition is a *synthetic truth.* "The dog is in the backyard," when true, states a synthetic truth because it is not a consequence of the definition of *dog, backyard,* or any other word in the sentence "The dog is in the backyard."

Rationalists and nonrationalists agree that analytic truths are known *a priori.* That the statement "Bachelors are unmarried" is true will be grasped by anyone who understands it. And anyone who thinks it is necessary to take surveys of bachelors to discover whether they are unmarried labors under an extreme misconception. However, rationalists—and only rationalists—hold that we have *a priori* knowledge of synthetic truths. Rationalists do not ordinarily claim to know *a priori* things like the dog is in the backyard; rather, they tend to belittle such knowledge as being hardly worthy of the name.

An example of something a rationalist might claim to know *a priori* is that *every event has a cause.* We must be careful to distinguish this from the analytic truth that *every effect has a cause.* If we do know *a priori* that "every event has a cause" or, in other words, that "every event is an effect," this would be an example of *synthetic a priori* knowledge.

Rationalism and Mathematical Reality

Nonrationalists regard the truths of mathematics as truths by definition (or as consequences of such truths). In the nonrationalist view, our knowledge of such truths is an instance of *a priori* knowledge of analytic truths. "$2 + 2 = 4$" is true because of the definitions of "2," "4," "+," and "=." In contrast, rationalists regard the truths of mathematics as synthetic truths. Mathematical truths, in the rationalist view, are about a separate, autonomous, and irreducible domain of mathematical reality about which humans, using reason in its purest form, can make discoveries.

Innateness

Although it is not part of the definition of rationalism, many rationalists have held that some part of human knowledge is *innate* (or *inborn*). What makes the *innateness* hypothesis (also occasionally called the *nativist* hypothesis) attractive is that it seems plausible to hold that a human being would have to know something in order to learn something. Starting from scratch and learning everything from experience doesn't seem possible. This is argued, for the important case of language, by the contemporary linguist Noam Chomsky (b. 1928).

It is probably not true that we are born with any knowledge, in the sense of "propositional" knowledge. It is reasonable, however, to claim that our brain/nervous system is structured at birth in a way that gives us a certain built-in know-how. Sometimes, experience is pictured as writing on a blank slate, or *tabula rasa*. The picture of the human mind as such a blank slate, devoid of innate ideas and principles, is associated with classical British empiricism, in particular with John Locke (1632–1704).

Empiricism

Etymology

The word *empiricism* comes from the Greek *empeiria*, meaning experience. Although the word *experience* is used in English in a variety of ways (even allowing us to speak of a purely internal "thinking something through" or "realizing something" as an "experience"), in discussions of empiricism, experience always means *sensory experience*—that is, experience that depends in some essential way on the operation of one or more of our senses.

Definition of Empiricism

An empiricist holds that experience is the source of all human knowledge. (There are also less extreme forms of empiricism that hold that experience is the main source of knowledge, or that experience is the source of the most important kind of knowledge.)

Empiricism and Observation

Empiricists start with the very plausible idea that knowledge of the world must be based on observation of the world. For example, no amount of thinking will let me know whether or not the dog is in the backyard; I find this out only through some form of observation. Commonly, I simply *see* that the dog is in the backyard; however, other senses might also play a role in my observation.

How Our Senses Work

Although we ordinarily take our senses for granted, empiricists— relying on science—offer an explanation of how our senses work. In so doing, they show why our senses provide us with information about the world. Let us sketch this explanation for *vision*, which is probably our most important sensory "modality," with respect to both the quantity and quality of the information provided. When I see the dog in the backyard, the process starts with light reflected from the surface of the dog. The rest of the story is somewhat complicated. In brief, though, light is focused by the eye's lens onto the retina, where receptor cells send impulses to the optic nerve. In the process, light energy has been converted into complexly patterned electrochemical signals. The optic nerve carries these signals to the brain where—in a manner still only imperfectly understood—they are decoded, and produce the appropriate visual experience. Seeing gives us information—in this case, about the dog's whereabouts—because the dog *causes* the experience.

From the point of view of the empiricist, the rationalist who thinks the mind by pure thought can come up with substantial knowledge of the world is asking us to believe in a kind of miracle. The empiricist, it must be granted, is giving an account in terms of processes that are familiar and—at least in broad outline—well understood. Although the empiricist view of the senses captures something that is obviously correct about the way experience is caused, there are still problems with which the empiricist has to deal.

Sensation and Perception

It is sometimes claimed, in objection to empiricism, that we do not really see particular objects such as dogs and cats, tables and chairs. All that vision delivers (in the dog case, let's say) is a brown patch that moves around in our visual field. Our senses, in this view, provide us with sense-specific sensations (colored patches, sounds, etc.) that are sometimes referred to as *sense data*, or *sensa*. From these sense data, we then "infer" or "construct" the ordinary world.

In fact, though, our senses do not operate in isolation from the rest of our nervous system. We really do see the dog, because *perception* involves not only "photographic" registration, but all our recognitional and classificatory abilities as well. My eyes don't see; *I* see, using eyes plus brain. The term *perception* is ordinarily reserved for "intelligent" seeing, hearing, and so forth. Sensation is then one—and only one— factor in perception.

Naive Empiricism

Contemporary empiricists generally acknowledge that sense experience is only one factor in the production of substantial knowledge; sensory experience is then viewed as a necessary—but not a sufficient—condition for such knowledge. Again, contemporary empiricists have generally abandoned the blank slate (or *tabula rasa*) picture: the mind (reason, intellect) is acknowledged as an active partner in the production of knowledge. The view that we are the passive recipients of information, and that knowledge arises whenever we simply open our eyes and look at the world about us, is today universally dismissed as *naive empiricism*. (*Naive* here is a pejorative term, often used polemically to denigrate views regarded as simplistic—views that do not take into account some essential subtlety or complexity.)

Logical Empiricism

Although some empiricists, including John Stuart Mill (1806–1873), have attempted to explain even the necessary truths of logic and mathematics as generalizations from experience, contemporary empiricists usually make a sharp distinction between analytic truths— which are *a priori*, or entirely independent of experience—and nonanalytic truths, which do depend on experience or observation. (See the definitions of *a priori* and *analytic* earlier in this chapter.)

A Posteriori

The term "*a posteriori*" is the antonym of *a priori*. In Latin, it simply means "after" (approximately), but in discussions of rationalism and empiricism it always means dependent on particular experiences, observations, or experiments. We can state the position of the contemporary logical empiricists as follows: All *nonanalytic* or *synthetic* or *substantial* knowledge is necessarily *a posteriori*.

Knowledge by Acquaintance/Knowledge by Description

In considering the role of experience in human cognitive life, philosophers have often distinguished between those things of which we are directly aware (and, accordingly, know in a first-hand way [*knowledge by acquaintance*]), and those things that we know based upon descriptions—that is, indirectly, or by hearsay (*knowledge by description*). This distinction is, at best, relative and imprecise, since the concept of *direct awareness* cannot be explained in precise, non-comparative terms: it is always a case of being more directly aware of one thing than of something else. It's interesting to note that some things really seem to require acquaintance for adequate knowledge— knowledge of colors, for example, or of works of art. Other things, we can know with various degrees of adequacy either by acquaintance or by description—people being a good example here. Finally, there are many things that we believe to exist, but of which we are not and cannot be directly aware. Electrons and viruses are obvious examples.

Science

Etymology

The word *science* comes from the Latin *scientia* ("knowledge"). At one time, science was used in English to cover every sort of knowledge; however, this is no longer the case. (It should be added that, in ancient Greek, the word *sophia* was similarly used to cover every sort of knowledge, including that which we associate with science in the modern sense. Until well into the modern period, the word *philosophy* itself was also used to refer to what is now a part of science; thus, Isaac Newton (1642–1727), whom we think of today primarily as a physicist, was in his own time referred to as a "natural philosopher.")

Definition of Science

Although most of us have a rough idea of what science is, and could even provide a listlike characterization—"things like physics, chemistry, and biology, plus, maybe, things like psychology, economics, and sociology"—there is no simple way of defining science. Certainly, there is no single feature, or even small set of features, common to all the sciences. From the beginning of this century through the end of the 1950s, philosophers of science tried to work out some abstract, all- embracing conception of science. Today, however, they tend to regard the concept of science as a *family-resemblance* concept—a concept that applies by virtue of many partially overlapping areas of similarity. This contemporary approach considers science in terms of four interrelated factors: the practice of science, its history, its existence as an institution, and its methodology.

Science as a Practice

Instead of thinking of science as a body of knowledge to be defined (fairly abstractly) in terms of vocabulary or subject matter, contemporary approaches to science stress the fact that science is something that human beings do—a human practice. We could indeed define science as "that which scientists do." This might seem purely circular, since we would have to go on and define a scientist as "someone who does science," but in fact there is little difficulty in picking out the scientists. Then, having picked them out, we can make detailed studies of what they do.

The Relevance of History

Science has a long and complicated history. Today, it is generally held that we cannot understand the nature of contemporary science without studying its history. In practice, this involves studying the histories of many particular sciences. Our best bet for gaining an understanding of a contemporary science is to look at its historical development. Similarly, if we wish to understand the relation between two sciences, the most fruitful approach is to look at their historical connections. In any case, it is important to bear in mind that, when philosophers speak of understanding a science, they are talking about an outsider's, or nonparticipant's, grasp of that science, which involves seeing its place in the whole range of human intellectual activities. That is to say, they are *not* talking about the kind of insider, or participant, understanding of science that scientists themselves possess.

Institutionalization

In the course of studying science as a historically developing practice, we cannot fail to notice that all sciences have become more and more institutionalized. A scientist is not an isolated thinker, after all, but a participant in a university or college science department, or in a research institute. He or she has colleagues with whom information is exchanged both formally and informally, and with whom he or she collaborates in experiment and research. There is also, for each scientific specialty, what is called the "invisible college"—the totality of scientists, wherever they may be located, who regard each other as doing the same kind of science. Members of the invisible college keep in contact by phone, by letter, by exchanging "preprints" of papers, and by contributing to and reading the same scientific journals.

Scientific Papers. Whatever else it may produce, scientific activity's common end product is scientific papers. In addition to their informal circulation prior to publication, these papers are sent to certain appropriate journals where they are subject to a process of evaluation known as "peer review." Papers that are judged worthy are then published. A paper's importance is determined by how often it is subsequently "cited" (or referred to) by other workers in the field.

It is only by actually reading a broad range of scientific papers, or—even better!—by visiting actual scientific laboratories and similar research installations that one can appreciate the *diversity* of scientific work. Short of that, a student wishing to get a sense of what contemporary science is up to might profit from a look at the wide range of papers in *Science*, the weekly publication of the American Association for the Advancement of Science, which is available in most libraries.

Consensus and Conspiracy Theories of Scientific Practice. It is sometimes suggested that the verdict as to what counts as scientifically valuable depends on nothing more than group agreement, or *consensus*. However, while it is indeed true that scientists aim at consensus, they achieve this by rationally persuasive arguments in support of their views. Conspiracy theories—which may be considered undemocratic versions of consensus theories—hold that a few powerful figures in each scientific field act as "gatekeepers," controlling access to journals, jobs, and research funds.

It is true that scientists as a rule are inclined to take recognized authorities very seriously, and that science is no more immune to "power brokers" who enjoy throwing their weight around than is any other area of human endeavor; nevertheless, given the way science is institutionalized, no individual or group within science could promote or shelter the effects of "bad" science even if he or it wanted to. (True, the power of a totalitarian state has occasionally been used to redirect or otherwise interfere with the normal process of scientific research, but this does not render suspect science as it is ordinarily institutionalized.) Work has to be published. It is then subject to scrutiny by individuals whose own careers will be enhanced by the detection of any errors or inadequacies. Thus, it is the institutional forms of science that keep its practitioners honest, and do so by relying on no higher motivation than ordinary human competitiveness. (All of this is not to deny that many scientists are motivated by a combination of disinterested curiosity and a single-minded devotion to problem-solving for its own sake.)

Methodological Pluralism

In the past, discussions of science tended to emphasize what was referred to as the *scientific method*. It turns out, however, that there is no single method shared by all the sciences. Of course, all scientists should be logical and careful, should check their results, should look always for the best explanation, should take note of whether their various predictions turn out to be correct, and so forth; but these general guidelines—which in any case apply to many nonscientific intellectual activities—do not amount to a scientific method. There are, rather, many methods, procedures, and techniques, existing at every level of specificity and detail: techniques for staining slides, procedures for dissecting out the hippocampus of a frog, methods for getting a supersaturated solution to crystallize. Techniques, procedures, and methods such as these are indispensable to the daily advancement of science.

There is, furthermore, no technique for coming up with new scientific theories. At a given time in a given science there are likely to be promising approaches, reasonable conjectures, experiments likely to produce interesting results: none of these, however, can provide a failureproof recipe for successful work.

Aims of Science

Although individual scientists may aim at nothing higher than advancing their careers, making money, or winning the Nobel Prize, the only way they can hope to do this is by advancing science itself. This means, in essence, that they have to discover something about nature that was not previously known. (Bear in mind that even a new explanation of a familiar phenomenon involves discovering something about that phenomenon that was not previously known.) It is customary to distinguish "pure science," which is interested in knowledge for its own sake regardless of whether it ever comes to have any practical application, from "applied science," which is interested in the practical/technical/engineering uses of knowledge. (We should add that much work that has been done in the spirit of pure science has later turned out to have great practical importance.) As to the aim of pure science, we can describe it as the creation of new knowledge.

Observation, Description, Theory

Naive empiricists—Francis Bacon (1561–1626), most famously—thought that what made science science was the fact that—unlike philosophers, who speculated about nature and concocted idle fantasies—scientists observed nature and patiently gathered their observations together to form a true account of things: a composite of all, and of nothing but, the facts. The problem with this view is that there is an infinity of observations that might be made and recorded. A true description of the world would be infinitely long, and about as interesting as the telephone directory. One could, for example, begin to describe the shape of each grain of sand on a particular beach. No one, not even Bacon, conceived of the task of science in quite those terms.

It did, however, take a while for scientists themselves (as well as philosophical science-watchers) to grasp clearly that observation, in order to be meaningful, has to be theory-guided. Many people continue to think that observations must always come first, after and based on which theories can be developed. It is generally the case, however, that it is some theory that tells the scientist exactly which observations are worth making. In addition, of course, theory also provides the vocabulary in terms of which observations are described. Objects, events, experimental situations, and the like have infinitely many observable (and describable) properties; it is theories that determine which of these many properties are *relevant* for a given unit of scientific work.

Theory and Explanation

Etymologically, the word *theory* comes from the Greek *theoria*, which means "seeing together." (In point of fact, theory is probably just as much a "family-resemblance" concept as science itself.) It is also the case, for better or worse, that *theory* is used, overlappingly, with such terms as *hypothesis*, *law*, and *model*. Still, we can venture this much of a definition: a theory is a set of general principles that explain a range of observed phenomena. For example, one may observe that polar bears are white. The whiteness of polar bears is a phenomenon. Further, the properties of being a polar bear and being white are *empirically correlated*. So far, so good, but no explanation, just description ("That's how the world is"). The theory of natural selection, among the many things it explains, explains the whiteness of polar bears: white bears have a competitive edge, and a survival advantage in their white world.

Having theories is very beneficial. This can be understood in terms of (1) anchoring empirical correlations in nomic regularities, and (2) enabling us to make intelligent predictions.

Empirical Correlation and Nomic Regularity

Property *A* and property *B* are "empirically correlated" just in case anything observed to have property *A* (being a polar bear, say) is also observed to have property *B* (being white). (Sometimes, particularly in the social sciences, two properties are said to be positively correlated if they co-occur not invariably, but simply more often than pure chance would warrant.)

The statement "All polar bears are white" is arrived at by *induction*. The "inductive argument" involved might be stated as follows:

All observed polar bears are white;

Therefore, all polar bears are white.

As in this example, all inductive arguments rely on premises stating truths about some *sample* or *subset* of a larger class in order to establish a truth about *all* members of the larger class. It is generally recognized that, by themselves, inductive arguments are rather weak, involving as they do something like a leap of faith. Two things can be done about the weakness of an inductive argument, however. One is to try to make sure that your sample is a *fair*, or *representative*, sample. (In the social sciences, which depend on the results of sophisticated samplings of public opinion, "representativeness theory" has been highly developed in an elaborate statistical form.)

A much better way of overcoming the weakness of inductive arguments (and the riskiness implicit in mere empirical correlations) is to discover a *nomic regularity* that supports the empirical correlation. *Nomic* comes from the Greek *nomos*, meaning law (and which, like *law* in English, can mean either "law of nature" or "law of the land"). Philosophers of science speak of "nomic necessity"; this is weaker than logical necessity, but much stronger than mere correlation. Mere correlation just tells us that certain properties happen to occur together, but they don't have to. Nomic necessity, where applicable, shows us why the properties observed as going together *have to* go together. Thus, if evolutionary theorists are right, polar bears have to be white. Even if it isn't a "law of nature" that polar bears have to be white, their being white is a direct consequence of laws of nature (the very laws of nature that make up the theory of evolution, as it happens). If we now understand why polar bears are white (that is, as a matter of nomic necessity), we don't have to worry that the next polar bear to be observed might not be white.

There are people (though few of them scientists) who think that the theory of evolution is (or might turn out to be) incorrect. For the benefit of these people, let's provide a totally uncontroversial example of nomic necessity. The physical/chemical properties of any element are explained as nomically necessary on the basis of the atomic structure of that element. It would be pointless—indeed, wildly misconceived—to test further samples of iron or lead or sodium to see whether they have the standard physical/chemical properties of that element. If a sample is a sample of iron (or lead, or sodium), it *must* have the standard properties of iron (or lead, or sodium).

Prediction

Another great advantage of theory is that it allows us to make predictions. Even before the development of science, humans were able to make some predictions: the regularity of night and day, of the phases of the moon, of the seasons, has allowed a degree of prediction from time immemorial. Nevertheless, science has, of course, greatly extended the range of our predictive abilities.

It is, furthermore, generally regarded as a criterion of good science to be predictive. (Of course, such sciences as geology and archeology are primarily *retrodictive*—reconstructing the past on the basis of present evidence.) Take the case of evolutionary theory. It not only explains such conditions as the whiteness of polar bears, but it also predicts a general fitness of organisms to their environment. Where environments change in ways that affect survival, evolutionary theory predicts a change in organisms. Since evolution is usually a slow process, it is not generally observable. In a particularly striking case within living memory, though, peppered moths in the industrial north of England darkened as their environment got sootier, just as evolutionary theory predicts.

Predictive success varies from science to science, however. Astronomy, for example, gives us very good predictions about the positions of stars and planets, of eclipses, and of such periodic phenomena as Halley's comet. Meteorology, the science of the weather, though based on the very solid and strongly predictive sciences of physics and chemistry, is notoriously unsuccessful, especially in terms of long-range forecasting. In the case of the weather, incidentally, there is almost nothing we don't understand; we even know why, in terms of the mathematics of incredibly complicated weather systems, we can't predict the weather.

Falsifiability

Generally speaking, we take for granted that prediction is a good thing, and that it confers a great survival advantage on the members of our species; however, this does not fully explain its importance to pure—as opposed to applied—scientists. For pure science, it is by way of its predictions that a theory is tested. If a theory can't be tested because it doesn't issue in testable predictions, the theory, so long as it remains untestable, is worthless. Traditional accounts of science emphasize *confirmation* of theory by observation and experiment. This is a legitimate way of thinking about the matter as long as we are careful to remember that "confirmed" really means "not falsified."

Confirmation and Falsification. We can explain the logical relations between confirmation and falsification as follows. (For the sake of simplicity, we will use an empirical correlation rather than a real theory.) The "theory" that polar bears have to be white predicts that the next polar bear I see will be white. Suppose, then, that the next polar bear I see is indeed white. I may say that this confirms the theory, but, of course, it doesn't conclusively *establish* the theory, since the polar bear after that one—the *next* next one—may after all turn out to be nonwhite. And, if the next polar bear I see turns out to be nonwhite, that one observation conclusively falsifies the theory. So we see that theories can't be confirmed all at once—on the contrary, our confidence grows bit by bit—but they can be falsified in one fell swoop.

The Paradox of Confirmation. The logic of confirmation is complex. This can be illustrated by the so-called *paradox of confirmation*, also known as the *ravens paradox*. The generalization "All ravens are black" is logically equivalent to "All nonblack things are nonravens." Since evidence that supports one statement should also support any logically equivalent statement, the existence of a white polar bear (a nonblack nonraven) should support the generalization that all ravens are black. Views that regard falsifiability, rather than confirmation, as fundamental avoid the paradox of confirmation. A polar bear's being white, unlike a raven's being white, fails to falsify the generalization in question.

The Best Explanation. It is sometimes remarked by those who have studied the history of science that scientists don't really give up theories on the basis of a single falsifier. This is correct. A scientist sometimes has a great deal of confidence in a certain theory—confidence that is fully justified rationally—and he or she would be foolish indeed to give up on the theory because of one apparent falsifier. It could be that a single observation was wrong; it could be that the experiment was not correctly performed. In the real world, scientists have hangovers and fights with their spouses; chemicals are mislabeled; there is dirt on the glassware; and so on.

That said, though, it is still true that a scientist should always seek the *best explanation* of what has happened. This involves taking account of such factors as simplicity, adequacy, and overall explanatory compatibility. In the case of an apparent falsifier, the explanation is not always that the original theory was wrong. Facts that don't agree with theory-based nomic necessity are referred to as *anomalies*. If anomalies build up against an established theory, scientists may at first try to explain the anomalies away. If the anomalies are stubborn, however, and refuse to go away, a search for a new and better theory may ensue. Such a new and better theory would be one that not only explained everything the old theory explained, but also showed that what looked like anomalies from the point of view of the old theory were nomically regular after all.

Paradigms, Normal Science, and Scientific Revolutions. Much of the contemporary discussion of science and its history carried on by both philosophers and historians of science makes use of the term *paradigm.* (The word comes from the Greek *paradeigma,* meaning pattern.) Thomas Kuhn (b. 1922), who introduced the term into contemporary discussion, meant by paradigm the total set of theories, habits of mind, intellectual and technical skills and abilities that, taken together, define a way of doing a particular science at a given time. Thus, "normal science" is science done under the governance of the dominant paradigm. The paradigm suggests the problems to be solved and sets the standards for normal (or more or less routine) science.

When enough anomalies build up against an established paradigm, a "scientific revolution" may take place. This involves the replacement of one paradigm with another. Although the terms introduced by Kuhn are widely used, there is less than full agreement about the similarities between scientific revolutions and political revolutions. There are, in any case, two interrelated questions under active discussion: *first,* how discontinuous is the history of science?; *second,* how much irrationality is involved in the shift from one paradigm to another?

Falsifiability and Pseudoscience. Genuine science is falsifiable. It has been suggested—most emphatically by Sir Karl Popper (b. 1902)— that certain intellectual systems that pretend to the status of science should be rejected as *pseudosciences,* on the grounds that they do not eventuate in falsifiable predictions. (A pseudo-X is anything that appears to be an X but turns out not to be.) The two systems Popper mentioned were Marxism and classical Freudian psychoanalysis. If they are genuine sciences, the thinking goes, they should be able to specify what would count as falsifying or disconfirming them. (Good theories have many potential but no actual falsifiers.) According to Popper (and it should be noted that many people strongly disagree with him), neither Marxism nor Freudian psychoanalysis passes the falsifiability test.

Whatever the final judgment on Marxism and Freudian psychoanalysis, it is worth remarking that both philosophers and ordinary people often make claims that seem to be about the world but are actually unfalsifiable. People sometimes claim, for example, that all human action is selfish. People who say this will not in general accept ordinary counterexamples (such as volunteering to serve in a hospital). In fact, they will not accept any possible evidence as showing that their view of human nature is mistaken. The way a counterexample might be dismissed is illustrated by the following: Mary is helping out at the hospital of her own free will, so helping out must be something she wants to do—and doing what you want to do is selfish. A claim that allows all potential counterexamples (or falsifiers) to be dismissed in this way is a pseudoclaim. Making such claims is, in fact, doing something very much like practicing "bad" science.

Theoretical Terms and Theoretical Entities

Almost all contemporary scientific theories contain terms that refer to entities that cannot be directly observed. Such terms are called *theoretical terms*, and the items they refer to are called *theoretical entities*. No one has ever seen an electron, or has had any other kind of direct experience of, or knowledge by acquaintance with, electrons. Yet contemporary physical theory confidently refers to electrons.

This might perhaps be surprising to a naive empiricist who thinks of science as simply coordinating and systematizing sensory experience. It is not surprising if we remember that science is supposed, not merely to describe our experiences, but also to explain them. Contemporary physics refers to electrons because the theory that best explains all observable phenomena is a theory in which electrons play an important role. In the laboratory, the scientists can see a track of droplets of water inside a Wilson cloud chamber. Why does that track appear? What caused it? The best explanation (given certain circumstances) is that the track of droplets was precipitated by the passage of an electron.

It should be noted, finally, that some entities—for example, certain single atoms and microorganisms—that were formerly postulated entirely on the basis of theory have been subsequently observed.

Status of Theoretical Entities

Philosophers of science do not agree about the status of theoretical entities. Are electrons real? Are they real, that is, in the same way that bricks and rocks and tables and chairs are real? Of course, parts of real things are real, but the question is whether we should view electrons as parts or components of such macroscopic objects as bricks and rocks. Many answers, some highly qualified, have been given to this kind of question, but all fall into two broad categories: *instrumentalist/pragmatist* and *realist*.

Instrumentalism/Pragmatism. According to this view (actually, a whole range of views), the main purpose of a scientific theory is to make predictions. Although theories may refer to various entities, this is in some way secondary—albeit picturesque and possibly psychologically helpful—compared to the mathematical equations on which predictions are actually based. Labeling the view *instrumentalism* is appropriate, since it views a scientific theory as an instrument, principally mathematical, for generating predictions; labeling the view *pragmatism* is also appropriate, because it emphasizes the *use of theories* in the generation of predictions. Although instrumentalist/pragmatist views were once popular, few contemporary philosophers of science (and almost no contemporary scientists) believe that anything in this range of views could possibly be correct.

Realism. The word *realism* is used in philosophy in a number of loosely related senses; however, we are concerned here only with *scientific realism*, according to which entities required by a successful (that is, established) scientific theory are real. So, electrons really exist. More, they exist in the same sense of "exist" that applies to bricks and rocks and tables and chairs. Working scientists are almost all scientific realists, as are most philosophers of science. There are many arguments for realism. We'll look at three that are important in current philosophical discussions of science.

1. Microbes and Microscopes. At a certain stage in the history of science, there was some speculation that invisible organisms existed in a variety of materials and places. The presence of these entities, it was suggested, might explain certain known phenomena. An amateur scientist and lens maker, Anton van Leeuwenhoek (1632–1723), was the first to report seeing such tiny creatures. Employing a crude, single-lens microscope, he saw what he called "animalcules" in a drop of rain water. What is more, later and better microscopes confirmed, extended, and refined his observations.

Before microscopes came along, what we now call microbes were but theoretical entities. In the realist view, this means that the microbes were there—in reality, in the world, in the pond—just as much as water-lilies and frogs were—only we did not have *perceptual access* to them. Microscopes provided us with that perceptual access. What was there all along could now be seen. With the development of better as well as new kinds of microscopes—for example, electron microscopes and acoustic microscopes—other entities that were postulated on the basis of theory came to be observed. (A similar story could be told in terms of the development of telescopes, including radio telescopes.)

The microscopy/microbes example is not intended to show that we should be realists about anything at all that someone guesses might exist, or is simply looking for and hoping to find; many claims on the order of There-must-be-such-and-such-out-there are false. All our example seeks to show is that a person who is a nonrealist about entities that we have good reasons to think exist (but which we cannot, presently, observe) should be prepared to argue why this case is different in principle from the microscopy/microbes case.

2. Artifacts and Real Phenomena. An *artifact* is defined as something that is made by humans. Scientists, when they are performing experiments, use the term *artifact* to refer to some effect produced by the experimental situation itself. (Here, artifacts are contrasted with whatever "real" phenomena the experiment may reveal.) The very conception of experiment as a way of *discovery* expresses a realistic view of the scientific project. Again, this is not a "proof" of realism, but rather an argument that realism better fits a contrast built into actual scientific practice than do competitive views.

3. The Argument from the Best Explanation. The most powerful argument for scientific realism is also the simplest. It holds that the best—i.e., most plausible, sensible, compelling—explanation of why the world behaves *as if* entities postulated by scientific theories existed is that these entities do in fact exist. It would be something of a miracle for a theory postulating the existence of electrons to be so successful in generating predictions about the world unless the world is indeed really composed of such things as electrons.

Theory-Ladenness and Incommensurability

The sophisticated picture of science that emphasizes the importance of theories has one curious consequence: the very language used to express observations and to describe experimental results is determined by a particular theory. The language used by a scientist committed to a particular theory is said to be *theory-laden* ("loaded with theory"). If this is so, it appears that there is no way to compare two scientific theories. Theory *A* has its vocabulary, which determines what it is talking about; theory *B* has *its* vocabulary, which means that theory *B* is talking about something else. Therefore, theory *A* and theory *B* cannot be directly compared, since that would only be possible if they were talking more or less adequately about the same thing.

Theory *A* and theory *B*, in this view, are said to be *incommensurable* ("not capable of being measured by a common standard or metric"). Despite concerns related to incommensurability, however, almost all scientists (and most philosophers of science) believe that science does indeed make progress. And of course this involves the idea that later theories can, after all, be compared with earlier theories.

One explanation of why theories can be compared is that incommensurability is only partial. Two scientists, one earlier and one later, committed to different theories, may nevertheless share a large extratheoretical vocabulary. They can, therefore, despite incommensurability, be talking about the same world.

Causality

We understand things by discovering their causes. This idea, which goes back at least to Aristotle (384–322 B.C.), is firmly entrenched in any common-sense view of the world. Does science explain the world by searching out the causes of natural phenomena? Views of science emphasizing empirical correlation (*positivism* is sometimes used as a vague label for this family of views) tend to hold that the concept of causality is not needed in science, and that any statement of the form A *caused* B goes beyond anything that evidence could support.

Perhaps the most famous expression of this view was by David Hume (1711–1776). Hume's example is also famous: If a billiard ball collides with a stationary ball that then begins to move, we may say that the first ball *caused* the second to move, but all we are *entitled* to say is that the movement of the second ball *came after* the movement of the first. When this is observed to happen on a great many occasions, we may come to expect the movement of the second ball, but the movement of the second is not really necessary.

Hume's account of the billiard balls and all subsequent "positivist" accounts of science simply leave out *explanation by theory*. In the case of the billiard balls, we have a physical theory—classical mechanics— that explains the movement of the second ball, given the movement of the first. It is not *logically impossible*, but it is *nomically impossible* for the second ball not to move when hit in a certain way by the first. Causes determine outcomes with nomic necessity. It is part of the standard conception of causality that, given a set of initial conditions and all the laws of nature, there is only one possible outcome. (A possible qualification is considered in the next paragraph.)

The Uncertainty Principle

Although much ordinary science proceeds on the basis of a *causally deterministic* view of nature, there have been developments in twentieth-century physics that challenge this view. In 1927, Werner Heisenberg (1901–1976) stated what has come to be known as the *Heisenberg uncertainty principle*: the position and momentum of a subatomic particle (for example, an electron) cannot both be known with certainty at any given time, since the process of establishing either always affects the other. Alternatively, variables specifying position and momentum of a particle cannot both take definite values simultaneously.

Understanding what this means, intellectual prudence suggests, is probably possible only for a physicist versed in the subtleties of quantum mechanics. However, it is often interpreted, both by physicists and outsiders, as making nature, in some essential way, indeterministic. We can't pin nature down, at least at the subatomic level, in the way we had long supposed possible. If the Heisenberg uncertainty principle gives us an ultimate insight into nature (and Einstein thought it didn't, although most contemporary physicists think it does), then it is *probability*, rather than necessity, that is at the heart of things.

Social Sciences

Are Social Sciences Possible?

It is sometimes asked whether there can be social (or, as they are sometimes also called, human) sciences. True, we are used to the idea of humans studying nature; but can humans study themselves? Perhaps the best way to answer this question is to point to the actually flourishing human sciences: psychology, anthropology, sociology, economics. Surely, what is actual must be possible.

Perhaps this is too facile, though: what looks like a science, what pretends to be a science, might turn out to be a pseudoscience. Can psychologists really predict human behavior? Can anthropologists explain the diversity of custom? Can sociology tell us anything about society that we didn't already know from reading the "important" novels? Can economics do *anything*? These may be framed as rhetorical questions, but each really deserves an answer based on a survey of the field in question. Here, however, we can consider only a few matters of principle.

Why Not?

Since science is a family-resemblance concept taking in a great many quite distinct cognitive styles and practices (even within the area of the physical sciences), there seems to be no good reason not to extend that concept to the social (or human) sciences. As already emphasized, there is really only one hard-core requirement for science: the construction of theories. We should remember, though, that nothing qualifies as a scientific theory unless it explains some domain of reality. We should also remember that no theory is worth taking seriously as a scientific theory unless it can be tested.

Explanation and Prediction

In the natural sciences, explanation and prediction go hand in hand. This is true even of the less predictive (i.e., historical and "retrodictive") sciences such as geology. Should the social sciences give up the attempt to predict and content themselves with "after the fact" interpretation? The answer is that most social scientists do not want to give up

prediction; they are concerned to offer something more than a historically compelling account of various human groups. This does not mean
that social scientists expect their disciplines to develop in the direction
of physics, say: an adequate, fully predictive social science will undoub-
tedly be statistical in character. What is crucial is not whether a science
produces laws that have the form "If A, then definitely B" or "If A, then
probably B," but whether the science can explain the relation between
A and B in terms of a satisfactory theory.

Choice

What is in the back of many people's minds when they wonder
whether there can be such a thing as a social science is the idea that
human behavior is the result of choice. We sometimes express this idea
by saying that humans are free, or have free will. (For a more detailed
discussion of human freedom, see *Free Will as a Metaphysical Problem*
in chapter 4.) There certainly appears to be some tension between the
idea of a causal explanation (which shows why something had to
happen) and the idea of choice (which at least suggests that there was
an available alternative). One way of dealing with this tension is to say
that our view of ourselves as having choices—choices in the sense of
genuinely alternative causal pathways branching out at the moment of
choice—is simply an illusion. Another way of dealing with this tension
is to admit choice, but to deny that choice requires alternatives in any
way that would violate causal determinism. There seems to be no
well-established consensus among philosophers about how to reconcile
explanation and choice, or—if irreconcilable—about which one should
be given up.

Prediction and Folk Psychology

Folk psychology is the term used for the theory we all share (even
if we are not scientists), and which we use to understand and predict the
behavior of the people around us. Unlike a full-fledged scientific theory,
folk psychology is mostly inexplicit or tacit. What is most striking about
folk psychology, however, is just how successful it really is. Though
we often say—though some people *predictably* say—that human nature
is unpredictable, most of our predictions, in the rough-and-ready way
folk psychology makes them, turn out to be correct!

Suppose you give a party. Most people you invite will probably show up. Although each person you invite could decide (that is, choose) not to come, and though most likely one or two *will* choose not to come, the majority of people will come. Or, consider that several million people use the New York City Transit System each day. Occasionally, a madman throws someone under a train, and this makes the papers. But on most days most people behave in entirely predictable ways. If they didn't, it would be impossible to have a transit system.

There is probably more than one moral to be drawn from the success of folk psychology. Here, though, the important lesson is that if folk psychology works, there is no reason why a scientific psychology could not work. It must be conceded that psychology aims to be more than a *social psychology* capable of predicting the aggregate behavior of groups. Psychology aims to predict individual behavior, and it has had some success in saying what an individual will *probably* do. How much success it will have (or can have) in saying what an individual will *definitely* do remains an open question.

Reasons and Causes

We sometimes find it useful to distinguish explanations of human behavior based on reasons from explanations based on causes. An ordinary thief has *reasons* for stealing what he steals. If we were to ask him, "Why did you steal that TV?" he might reply, "Because I know someone I can sell it to." There is presumably much more to it than that, of course, but then most reason-giving is *elliptical* or *incomplete*.

Two things should be noted about explanation by reason. *First*, the agent whose action is explained must be aware of the reason. It must be a reason-for-him. *Second*, we have to assume that the agent whose action is explained is rational. A store that installs conspicuous security is trying to give potential thieves reasons not to steal, but this only works for rational thieves. A kleptomaniac, unlike the ordinary thief, is caused to steal by a psychological compulsion. If we ask him, "Why did you steal those worthless trinkets?" his honest answer would be, "I don't know; something came over me." Of course, in the case of the kleptomaniac, because he is caused to steal, we are inclined to say that the stealing wasn't something that he *did*. (It's more like something that happened to him.) If I fall down the stairs (caused by a banana peel plus gravity), falling down the stairs isn't something that I *do*.

We certainly try to explain people's actions by trying to figure out the reasons that moved them to act in such and such a manner. Philosophers speak of "ascribing" or "attributing" reasons to agents. However, this only works to the extent—greater than is sometimes imagined—that agents are rational.

There are two views among philosophers concerning the necessary conditions for the success of explanations by reasons. According to one view, reason-based explanations can work only if the reasons are causes. (This, of course, makes reason-based explanations a subtype of causal explanations generally.) According to the other view, reasons cannot be reduced to causes, but they don't need to be in order for reason-based explanations to work. In other words, reason-based explanations are autonomous.

Is That All There Is?

Reduction

Science generally—and the various special sciences, both physical and social—are sometimes accused of *reductionism. Reductionism* is a term (always pejorative) used to label a view judged unacceptable. Let's begin by defining the more neutral term, *reduction.* A reduction is a claim of the form: *A's are nothing but B's.* Reductions are expressed by *reduction sentences.* Two examples are: "Lightning is nothing but a discharge of static electricity" and "Water is nothing but two atoms of hydrogen and one atom of oxygen." Reduction as illustrated by these two examples is a fundamental part of all good science. Strictly speaking, "is nothing but" means the same thing as "is identical with," so that reduction sentences really express identities. And discovering identities—sometimes, quite unexpected identities—has always been an important part of scientific research.

Reductionism

Perhaps no one would quarrel with the two reductions—lightning to electricity, water to H_2O—mentioned in the previous paragraph. The charge of reductionism is leveled when it is thought that there is more to the item reduced than the reduction specifies. Consider the following ancient—indeed Presocratic—example: some Presocratic philosophers said that the earth, though worshiped by many as a goddess, was nothing but a big rock. This was clearly felt by many traditional believers to be both reductionist and irreligious. As it happens, the earth *is* a big rock (or at least certainly closer to being a big rock than a goddess), and it would seem that Presocratic "proto-science" was entitled to announce this, whether or not it pleased their fellow citizens.

Perhaps the most important modern example is the claim that humans are nothing but biological organisms—that is to say, nothing but complicated biophysical systems. This has been felt by many to involve unwarranted reduction—in other words, to involve reductionism. Science can, in fact, make progress without committing itself to such controversial "nothing but" positions. Biology can say, for example, that it studies humans *as if* they were biophysical systems; the question of whether there is anything left over that biology does not study is not a claim *internal to biology*, but a claim *about* biology. For example, a person who believes, on religious grounds, that humans have souls can still study humans as biophysical systems. Such a person will, of course, believe that there is something humans have that biology does not consider.

What the World Is Made Of—and What We Make of That

There is an elementary distinction that is frequently forgotten in discussions of scientific reductions. Again, this distinction can best be explained in terms of examples. Lightning is the discharge of static electricity. Static electricity is studied in a physics subfield known as electrostatics. Lightning is also studied in meteorology. Both electrostatics and meteorology have a certain theoretical vocabulary. But there is a question as to whether everything that *we* want to say about lightning can be expressed either in the vocabulary of electrostatics or the vocabulary of meteorology. Whatever lightning is composed of, and whatever its role in weather systems, we may feel it is "awe-inspiring"—and *awe-inspiring* does not belong to the vocabulary of either electrostatics or meteorology.

Again, it is very clear that a painting (to turn to another example) is made out of chemicals: whatever chemicals compose the canvas, plus the pigments and so forth applied to the canvas. However, this does not mean that art criticism is a branch of chemistry, or that the vocabulary—

"beautiful," "ugly," "clumsily drawn," "striking," "sensuous," whatever—that we require in our discussions of art has, or should have, anything to do with the language of chemistry. So, the reduction sentence "Paintings are nothing but chemicals," while true, may be misleading if understood to exclude beauty and other aesthetic characteristics.

The Most Basic Science

Despite the fact that "science" covers an enormous range of activities, similar and dissimilar, convergent and divergent, most scientists operate with the following "map" of how the sciences abut and interlock. Biological organisms are composed of chemicals, so that chemistry is, in some sense, more fundamental than biology. Chemicals, in turn, are combinations of atoms, which are composed of the particles and forces studied in physics; consequently, physics is, in some sense, more fundamental than chemistry.

There is nothing more fundamental than physics: physics provides the ultimate inventory of the universe. According to contemporary physical theory, that ultimate inventory consists of four basic forces and seventeen particles. That's all there is. But, of course, there are also tables and chairs, clouds and rainbows, nervousness and jet-lag. A table may be made out of wood, the wood out of chemicals, the chemicals out of just what basic physics says they're made out of; but this does not mean either that there are no tables or that what we want to say about tables can be entirely captured by the theoretical vocabulary of chemistry or physics.

Relations Among Sciences

Relations of dependence among the various sciences is a complicated story that could really only be told in the form of a detailed history of all the sciences. Here, though, only two general principles can be noted. *First*, a relatively less basic science—for example, chemistry in relation to physics, geology in relation to chemistry, or meteorology in relation to physical chemistry—is still an independent science with its own theories, theoretical vocabulary, and predictive power. *Second*, the less basic science cannot make claims that are incompatible with the claims of a science that is more basic relative to it. Should claims be made that are (or appear to be) in conflict with those of the more basic science, they must either be abandoned, modified, or demonstrated to be in conformity with basic science.

Emergent Properties

We can rarely deduce the properties of more complex items from the properties of their constituents. For example, the properties of water—fluidity, liquidity—are nothing like the properties of hydrogen and oxygen. Such new properties that arise in more complex combinations or systems are referred to as *emergent properties*. Another example: crystals have all sorts of properties, both geometrical and optical, that the molecules that compose them do not possess.

Supervenience

A property that depends on some other property is called a *supervenient*, or *consequential*, property. Two things cannot differ in that one has a supervenient property and the other does not, unless they also differ in other properties. Colors are supervenient properties because they depend on, and can finally be explained in terms of, other more basic physical properties. Two things cannot differ in color without also differing in their surface microstructure. It has been suggested (controversially) that psychological properties are supervenient relative to (or, as it is also put, "supervene on") the neurophysiological properties of organisms.

Emergence and Supervenience

One question bearing on our understanding of science and its relation to everything we believe we know outside of science is whether all *emergent* properties must be *supervenient* properties. One thing that we do know is that not all the properties we have occasion to talk about can be explained by current science. Some people believe that science can enlarge its explanatory scope without limit; others are doubtful. This is another place where intellectual prudence would suggest adopting a wait-and-see attitude.

Extrascientific Knowledge

Science may tell us what the world is made out of; however, much of our ordinary knowledge of the world does not belong to science. All of the things I know about my own life or about the lives of my parents, spouse, children, and friends are simply not part of the big scientific picture. One feature of science (implied in much of the above) should here be made explicit: its *generality*. General statements (or *generalizations*) refer to all members of a given class. All basic scientific descriptions and laws are general. When, for example, a scientist says that an electron has such and such a property or behaves in such and such a way, it makes no sense to ask: "Which electron are you talking about?" An electron is a *type* of natural object, and what a scientist says about it is supposed to be true of any and every individual of that type. Even a science such as geology, which talks about particular natural features like mountains and canyons, does so by treating them as instances of types governed by the laws of nature.

Much of what we know and care about is irreducibly particular. Much of our knowledge of the world is—to stretch standard terminology slightly—"knowledge by intimate acquaintance."

Experience

In the context of the philosophy of science, one might wrongly assume that the whole point of having experience is to provide a data-base for the construction of explanatory theories. Although experience does sometimes inspire theory construction, and is also sometimes deliberately provoked—for example, by arranging experiments—in an effort to test theories, experience is also enjoyed for its own sake.

Perhaps the clearest, though by no means the only, examples are provided by our experience of works of art. When I look at a series of paintings by Picasso, I may not be testing any theory. I may simply be interested in the highly specific pleasure paintings can provide. Interestingly, I also acquire, as my acquaintance with the paintings grows, a wholly nontheoretical knowledge: what the paintings of Picasso are like at different periods. This *knowing what something is like*, whether it arises from our own experience or from our imaginative engagement with works of art, is an important part of what we know. This does not detract from the importance of scientific knowledge; it simply makes the point that not all important knowledge is scientific.

We began this chapter by considering skepticism which, in various limited forms, denies that humans have knowledge of particular topics or domains; and, in its global or radical form, denies that humans have any knowledge whatsoever.

We next considered the two major views about the source of knowledge: rationalism, which holds that all knowledge (or at least all important knowledge) comes from reason, or intellect; and empiricism, which holds that sense experience is the only (or at least the most important) source of knowledge.

Reflection shows that our senses never work alone. We do not passively register sense experiences. Rather, human sense experience is an active—and thoughtful—perception of the world. Any realistic account of human knowledge shows reason and sense experience in intimate cooperation. This is, in fact, precisely what we see when we turn to science, the most important source of new knowledge.

Sophisticated contemporary accounts of science do not look for a single essence or nature shared by all the sciences. Science is, in fact, best viewed as a "family-resemblance" concept. There are four main reasons for viewing science this way:

(1) Science is not an unchanging body of knowledge, but a human practice, something that scientists do. Like other practices, it is guided by rules, or norms, stated and unstated. (Scientists themselves constantly distinguish "good science" from "bad science.")

(2) The practice of science has a long and complicated history, which must be studied if the development of science is to be understood. In fact, since there are many distinct sciences, science has many histories—many (sometimes overlapping) research traditions.

(3) Contemporary science is fully institutionalized. Scientific work is done by scientists who function as members of concrete institutions and groups—for example, universities and scientific societies; even more important, though, scientists operate within particular disciplines.

(4) The sciences display extreme methodological pluralism. There is no such thing as the scientific method: each science uses many specific and detailed methods designed—and constantly redesigned—to accomplish some often fairly narrowly defined objective.

There is one hard-core requirement for science: the construction of scientific theories. Nothing is counted as an acceptable scientific theory unless it explains some range of phenomena, and is also testable. Theories allow us to go beyond the mere correlation of observations, by enabling us to explain our observations and their correlation in terms of nomic, or lawful, necessity. Science does more than simply saying that A and B always go together: it explains why A and B go together— why, given the laws of nature, they must go together.

Theories, as we have seen, also enable science to make predictions. It is obvious that making predictions quite often has great practical importance, but, even in "pure" science, predictions are important because it is by virtue of its predictions that a theory can be tested. Although older accounts of theory-testing emphasized confirmation of (or the extent of empirical support for) theories, modern accounts are more likely to emphasize falsifiability: a good theory is viewed as one with many potential, but no actual, falsifiers.

Contemporary science commonly constructs theories that refer to entities that cannot be observed—entities to which we lack, whether temporarily or permanently, anything like "perceptual access." Electrons are an example from contemporary physics. There are two main views about the existence of unobservable entities such as electrons: the instrumentalist/pragmatist view and the realist view. The instrumentalist/pragmatist view denies the existence of unobservables. The point of science, in this view, is not to map reality, but to generate predictions using a theory's equations, whereas the realist view of science holds that any entities referred to by successful theories are fully real.

A consequence of viewing science as theoretical is that, since each theory has its own language for describing observations and experimental results, theories seem to be "talking past" each other. To put it another way, theories don't seem to clash head on. This alleged feature of theories is referred to as incommensurability.

Ordinary explanations are often causal. Does science need the concept of cause? Those who emphasize correlation (a position known as positivism) think that science does not need to specify causes. According to the standard view that science offers a deep explanation of surface phenomena, scientific explanations are typically causal. It is nevertheless true that certain developments in modern physics have suggested that causal necessity (sometimes called causal necessitation) *does not apply to the very minute structure of the physical world (the level of reality studied by quantum mechanics).*

In addition to the physical sciences, there seem to be flourishing social, or human, sciences. Yet doubt remains as to whether there can be such a thing as a social or human science. The main reason for this doubt is the feeling that human actions, arising as they do from choice, are intrinsically, or in principle, unpredictable. In fact, even outside of science, all of us use "folk psychology" to predict the behavior of those around us with great (though not perfect) success.

Although there are many sciences—each with its distinctive theoretical structure, theoretical vocabulary, and predictive power— there is still some reason to think of physics as the basic science. Biological organisms, though subject to the distinctive laws of biology, are made out of chemicals. Chemicals, though subject to the distinctive laws of chemistry, are made out of the forces and particles studied by basic physics.

Recommended Reading

Several standard reference works that have been already mentioned contain useful material on the philosophy of science. The *Encyclopedia of Philosophy* has two brief general articles under the headings "Philosophy of Science, History of" and "Philosophy of Science, Problems of." For more on confirmation (referred to only dismissively here), the student should see the articles headed "Confirmation: Qualitative Aspects" and "Confirmation: Quantitative Aspects." Along similar lines, the student may wish to consult the article on induction. The *Encyclopedia of Philosophy* also has good general articles, with extensive bibliographies, on rationalism and empiricism.

The Handbook of Western Philosophy has useful articles under the following headings: "Induction and Probability," "Science as Conjecture and Refutation," "Science and the World," "Our Knowledge of Causality, Space, Time and Motion," and "The Philosophy of the Social Sciences."

Among the many books on skepticism, particularly worthwhile are Arne Naess's *Scepticism* (1968), *The Modes of Scepticism: Ancient Texts and Modern Interpretations* by Julia Annas and Jonathan Barnes (1985), and Nicholas Rescher's *Scepticism* (1980). A very good contemporary philosophy of science text that views science as a way of overcoming skepticism is John Watkins's *Science and Scepticism* (1984).

In addition to the articles in the *Encyclopedia*, a good idea of rationalism can be derived from a number of primary texts. The most accessible is Descartes' *Meditations on First Philosophy* (originally, 1641; many reprintings). Hume's *A Treatise on Human Nature* (London, 1739–40; many reprintings) provides a good idea of the empiricist temperament, and is the source of the billiard-ball example. A relevant collection of essays is "Rationalism, Empiricism, and Idealism," edited by Anthony Kenny (1986).

There are a great many textbooks and more specialized books about the philosophy of science. A text that provides a clear and now classic presentation of what was the "received view" when it was published is Ernest Nagel's *The Structure of Science: Problems in the Logic of Scientific Explanation* (1961). Two texts that similarly encapsulate views prevalent when they were published (and which are aimed at the beginning student) are Carl G. Hempel's *Philosophy of Natural Science* (1966) and Richard S. Rudner's *Philosophy of Social Science* (1966).

For an overall, up-to-the minute account of what science is all about, the single best book is John Ziman's *An Introduction to Science Studies: The Philosophical and Social Aspects of Science and Technology* (1984). Ziman has the great advantage of being a working scientist—a Fellow of the Royal Society who knows science from the inside.

Five books, each of which in some way represents an improvement on the earlier generation of philosophers of science, are Ian Hacking's *Representing and Intervening: Introductory Topics in the Philosophy of Natural Science* (1983); Mary Hesse's *The Structure of Scientific Inference* (1974); Richard W. Miller's *Fact and Method: Explanation, Confirmation and Reality in the Natural and the Social Sciences* (1987); Dudley Shapere's *Reason and the Search for Knowledge: Investigations in the Philosophy of Science* (1984); and Marx Wartofsky's *Conceptual Foundations of Scientific Thought: An Introduction to the Philosophy of Science* (1968). More advanced students may also wish to look at Wartofsky's *Models: Representation and the Scientific Understanding* (1979). To these may be added three recent books which are unusually clear: Alan Chalmers's *Science and its Fabrication* (1990); Brian Ellis's *Truth and Objectivity* (1990); and Larry Lauden's *Science and Relativism: Some Key Controversies in the Philosophy of Science* (1990).

The one book that probably did more than any other to shake up earlier views of science is Thomas S. Kuhn's *The Structure of Scientific Revolutions* (1962). Later thoughts by the same author on the same themes can be found in *The Essential Tension* (1977). Further discussion of Kuhn (or work inspired by Kuhn) can be found in *Criticism and the Growth of Knowledge*) edited by Imre Lakatos and Alan Musgrave (1970), and in *Scientific Revolutions*, edited by Ian

Hacking (1981). A thorough historical study, and one which is aware of recent philosophy of science, is J. Bernard Cohen's *Revolution in Science* (1985).

One of the most interesting recent developments is the anthropological study of science and the scientific community. The associated literature is sometimes described as the new ethnography of science. A few of the best books are Karen Knorr-Cetina's *The Manufacture of Knowledge: An Essay on the Constructivist and Contextual Nature of Science* (1981); H. M. Collins's *Changing Order: Replication and Induction in Scientific Practice* (1985); Michael Lynch's *Art and Artifact in Laboratory Science: A Study of Shop Work and Shop Talk in a Research Laboratory* (1985); Bruno Latour and Steve Woolgar's *Laboratory Life: The Construction of Scientific Facts* (1986); Bruno Latour's *Science in Action: How to follow scientists and engineers through society* (1987); and Steve Fuller's *Social Epistemology* (1988). A related study is Derek J. De Solla Price's *Little Science, Big Science . . . And Beyond* (1986).

Two recent books that argue well for particular ways of viewing science are Rom Harré's *Varieties of Realism: A Rationale for the Natural Sciences* (1986), and Paul A. Roth's *Meaning and Method in the Social Sciences: A Case for Methodological Pluralism* (1987).

The concept of *family resemblance* used throughout this discussion of science derives from Ludwig Wittgenstein's *Philosophical Investigations*, translated by G. E. M. Anscombe (1958), sections 66 and 67. The concepts of *falsifiability* and *pseudoscience*, as they are used in this chapter, derive from Sir Karl Popper's *The Logic of Scientific Discovery* (German original, 1935; English translation, 1959, and many reprintings).

Derek Gjertsen's *Science and Philosophy, Past and Present* (1989), which is designed for the general reader, discusses the following questions: When did philosophy and science diverge? How do philosophy and science differ? Is science really the art of the soluble? Do scientific problems begin in philosophy? Do philosophical problems end in science? Is there a scientific method? Can philosophy learn from science? Is science open to philosophical criticism? Can science and philosophy conflict? Could science have developed differently? Are scientific theories rational? Are they true?

A few books on special topics are also of interest. About observation and perception, see Norwood Russell Hanson's *Patterns of Discovery: An Inquiry into the Conceptual Foundations of Science* (1965), which is actually very good on all philosophy of science topics; Godfrey Vesey's *Perception* (1971); and *The Philosophy of Perception*, edited by G. J. Warnock (1967). About evidence, induction, confirmation, and kindred topics, see *The Concept of Evidence*, edited by Peter Achinstein (1983), and *The Justification of Induction*, edited by Richard Swinburne (1974).

A good idea of how difficult it is to analyze the concept of cause is provided by *Causation and Conditionals*, edited by Ernest Sosa (1975). The single best book on causal determinism, which discusses everything from Hume's billiard-ball example to the latest developments in physics, is John Earman's *A Primer on Determinism* (1986).

A good selection of papers on explanation, both inside and outside science, is *Explanation*, edited by Stephan Korner (1975). An up-to-date survey of philosophical views concerning scientific explanation is Wesley C. Salmon's *Four Decades of Scientific Explanation* (1989; additional material, 1990). A clear, sophisticated, but demanding book on the methodological problems related to biological evolution is Elliott Sober's *Reconstructing the Past. Parsimony, Evolution, and Inference* (1988).

The uses of experiment: Studies in the natural sciences, edited by Gooding, Pinch, and Schaffer (1989), is a useful collection of essays by philosophers and historians of science that focuses on the role of experiments in the development of science. Two other books about experiments are also useful: Rom Harré's *Great Scientific Experiments: Twenty Experiments That Changed Our View of the World* (1981), and Allan Franklin's *The Neglect of Experiment* (1989). The latter, written by an experimental physicist, focuses on experiment in contemporary high-energy physics.

All of the books above were written in what is loosely called the "Anglo-American tradition." A good sample of contemporary European writing on the philosophy of science is provided by Karl-Otto Apel's *Understanding and Explanation: A Transcendental-Pragmatic Perspective*, translated by Georgia Warnke (1984).

CHAPTER 4

Metaphysics

The term metaphysics *is used to cover two distinct but closely related areas of inquiry: (1) any attempt to give a systematic account of "basic" categories, and (2) any systematic attempt to answer the question "What is there?" We shall see how these two areas of inquiry are related, and also consider the sense of "basicness" common to both.*

In the twentieth century, those philosophers concerned with metaphysics may be divided into two groups: those who seek to clarify and explain categories already in use (and who are said to be doing descriptive metaphysics), and those who advance new categories and concepts (who are said to be doing revisionary metaphysics).

Any adequate contemporary discussion of metaphysics has to consider why—indeed, whether—metaphysics is useful. A special case has to be made for the usefulness of revisionary metaphysics; it would have to show why revisions of the common-sense picture of the world arising from science are not enough. In fact, whether the basic inventory of science covers all reality is perhaps the *crucial metaphysical question.*

Also to be considered in this chapter are views that seek to downgrade the importance of metaphysical questions, or even attempt to eliminate metaphysics altogether. To the question "What is there?"

one possible answer is "Everything!" This answer—which is associated with what is sometimes called the "cheap-ontology" view of metaphysics—deliberately trivializes both the question and "ontological commitment" itself.

The most important metaphysical problem is the mind/body problem: in essence, do we have minds that belong to a category that is fundamentally different from everything studied by the physical sciences? Materialists (now generally called physicalists) answer no; psychophysical, or Cartesian, dualists answer yes. We will consider the main arguments for and against each position.

One closely related issue is the metaphysical status of free will: whether or not human beings are able to choose between two or more alternatives at particular times in their lives. If humans are physical systems, governed by the laws of nature, the question arises as to whether they can have free will as free will is commonly understood.

We will also consider the reality of "abstract" objects. Do such things as numbers and propositions exist independently of human thought, so that they would exist—would be "out there"—even if we humans did not exist? This question can also be framed as: Is the domain of abstract objects discovered or invented?

Finally, we will look briefly at a special development known as formal ontology. *Formal ontology is the attempt to construct an almost mathematical system of categories with definitions, axioms, and derived theorems—something like Euclidean geometry applied to all reality.*

Etymology

The word *metaphysics* derives from the Greek *meta*, a prefix meaning after or beyond, and the noun *phusis*, meaning nature. It is interesting to note that it is from the Greek *phusis* and its exact Latin equivalent, *natura*, that we derive the interchangeable labels *physical* (sciences) and *natural* (sciences). There is, however, some uncertainty about how the combination of *meta* and *phusis* came about. According to one view, they were combined to indicate that metaphysics studies whatever lies beyond the physical. According to the other explanation, metaphysics is simply the label applied by the scholar Andronicus of Rhodes (flourished *c*.80 B.C.) to those writings of Aristotle (edited by Andronicus) that came after Aristotle's works on physics.

The Nature of Metaphysics

Like the term *science, metaphysics* does not designate a homogeneous subject matter, but rather a collection of "family-resemblant" intellectual activities. It is nevertheless possible to organize these activities under two main headings: the analysis of basic categories, and the inventory of basic kinds of things.

The Analysis of Basic Categories

Systems of Classification

To classify an object is to assign it to a category or class with other things of the same type or kind. (Note that a single object may belong to many such categories at the same time.) All human groups employ elaborate systems of classification. In addition, every language embodies such a system, and speakers of a given language also develop new systems of classification for special purposes. Two different languages—English and French, for example—may express almost the same classificatory scheme, in which case it is easy to translate from either language into the other. Both English and French have very elaborate systems for classifying colors, for example, while certain other languages have many fewer such color words. Not surprisingly, certain Eskimo languages have many more words than does English for classifying kinds of snow. (Of course, not all of these categories are *basic* categories.)

Although there is a close connection between a given language and a given system of classification, two speakers of the same language need not employ the same system of classification. For example, a religious person may classify people as either pious or not pious, while a non-religious person—although speaking the same language—may have no need for this particular classification. It should also be remembered that linguistic resources are flexible, rather than frozen: it is always possible to invent a new word, to "coin a phrase," in order to capture some newly noticed similarity or difference.

Generality/Specificity

Most of the categories that humans use are not basic categories. We can demonstrate this by means of the following exercise: Go through a dictionary and extract every word that names a kind of dog. One would come up with a very long list, from afghan hound to wolfhound. But categories for dogs are not basic categories. This can be shown, diagrammatically, as follows:

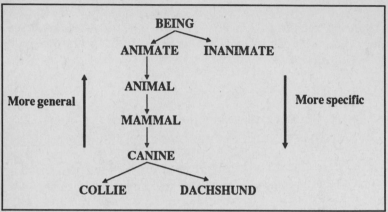

This way of ordering categories, which goes back to the time of Aristotle, is generally known as ordering in terms of *genus* and *species*. These are the Latin words for *class* and *subclass* (or *kind* and *subkind*), respectively. A collie is a kind of canine. A canine is a kind of mammal. A mammal is a kind of animal. An animal, finally, is a kind of being. There is no higher genus of which being is a subkind, a fact that is expressed by describing *being* as the *summum genus*, or, literally, "the class at the absolute top." (At the other end of the ordering, it would be very easy to construct subkinds of collies: male collies are a subkind of collie, for example.)

Two obvious principles govern the use of the terms *general* and *specific*. (1) The "more general" is always the "less specific" (and the "more specific" is always the "less general"). (2) With the exception of *being*, judgments of generality and specificity are always comparative. *Animal* is specific compared to *animate*, but general compared to *mammal*. It therefore makes no sense to ask whether, for example, *mammal* is genus or species. It is genus relative to *canine*, and species relative to *animal*.

Basicness as Generality

Basicness can be defined in terms of generality. Of two categories, the more basic is simply the more general. This means, of course, that there are degrees of basicness corresponding to degrees of generality. How basic (or general) does a category have to be to be of interest to metaphysics? There is probably no absolute rule here. Aristotle regarded metaphysics as the study of being, or of "being *qua* (as) being" (that is, being "as such"). Since there is really not very much to say about being *qua* being, even Aristotle ended up talking about many other less general (i.e., less basic) categories.

Basicness as Topic Neutrality

An alternative way of approaching basicness uses the idea of *topic neutrality*. A topic is, as we know, simply a subject of discussion. The weather, the stock market, particle physics—all of these phrases indicate topics. Some concepts (and their associated terms) are specific to a given topic. The concept *low-pressure area*, for example, belongs to a discussion of the weather, and is very unlikely to be used in connection with any other topic.

Other concepts (and associated terms) are used in connection with a host of different topics. Logic is said to be *topic-neutral*, because the arguments studied by logic can be used with all sorts of different topics or subject matters. Certain categories are also used with topic neutrality. Cause and effect, for example, are likely to come up in connection with virtually any topic. (It should be noted that topic neutrality is a matter of degree: causal [i.e., cause-and-effect] categories, though comparatively topic-neutral, do not apply to such objects of pure mathematics as numbers.)

The more topic-neutral a category is, the more basic it is. Metaphysics, then, as the branch of philosophy concerned with basic categories, is obviously concerned with relatively topic-neutral categories. *Space* and *time* are examples of big, topic-neutral categories. Almost everything is in space. It is indeed an interesting metaphysical question: What might exist that is not in space? Similarly, almost everything is in time, which leads us to another interesting metaphysical question: What might exist that is not in time?

Categories like space and time and cause and effect are used both in ordinary life and in science. Metaphysics attempts to provide philosophically illuminating analyses of these and similar categories.

The Inventory of Basic Kinds of Things

Metaphysics has also been described as the inventory of basic kinds of things. From this point of view, a metaphysical system is regarded as providing a very general answer to the question: What is there? What basic kinds of things exist? Of course, a metaphysician does much more than provide a mere inventory or list; he or she tries also to explain why the proposed inventory or list is superior to others. Finally, the metaphysician tries to show that his or her inventory or list provides a place for everything that really exists.

There is a close relationship between attempts to understand basic categories and attempts to provide basic inventories. Ideally, we would expect one basic category for each item included in the basic inventory. In practice, however, these two approaches to metaphysics diverge. This happens because categories are most naturally interpreted as human inventions—classificatory systems developed by various human groups and therefore embodied, to a large extent, in the languages they use. There is no guarantee that the categories used by any group of humans accurately reflect the kinds of things that exist *in reality*.

We can see this most clearly, perhaps, by looking at certain categories and classifications no longer in use. The once-popular psychological classification of humans into four temperaments, or *humors* (choleric, phlegmatic, sanguinic, and melancholic), though it continues to inspire artists to some degree, is no longer regarded as corresponding to any four basic psychological types displayed by actual human beings. Ideally, what we seek are categories and classifications that exactly map the real similarities and differences found in the real world. What we probably have, then, and will probably continue to have, is a somewhat imperfect match. Even though science, as it develops, quite clearly upgrades the quality of our inventory, there is nevertheless room for worry about whether science—that is, all the sciences, collectively—in fact captures everything that exists.

In the following sections we will examine some items that have occurred more or less frequently on traditional basic inventories: substance and accident, spatiotemporal particulars, abstract particulars, necessary and contingent beings, and events and processes. Note that all of these items have also been regarded as basic categories.

Substance and Accident

Substance. A *substance* is most commonly defined as "that which is capable of independent existence." The phrase *capable of independent existence* is not easy to interpret, but it is usually taken to mean not that which could *really* exist by itself (things being as they are), but rather that which can be *conceived of* as existing by itself and independent of all else.

Consider a red ball. As things are, red balls have to be made by someone, so in that sense they can't be said to exist by themselves. Nevertheless, a red ball can be conceived of, or imagined, as existing by itself. This can be shown by either of two thought experiments. In the first, imagine the universe being progressively destroyed. Could the last thing to go be a red ball? Thinking this through, there seems to be no reason why not. In the second thought experiment, imagine God creating the universe. *Could* He have created a single red ball and nothing else? Here, one might worry, quite properly, about the ball being red without there being any light or without perceivers, but there seems to be no reason why God could not have created something identical, molecule for molecule, with what we think of as a single red ball.

Try a similar thought experiment with *red*. Could the universe be destroyed, leaving only red? Could God have created red and stopped? The answer seems to be negative in both cases, and the reason is simple: there has to be something—a ball, an apple, whatever—to *be* red; red can't exist by itself. Therefore, a ball (but not red) is a substance—that is, something capable of independent existence.

Accident. *Accident* is used as a technical term in philosophy. Items like *red*, which cannot exist by themselves, are referred to as *accidents*. Other, perhaps more familiar words used instead of *accident* in this sense are *property*, *quality*, *characteristic*, and *feature*. Accidents (or properties, qualities, characteristics, or features) are said to *inhere in*—or *qualify*, or *be true of*—substances. Even a property that something *has* to have is, in this technical sense, referred to as an accident.

Essence. The *essence* (or *nature*) of anything is defined as that which it has to be to be a thing of that kind. It is part of the essence or nature of a horse to be a mammal, for example, but not a part of the essence or nature of a horse to be lame—though, in fact, some horses are indeed lame. A horse is necessarily a mammal; no horse is necessarily lame.

Although *accident* is used, as in the previous paragraph, as a synonym for *property*, in discussions of essence or nature *accidental* properties are sometimes distinguished from *essential* properties. (The traditional terminology *is* tricky: *accidents* are what substances are said to have; there are both essential and accidental properties, but *accidental* is the antonym of *essential*.) A given human may have such accidental properties as being blue-eyed, weighing 150 pounds, or having been born in Missouri. That same human will also have properties that must be had in order to be human: being an animal, being a mammal, and—perhaps—being rational. (It is not always clear whether a given property is essential or accidental. The debate continues, for example, about human nature—that is, about just what properties are necessary for being human and accordingly possessed by all humans.)

Spatiotemporal Particulars

Closely related to the idea of substance is the idea of spatiotemporal particulars. Some examples of spatiotemporal particulars include people, tables and chairs, stars, rainbows, and clouds. Spatiotemporal particulars are so called because, at any moment of time, they have a particular location in space. (Or, if you prefer, spatiotemporal particulars are always somewhere in space-time.) Each spatiotemporal particular has its own history, which is the sum total of the changes that have happened to it while it has remained the same "it."

Spatiotemporal particulars are sometimes also referred to as *individuals*, or *concrete individuals*. Some individuals are relatively hard-edged, and thus easy to distinguish from other individuals of the same or of a different kind. Tables and chairs are examples of individuals of this kind. Other individuals are much less hard-edged, much less firmly bounded, and correspondingly harder to distinguish from other individuals. Clouds and rainbows are examples, and an individual ocean wave seems hardly to be a spatiotemporal particular at all.

In any case, not all philosophers equate being an individual with being a spatiotemporal particular. (All spatiotemporal particulars are individuals, but it doesn't follow that all individuals are spatiotemporal particulars.) Consider angels, for example. An angel, though an individual, is not a spatiotemporal particular. Or, suppose the number three is an individual—that is, just the number it is, and not another. It is certainly wrong-headed to ask where, at a given time, the number three is located. (One might respond that the number three is located in the realm of numbers, but this is not a spatial location—not a "where" in the ordinary sense.)

One answer to the question "What is there?" that some philosophers have given is simply "spatiotemporal particulars." That way, anything that seems not to be a spatiotemporal particular has to be analyzed in terms of spatiotemporal particulars. There is, for example, no *red*, but only red spatiotemporal particulars. Similarly, there is no number three, but only the class of all triplets of spatiotemporal particulars. And so forth.

This view is sometimes called *materialism*, because spatiotemporal particulars seem very like what are ordinarily called *material* objects. It is also associated with *nominalism*, defined as the view that only *particulars* (or *particular existents*) are real. The word *nominalism*, which derives from the Latin *nomen*, meaning name, is appropriate for this position because general terms—terms that apply to many individuals—are regarded as "mere names" that derive their whole meaning from the similarities and differences of concrete individuals.

Abstract Particulars. Some metaphysicians have maintained that such properties as being red and being rectangular can exist at particular locations in space-time without inhering in or qualifying substances. Properties thought of in this way are referred to as *abstract particulars*. In contrast, *concrete particulars*—e.g., a red ball, a green leaf, a table—would then be regarded as sets of co-occurrent abstract particulars. Co-occurrent abstract particulars are said to be *compresent*. Each green leaf contains its own particular instance of green. An instance of green is called an abstract particular because it is being abstracted from—or isolated in thought from—the instances of other properties that, taken together, make up the concrete leaf. Abstract particulars, or cases of kinds, are also sometimes referred to as *quality-instances* or *tropes*.

Necessary Beings and Contingent Beings

Some metaphysicians divide all things that exist into two categories: necessary beings, defined as beings that could not not exist, and contingent beings, beings that could fail to exist.

Necessary Beings. The double negative in the above definition of necessary beings is, of course, deliberate. And to say that a necessary being cannot not exist is, also of course, the same thing as saying that it must exist—that it has to be. There is no general agreement among metaphysicians as to whether there are indeed any necessary beings. God, if He exists, is the most plausible candidate, and indeed many philosophers hold that, while there are indefinitely many contingent beings, there is a unique necessary being. There are, however, other candidates for inclusion in the category of necessary beings. Numbers and other mathematical items, viewed as existing in their own realm independent of human thought or invention, have sometimes been regarded as such necessary beings.

Contingent Beings. Almost all metaphysicians agree that we ourselves, that other people, and that all the ordinary objects we encounter in the world are contingent beings. All these beings, or *existents*, could have failed to come into existence. If things had been different, any or all of these beings might never have been. It is easy to see this if we look at particular cases. *First*, our existence and the existence of the beings that surround us, both other people and physical objects, depend on certain large-scale factors in the history of the universe. If our sun had not formed with its particular system of planets, for example, it is a safe bet that the particular table in my study would not have existed.

Second, there are always relatively localized factors that affect the existence of particular things. The company that made my table might have gone bankrupt before they made it, or they might have decided to discontinue making that kind of table. A fascinating exercise, and one that provides much insight into contingency, is to try to think of all the "might-have-been-differents" that would have resulted in your not having come to be. Certainly, it was not necessary that your parents met, married, and had the children they did. That you exist, then, means that you've had a bit of metaphysical luck! (Oddly enough, had you not come into existence, you would not have been *un*lucky, since in that case there would have been no you to be unlucky. Strictly speaking, had you never come into existence, we could not speak of *your* not having come into existence.)

Events and Processes

It has been argued by many metaphysicians that picturing reality in terms of discrete substances with their static properties provides a very inadequate basic inventory. To remedy this inadequacy, it is urged that we talk in terms of *events* and *processes*, which are, in this view, more fundamental than substances or spatiotemporal particulars.

Events. *Event* comes from the Latin verb *evenire*, meaning to happen or to occur. The ball's *being red* is not an event, but the ball's *being squashed underfoot* is an event, because it is something that happens. The ball's *becoming red*—for example, by being painted—is likewise an event. Events can be very short or they may go on for quite a while, but there is always a time when they happen.

There is no universal agreement about how to analyze the concept of an event. Do events always happen to individuals? Some certainly do. The event of my blushing happens to me. A thunderstorm or a traffic jam is also an event (a complex event, composed of many smaller events), but it is not clear that these events happen to some specifiable individual. (Perhaps they should be viewed rather as changes affecting space-time regions.) Events, it is also sometimes suggested, should be understood in terms of a change in properties: a blush is, among other things, a change in the color properties of a certain area of the face.

One very special kind of change is known as a *Cambridge change*. A Cambridge change in X is one in which there is no alteration of any of X's own real properties. X's becoming shorter than Y because Y has grown taller is a good example of a Cambridge change. Becoming shorter because someone else has grown is a very different kind of change than becoming shorter by shrinking. (See *Cambridge change* in the Glossary for an explanation of the origin of the term.)

Processes. The line between events and *processes* is not rigid. A process may be defined, roughly, as an interrelated series of events. There is a distinct movement in metaphysics known as *process philosophy*, to which Alfred North Whitehead (1861–1947) was the most eminent adherent. Process philosophers emphasize: (1) the continuously changing character of the universe, which is referred to as its *creative advance*; and (2) the basic character of process, understood to mean that individuals are (or are composed of) processes. Paraphrasing Whitehead, this means that how an entity *becomes* (or changes), constitutes what that entity *is*.

Descriptive versus Revisionary Metaphysics

Philosophers in all periods who attempted to clarify basic categories or develop systematic inventories of the basic kinds of things can be classified in terms of how far they depart from "common-sense" conceptions of the world and our ordinary ways of talking about it. In our own time, P. F. Strawson (b. 1919) introduced the terms *descriptive metaphysics* and *revisionary metaphysics* to cover the two extreme points on the scale of departure from common sense and ordinary language.

Descriptive Metaphysics

Descriptive metaphysics sees its task as providing an elucidation, or clarification, of categories already in use. These categories are embodied in the common-sense picture of the world and in ordinary language. Descriptive metaphysics aims to generate more clarity about familiar concepts by making our grasp of such concepts more reflective or explicit. Those who think of metaphysics as the analysis of basic categories are likely to approach their task "descriptively."

Revisionary Metaphysics

Revisionary metaphysics is based on the assumption that the categories in use, expressed by ordinary languages, are too flawed to salvage, and should be replaced by new and better categories developed by philosophers themselves. Many great philosophers have produced revisionary metaphysical systems, systems that aim or aimed to provide a better basic inventory than that expressed by ordinary categories.

Not surprisingly, those who think of metaphysics in terms of the basic inventory of reality are likely to approach their task in a revisionary spirit. This is because the question of what the basic inventory should contain (which is a question about reality itself) has nothing to do with the categories or concepts that happen to be in use in the particular revisionary metaphysician's society. Baruch Spinoza (1632–1677), who held that there is only one substance that could be called either God or Nature (*deus sive natura* is the actual Latin term he used), is the classic example of a revisionary metaphysician.

The Utility of Metaphysics

Metaphysics and Science

Although metaphysics has had a long and distinguished history, it has—particularly in the twentieth century—come under attack by antimetaphysical philosophers. (The most famous group of antimetaphysical philosophers belonged to a philosophical movement called *logical positivism* that flourished in the 20s and 30s, and some of whose views are still influential.) This attack has been developed along various lines, but always in respect to the perceived success of the natural sciences. (In considering the challenge to metaphysics posed by science, we must bear in mind that, despite its obvious success, science cannot be assumed to provide the only path toward an explanation of reality.)

One argument for the uselessness of metaphysics runs as follows: Metaphysics either stays close to ordinary categories or it doesn't. If it stays close to ordinary categories, all it does is recycle platitudes in fancy dress. To say there are substances and accidents is just an elaborate way of saying we talk about the world with nouns and adjectives; to emphasize events and processes is just a pretentious way of saying we can't tell reality's story without using some verbs. If, on the other hand, metaphysics gets away from ordinary categories, it becomes *speculative*—a kind of fairy tale that tries to pass itself off as science. Speculative metaphysics is dismissed as armchair pseudo-science, an attempt to penetrate the secrets of the universe without observation or experiment.

Another argument for the uselessness of metaphysics applies most directly to revisionary metaphysics. Given that, *under pressure* from science, we are obliged to alter and correct the common-sense picture of the world—that is, that picture embodied in the categories and concepts of everyday life—why should we also consider suggested alterations and corrections proposed by nonscientists? This question is based on the assumption that corrections forced on us by those who have observed and experimented are more likely to be compelling than those forced on us by "speculative" metaphysicians.

Although the attacks on metaphysics probably served a useful purpose in taming its more extravagant pretensions to being a purely thought-based source of knowledge about the world, such attacks are generally based on the questionable assumption that the natural sciences provide a complete and fully adequate inventory of reality. That there is a questionable assumption involved can be seen by considering the following simple argument:

> Science does not study souls;
> So souls do not exist.

There may or may not be souls, but this argument certainly does not establish that there are not. It rests on the hidden—and question-begging—premise that if something is not studied by science, it does not exist. An adequate metaphysics is supposed to provide a place for everything that we know, whether from science, religious tradition, art, or ordinary life. Perhaps, what we really know from all of these sources is the same as what we know from science alone; however, this is not something that can be cavalierly assumed.

Ontological Commitment

A rather more subtle criticism of metaphysics (and one that does not rest on "the triumph of the natural sciences") can be put as follows: although it is not true that everything human beings have ever mentioned or talked about is real—Santa Claus and Zeus do not exist, there are certainly no griffins or unicorns, and there *may* be no ghosts or honest politicians—we still derive our inventory of what is real from what we find it convenient to talk about. If we have good reasons for talking about X's, then there are X's. Philosophers use the phrase *ontological commitment* to refer to commitment to the existence of something. (*Ontos* is Greek for "being.") How much is involved in such commitment is something about which philosophers disagree. This amounts to a criticism of metaphysics, since it challenges the idea that there are either basic categories or basic inventories.

Expensive Ontology

Expensive ontology regards ontological commitment as a matter of great importance. For example, "Are there really unconscious desires?" is a question that, in the expensive-ontology view, would require a great deal of thought to answer. According to the expensive-ontology view, what is out there in reality does not reduce to the question of what we find it convenient to talk about. In this view, it makes sense to ask how it is even possible (not to mention useful) to talk about what does not exist.

Cheap Ontology

Cheap ontology is referred to, in contemporary philosophical discussion, as a deliberately *deflationary strategy*. According to the cheap-ontology view, the question of whether there are unconscious desires is easy to answer. There are unconscious desires because it is helpful, in understanding human behavior, to use theories—Freudian psychoanalysis, for example—that talk in terms of such desires. We needn't assume there are no unconscious desires: the question of whether there are or aren't may not be separate from the question of what theories have explanatory power.

The Natural Ontological Attitude

In the early twentieth century, many people who wrote about science worried about whether or not there actually were tables and chairs: perhaps only their *microcomponents*—electrons, protons, etc.— were really real. There was also some concern about whether or not there *were* electrons and protons, since no one had ever seen them. In fact, we have very good reasons for talking about tables and chairs, *and* we have very good reasons for talking about electrons and protons. How these various things we have good reasons to talk about relate to each other is a complicated story involving both analysis and empirical research. The view that *our best talk is our best access to what is real* is sometimes referred to as the *natural ontological attitude* (abbreviated NOA).

Dualism: The Mind/Body Problem

The mind/body problem is perhaps the most important of all metaphysical problems. In its contemporary form, it is closely related to the question of whether the physical sciences provide a complete account of reality. Essentially, the mind/body problem is the philosophical problem of whether there are nonphysical minds, souls, or spirits. The main form in which the problem arises is in understanding the nature of human beings.

The mind/body problem brings together a number of deep perplexities. We feel that we have access—from the inside—to a qualitatively distinctive realm when we are aware of our own mental life, our thoughts, feelings, and desires. How can we relate this to the picture of ourselves presented by science, especially by neurophysiology? From the subjective point of view, I find myself at the center of the world. From the scientific point of view, the world has no center, and there is, accordingly, some kind of illusion built into the way I experience my own life. When science tells me that water is really H_2O, I can accept this without any problem. But when science tells me that I am a complicated organism whose inner life can be explained in terms of biology, chemistry, and physics, I worry that something important is being left out.

Souls

According to many traditional religious views, what is being left out of the scientific account is the soul. Many people still believe that they have—or maybe even are—souls. The soul, though related to the body in some mysterious way, is thought to be separate from it, and able to survive after the body has perished. People who believe in souls—or, as we can now express it, are ontologically committed to souls—on the basis of religious faith are not likely to be either affected by purely philosophical arguments for or against souls, or much troubled by perplexities generated by commitment to souls. From a purely philosophical point of view, it is very unclear how the soul helps explain the existence and nature of our mental life, and equally unclear how the soul is related to its companion body.

Dualism

The term *dualism* derives from the Latin *duo*, meaning two or twofold. *Dualism* is the view that there are two fundamentally distinct and irreducibly different kinds of stuff. (*Stuff* here just means *the raw material reality is made out of*.) One can also define dualism in terms of categories. So defined, dualism is the view that we cannot talk about all of reality without employing two distinctive sets of categories, neither of which can be analyzed in terms of the other. The single most influential formulation of dualism was made in the seventeenth century by René Descartes (1596–1650), and has come to be called *Cartesian dualism.*

Psychophysical Dualism

Cartesian dualism is a form of what is called *psychophysical dualism.* This form of dualism says that one fundamental kind of stuff is mind or spirit. The other fundamental kind of stuff is body (or matter, or the physical). Although the most interesting application of psychophysical dualism is to human beings, it is important to understand that psychophysical dualism (or simply *dualism*, for short) is a perfectly general answer to the question "What is there?" Again, a thought experiment will illustrate. Suppose God had created angels and rocks and nothing else. Dualism would provide the correct metaphysics for such a universe, because the category of spirit would be needed (for God and the angels) and the category of body would be needed (for the rocks). This is true even though, in that universe, there would be nothing that was both spirit and body.

Cartesianism

Descartes was the inheritor of a long religious tradition, Roman Catholicism, which taught (and teaches) that humans have a non-material, and indeed immortal, soul. However, Descartes wanted to provide a purely philosophical basis for belief in soul or mind. He was concerned also to find a place in his metaphysical system for the newly emergent scientific picture of the world. For in Descartes' time science was able, for the first time in history, to provide a comprehensive physics that, in a single explanatory package, accounted for the motions of bodies on or near the surface of the earth and for the motions of the heavenly bodies. Descartes, as an enthusiast of the new science, accepted a mechanical explanation of all of nature with one important exception: the human mind. This involved rejecting the traditional view that animals and plants have souls (though souls of lower grade than human souls), and replacing it with the view that animals and plants are just complicated, soft-tissue machines.

Arguments for Dualism

Purely philosophical arguments of the sort put forward by Descartes are meant to be persuasive independent of religious conviction. (We should add that, even if these arguments are unsuccessful, the religious person—who is in any case not relying on argument—need not give up dualism.) Let us look at two arguments orginally put forward by Descartes and later, in various forms, by many subsequent thinkers.

Argument 1
The first argument is formulated as follows:

> I can think;
> Bodies cannot think;
> Therefore, I am not a body.

Although this argument has seemed compelling to many people, it is not so obvious that we should accept the second premise. Of course, if we think of bodies—and *body*, here and in discussions of this kind generally, just means "physical object"—of a relatively low-grade sort, such as rocks and sticks, it may seem obvious that bodies cannot think. But if we think of bodies such as our own, it is not so obvious that a body cannot think. On the basis of such consideration, some thinkers have formulated the following *anti-Cartesian* argument:

> I am a body;
> I can think;
> Therefore, some bodies can think.

How should the Cartesian and the anti-Cartesian arguments be evaluated comparatively? This is not something everyone will agree about. The very fact that one can formulate a valid Cartesian argument and a valid anti-Cartesian argument shows how difficult these issues are to resolve. Which of the two arguments will be found the more compelling will depend on intuitions about the obviousness (more precisely, the comparative obviousness) of their respective premises. Those who think it is more obvious that bodies can't think than that they are bodies are likely to accept the Cartesian argument; those who think it is more obvious that they are bodies than that bodies can't think are likely to accept the anti-Cartesian argument. Descartes thought the essence of mind is to think. His official term for mind, the Latin phrase *res cogitans*, means "thinking thing." He thought that the essence of body is to be extended, or spread out in space, and his official term for body, the Latin phrase *res extensa*, means "extended thing."

Argument 2

The second argument for dualism may be formulated as follows:

> I cannot doubt that I have a mind;
> I can doubt that I have a body;
> _____
> Therefore, my mind and body are nonidentical.

It seemed to Descartes that, no matter what he might come to doubt, he could not doubt that he had a mind (that is, something that thinks), since doubting is itself a form of thinking. I might think that I am walking but turn out to be wrong, because I am asleep or hallucinating; but I cannot think I am thinking and then turn out to be mistaken, because if I think I am thinking, I am thinking. These reflections led Descartes to formulate his famous *Cogito ergo sum:* "I think; therefore, I am."

Although most of us find the idea that we might not have bodies rather silly, Descartes did think that he could generate doubt about even such an obvious matter. Suppose, for the sake of discussion, that we grant that both premises of this argument are—or at least might be— true. Does its conclusion follow? It is supposed to be supported by the following idea: if *A* has a certain property and *B* does not, *A* and *B* must be nonidentical; that is, *A* and *B* can't be one and the same. The following valid argument is based on this principle:

> The murderer has a tattoo of an anchor on his forearm;
> The butler does not;
> _____
> Therefore, the butler is not the murderer.

We all understand why the butler can't be the murderer. However, although this form of argument works for most ordinary properties, it does not work for certain properties involving knowledge, belief, and doubt. An example will make this clear.

There was a time when no one knew that the morning star and the evening star were one and the same heavenly body—namely, the planet Venus. Some one might once have argued:

> I am sure that I have seen the evening star;
> I very much doubt that I have ever seen the morning star
> (since I never get up early);
> _____
> Therefore, the morning star can't be the evening star.

This clearly invalid argument shows that the general principle that argues from property divergence to nonindentity does not work for properties involving belief or doubt.

Arguments from Nonsynonymy

Between Descartes' time and our own, many of the arguments put forward in defense of dualism really amount to new versions of the second argument. Collectively, they can be called *arguments from nonsynonymy*. Such arguments rest on the idea that the terms we use to describe our inner life—"feeling depressed," "remembering my trip to Paris," "experiencing a sharp pain," "enjoying the taste of that ice cream"—do not mean the same as (or are *nonsynonymous with*) any of the terms that describe our bodies—for example, the language of neurophysiology. This is perfectly true. It does not follow from this fact, however, that our inner life cannot be identical with events in or states or conditions of our bodies. Again, an example will show this. The word *lightning* is nonsynonymous with "discharge of electricity," and the word *water* is nonsynonomous with "H_2O." All the same, lightning is a discharge of electricity and water is H_2O. Everyone, then, will recognize that the following is an invalid argument:

> I cannot doubt that water is water;
> I can doubt that water is H_2O;
> _____
> Therefore, water is not H_2O.

"Water" plays one role in our lives and thoughts, "H2O" another; *they don't have the same meaning*. But the meanings of words and phrases in our language are not always good guides to underlying reality. This does not mean that our inner life is identical with events in, or states or conditions of, our bodies. All it means is that arguments from nonsynonymy do not work.

Evaluation of Dualism

Dualism is an enormously appealing position for two main reasons. *First*, it agrees with an idea of human life that is advanced by many religions. If mind and body are distinct (nonidentical), then it is at least possible that mind may survive the death of the body. But if mind and body are identical, the death of the body will be the death of the person. (It is, of course, possible that my memories could be transferred to a new brain sometime before I die, and that this might count as my survival; however, few people would derive much comfort from this far-fetched possibility.)

Second, dualism fits in very well with the idea that we have immediate access, in our own case, to a qualitatively distinct inner realm of experience.

Nevertheless, dualism is faced with a serious problem. Dualism means absolute separateness, and, as Descartes realized, this means both that mind can affect mind (a thought triggering another thought) and that bodies can affect bodies (motions being communicated to adjacent parts of a single body, or to adjacent bodies). But conceived dualistically, in terms of strict separation, minds cannot affect bodies nor bodies minds. This is a problem because it makes many familiar phenomena mysterious if not downright impossible.

Two examples will make this clear. *First*, my idea that I want to go for a walk seems, under ordinary circumstances, to lead to the movements of parts of my body—for example, my legs. But according to dualism, this should not be possible. *Second*, when I've had too much to drink, my thoughts get fuzzy. But according to dualism, this should not happen. After all, the drinking involves only my body, whereas my thoughts involve only my mind.

Psychophysical Parallelism

Opinions differ about whether dualism can solve the problem of mind/body interaction. One attempted solution is referred to as *psychophysical parallelism*. This is the idea that the realm of the mental (or the *psychical*, from the Greek *psyche*, mind or soul) and the realm of the physical run on parallel tracks, but do not affect each other. When I stub my toe I feel pain, but what happens in my body does not cause the experience of pain. Why the parallelism, then? This is said to result from a *preestablished harmony* set up by God. However, even most people who believe that God created the universe find the idea of preestablished harmony rather implausible. The parallel-but-strictly-separate-tracks view seems implausible for two main reasons: (1) it runs counter to felt intimacy, or connectedness, of mind and body; and (2) it seems to rule out the possibility of a person having a real effect on what happens in the physical world.

Monisms

The word *monism* derives from the Greek *monos*, meaning single. Monism is the view that there is only one fundamental kind of stuff out of which everything is made. Monism can also be defined in terms of categories. So defined, monism is the view that everything can be talked about in a single fundamental vocabulary. Major monisms are as follows:

Panpsychism

Panpsychism (or idealism or objective idealism) is the view that everything that exists has the character of mind/spirit/psyche. Though it has been proposed by a number of important philosophers in the past, panpsychism is not taken seriously by any influential contemporary thinkers. One reason is that few people are willing to accept the idea that a rock might be a kind of mind, or be made out of something that is mindlike in character.

Pantheism

According to pantheism, everything that exists is part of the being of God. Like panpsychism, pantheism has been put forward by a number of prominent philosophers—most notably, Baruch Spinoza (1632–1677)—but, like it, can claim no adherents among modern professional philosophers.

Neutral Monism

Neutral monism is the view that there is one fundamental stuff, neither mindlike nor material, but rather capable of becoming either. Neutral monism, though it had at least one distinguished proponent in the philosopher William James (1842–1910), strikes most thinkers today as something of an unhappy compromise.

Materialism

Materialism—the view that everything that exists has the character of body or matter—has been influential over a long period of time. Some Presocratics—specifically, those who believed that the world is composed of material atoms—were materialists, and there were influential materialists up to the turn of the twentieth century. Modern materialists—roughly, those who lived from the seventeenth century through the end of the nineteenth—were willing to be guided by the natural sciences in answering the question "What is there?" (At one stage, there were many scientists who did hold that the universe is, in the final analysis, made out of matter.)

Physicalism

In our own time, the conception of the universe put forward by the natural sciences is no longer expressed in terms of matter; such things as energy, fields, and forces have come to occupy a more and more fundamental place in the picture of reality offered by contemporary science. Accordingly, thinkers guided by science have begun to think of themselves as *physicalists*, with physicalism defined as the view that everything comes down to the sorts of things studied by the physical sciences.

Arguments for Physicalism

Part of the appeal of physicalism is that characteristic of any monism: it avoids the problems that seem to be built into any dualism. These problems arise from the fact that dualism defines its two irreducible categories as strictly separate and noninteractive, and then has to try to explain interactions of minds and bodies (or explain away *apparent* interactions).

The primary intellectual motivation for physicalism, however, comes from the success of the natural sciences. Now, as already emphasized, the success of the natural sciences cannot be taken to prove that no fundamental realities exist that are not studied by science; religious experience, for example, may give us access to a realm of reality lying outside the scope of science. Nevertheless, after studying in detail the progressive extension of the range of phenomena science is capable of explaining, many thinkers have concluded that there is nothing which, in principle, falls outside the scope of scientific theory and explanation.

Mind-Brain Identity Theories

Although physicalism is a general metaphysical doctrine, it is, of course, particularly relevant to human self-understanding. What is a human being? Popular answers, throughout the ages, have favored answers such as "spirits" or "combinations of spirit and body." These popular views must be rejected by the consistent physicalist, however; the physicalist must hold that the mind is identical with the brain (or with the brain and the central nervous system). Such a view is called the *theory of mind-brain identity*, or *central-state materialism*. (Note that mind-brain identity views must be sharply distinguished from those more traditional views that picture the brain as a necessary condition of mental life.)

A fair guess would be that contemporary philosophers divide, in about equal numbers, into mind-brain identity theorists and psychophysical dualists. (There are, of course, many philosophers who haven't yet made up their minds between these competing views, or—committed to other specialized topics—do not feel an obligation to have an opinion about mind-brain identity.) This split can be explained in at least two ways. One might say that so many philosophers have converted to the identity theory because of the enormous contemporary success of brain science in explaining mental phenomena. Or one might say that so many philosophers remain unconverted because it is still mysterious how *consciousness*, as humans enjoy it, can be understood in terms provided by neurophysiology.

Free Will as a Metaphysical Problem

The natural sciences in general provide *causal explanations*. A given event is shown to be nomically necessary, given certain prior events and background conditions. (As you will recall from the discussion of nomic regularity in chapter 3, *nomically* means on the basis of laws of nature.) There may, at the microphysical (or quantum) level of reality, be something like a breakdown of causal determination; for large-scale events and processes, however, causal determinism operates. This is illustrated by the motion of billiard balls, each of which causes another to move in ways determined by initial positions, impacts, and the appropriate laws of mechanics.

From a physicalist—in this context also called a *naturalistic*—perspective, there seems to be no reason why human actions should be exempt from causal determination. Humans are, after all, part of the physical world, part of nature. Yet the most popular conception of free will seems to require exempting free human actions from the general causal order.

The Path of a Rock/The Career of a Human

As our lives go on, we ordinarily contrast how it is with us with how it is with ordinary physical objects as they move through space time. This can be illustrated by the following diagram:

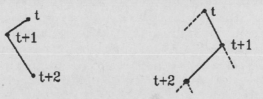

THE PATH OF A ROCK   THE CAREER OF A HUMAN

Almost everyone would agree that the position of the rock at time *t* (the intitial moment we happen to be considering), along with all the forces acting on the rock and the relevant laws of physics, *completely determines* the position of the rock at *t* + 1, *t* + 2, or any subsequent moment. Suppose the rock is rolling down a fairly complicated hill. We may not, *in practice*, be able to predict its final resting place, but we still feel its final resting place is, *in principle*, predictable. All that stops us from actually predicting are the difficulty of providing a suitably fine-grained description of the initial conditions and the complication of the necessary calculations. There are no branches in the pathway of the rock because there is no way compatible with nomic necessity that the rock did not go but might have gone. In short, the rock's path is causally determined. (We can, of course, set up experiments in laboratories, using such smooth things as balls and inclined planes, where what is predictable in principle becomes predictable in practice.)

Let us now turn to the picture of the segment of a human's career. Each of the places where the lines branch is a moment of choice. Solid lines indicate what was actually done, while dotted lines indicate certain *real alternatives* that were not pursued. If our picture captures the reality of the human situation, then the human's position at *t* does not determine his or her position at *t* + 1, *t* + 2, or any later moments. This is because human life contains real moments of choice—moments when alternatives are really open, really available. That human lives contain moments of choice is generally expressed by saying that humans are free or have freedom.

Choice: Real or Illusory?

Not everyone believes that human lives do contain the moments of choice illustrated in our diagram. A committed physicalist or naturalist is likely to deny that we have any kind of choice that requires a suspension of the general causal order. According to this view, our own experience of our lives as containing moments of choice—moments when there were things we might have done but did not do—is a *subjective illusion*. On the other hand, those who think that choice is real and not an illusion have difficulty formulating a metaphysics of choice that is not deeply mysterious or frankly miraculous.

Compatibilism/Incompatibilism

It is hard to see how choice and causal determinism are mutually compatible. It would seem that what I cannot not do because I am caused to do it is not something that I can be choosing to do. Nevertheless, many philosophers hold that choice and causal determination are compatible. Their position is known as either *compatibilism* or *soft determinism*. Compatibilists try to define freedom in such a way that its exercise does not involve the suspension of causality. A person acts freely, in the compatibilist account, just in case what he does is what he wants or desires to do. Free action is not uncaused action, but rather action caused by the agent's own wants or desires. Those who deny that choice is compatible with causality, and as a consequence reject the compatibilist definition of freedom, are known as *incompatibilists* or *hard determinists*.

The Reality of Abstract Objects

One important metaphysical question concerns the status of such abstract objects as numbers, concepts, and propositions. Should the full answer to the question "What is there?" include these items? Do we have good reasons to commit ourselves, ontologically, to their existence? Before attempting any clear discussion of the ontological status of abstract objects, we must say something about their nature.

Numbers and Numerals

The word *abstract* has a number of meanings in philosophy; here, however, it means separate from matter. Why are numbers abstract? To begin with, we must distinguish numbers themselves from their names. The names of numbers are known as *numerals*. There is one number three, which has many names: the Arabic numeral 3, the Roman numeral III, the English word *three*, the German word *drei*, and so forth. Number names are part and parcel of human language-using activity. Each *inscription* (also called a *token*) of a numeral is a physical object made out of chalk or ink or whatever. Each such inscription is located somewhere; but the number three is not located anywhere.

Again, humans may think of the number three from time to time, and their thoughts (if physicalists are right) may be located in their heads; but what they are thinking of—the number three—is not located in their heads. Everyone who has thought carefully about numbers, and has been able to avoid certain elementary confusions, will admit this much. Differences of opinion about the metaphysical status of numbers (and other abstract objects as well, such as concepts and propositions) nevertheless persist.

Platonism

One ancient view that still has many adherents is *Platonism*, or *realism*. Plato believed in a realm of immaterial, nonpsychological, mind-independent reality comprising all mathematical entities (including numbers and such geometrical entities as triangles) and all concepts (for example, redness and tablehood). (This realm is sometimes called the world of ideas.) According to Plato, we cannot learn about this realm by using our senses. Only the vision of the mind, purified of sensory distractions, can access this "ideal" realm.

The basic Platonic argument for the existence of this realm—using the case of numbers—might be formulated as follows:

> There are numbers;
> Numbers cannot be physical objects;
> Therefore, there are nonphysical objects.

Although this argument has persuaded many thinkers, there is—as often happens in philosophy—a competitive argument that cuts in the opposite direction:

> There are numbers;
> There cannot be nonphysical objects;
> Therefore, numbers cannot be nonphysical objects.

How should the Platonic and the "anti-Platonic" arguments be comparatively evaluated? Again, this is not something everyone will agree on. Those who think it is more evident that numbers cannot be physical objects than that there cannot be nonphysical objects will embrace the Platonic argument; those who think it is more evident that there cannot be nonphysical objects than that numbers cannot be physical objects will opt for the anti-Platonic argument. In fact, arguments in the philosophy of mathematics that discuss this topic are specifically designed to produce reconsiderations of these intuitions about comparative evidentness.

Non-Platonic Positions

Those who deny that there is a realm of ideas independent of humans and about which humans (if they are lucky) make discoveries must attempt to analyze numbers, other mathematical realities, and other abstract objects in terms of human intellectual practices, symbol systems, and languages. In the Platonic view, if humans did not exist, there would still be abstract objects; according to all non-Platonic views, by comparison, if humans did not exist, there would be no abstract objects.

Varieties of Non-Platonism

There are many varieties of non-Platonism, since there are many conceptions of how the analysis of abstract objects, in terms of human intellectual processes, should be carried out. There is, for example, mathematical *intuitionism*, or the view that mathematics should be limited to what can be *intuited*, or cognitively grasped, by humans. This view is generally regarded as eliminating the possibility of transfinite mathematics, and is accordingly also known as *finitism*. Intuitionism (or finitism) is a form of *constructivism*, so called because it seeks to limit mathematics to that which humans can actually *construct* (that is, specify systematically in terms we already comprehend). One further non-Platonic position is *formalism*, which seeks to understand mathematics in terms of formal systems invented by humans. This view is discussed in the following section.

Formal Ontology

The term *ontology* derives from the seventeenth century Latin word *ontologia*, which in turn derives from the Greek *ontos*, meaning *being*. Many writers use *ontology* interchangeably with *metaphysics*, though it has tended to acquire the distinctive meaning *science of being*, which suggests a particularly rigorous approach.

Formalism

A *formalism* is any system inspired by pure mathematics—especially by mathematics in explicit axiomatic form. Philosophers interested in metaphysics have often been drawn to systems that had some of the characteristics (and virtues) of mathematics. For example, the seventeenth-century Dutch philosopher, Spinoza, presented his metaphysics "*more geometrico*," or "in the manner of geometry." In the twentieth century, inspired by—and indeed made possible by—developments in mathematical logic and set theory, a number of philosophers have produced systems of formal metaphysics. Each such system is called a *formal ontology*.

Axiomatization

Putting ideas into mathematical form is called *axiomatization* and involves the following elements: (1) dividing key terms into *undefined* terms (also called *primitive* terms), and using these to explicitly define all other terms; (2) beginning with a small set of *axioms* (or *basic principles*); (3) adopting a set of *transformation rules*, or *purely logical principles*; and (4) using the transformation rules, deriving from the *definitions* and *axioms* all the *theorems* of the system in question. (You will probably have encountered all of these elements and procedures in high-school geometry.)

Applications of Formal Ontology

The formal approach to metaphysics has resulted in a number of interesting systems. Some have attempted to define abstract entities in terms of concrete entities; others have attempted to define events in terms of change-in-property, with *property* taken as a primitive term. One interesting development is a formal ontology of parts and wholes known as *mereology*.

Metaphysics, as we have seen, is the name for those intellectual activities that attempt to provide basic inventories or to clarify basic categories. Metaphysics aims to clarify and improve our thinking about reality. Some metaphysicians regard their task as the clarification or elucidation of basic categories already in use and expressed by languages actually spoken. Metaphysics approached in this spirit is called descriptive metaphysics. Other metaphysicians reject ordinary or pretheoretical categories, and seek to replace them with new categories designed by philosophers. Metaphysics approached in this spirit is called revisionary metaphysics.

Most philosophers acknowledge that the physical sciences help us answer the question "What is there?" However, they consider it unphilosophical to assume, without argument, that only what science studies is real. The adequacy of science to account for all reality comes up, in a particularly vivid way, in connection with human self-understanding. Should we think of ourselves as complicated biophysical systems, or do we have souls (or spirits, or minds)?

These problems are known, collectively, as the mind/body problem. One view is that mind *and* body *name two fundamentally distinct kinds of stuff, and that neither can be analyzed in terms of the other. This view is known as psychophysical dualism, Cartesian dualism, or simply dualism. What dualism really claims is that not everything that exists is of the right sort to be studied by the physical sciences. Another view claims that everything that exists—including the mental lives and inner experiences of human beings—is or can be, in practice or in principle, studied by the physical sciences. This view is known as physicalism, that form of monism which holds that all there is is physical—that is, of the sort that the physical sciences study.*

One problem for physicalism is that choice, as it is most naturally understood, seems to involve a suspension of the general causal order of nature. The physicalist has, accordingly, either to deny that human lives contain moments of choice, or to show how choice is, after all, compatible with the causal necessitation which seems to operate throughout nature.

Another problem for the view that everything is physical is suggested by the special character of such abstract objects as numbers. We saw that we cannot identify numbers with number names (numerals). Does this mean that, in addition to ordinary objects (which are both physical and concrete), we must commit ourselves, ontologically, to the existence of nonphysical abstract objects? This is a question, as we have seen, that not all philosophers would answer in the same way.

Finally, attempts to apply mathematics to our understanding of metaphysics (and in particular to produce axiomatic systems) have, especially in recent times, given rise to a number of systems known as formal ontologies.

Recommended Reading

As in the case of previous chapters, the student might well begin with the standard reference works. The *Encyclopedia of Philosophy* has useful articles under the headings "Metaphysics, History of," "Metaphysics, Nature of," "Ontology," "Mind-Body Problem," "Materialism," and "Monism and Pluralism." The article on the philosopher Stanislaw Lesniewski (1886–1939) is the most accessible source for information on both formal ontology and mereology.

In *The Handbook of Western Philosophy*, the student may wish to consult the articles entitled "Substance, Space, Time and Motion," "Mind and Body: Non-reductionist Theories," "Mind and Body: Some Forms of Reductionism," "and Freedom of the Will."

A very broad, intellectually distinguished survey of the whole field of metaphysics is provided by Anthony Qunton's *The Nature of Things* (1973). A much more modest book, but one written with the beginning student in mind, is Richard Taylor's *Metaphysics* (1963). A more recent book, which supplements Taylor, is Brian Carr's *Metaphysics: An Introduction* (1987).

Several classic works should at least be noted. Two that will give the flavor of bold speculative, or revisionary, metaphysics are Gottfried Wilhelm Leibniz's *Monadology* (written 1714; first published 1840; many subsequent reprintings) and Baruch Spinoza's *Ethics* (originally published shortly after his death in 1677; many subsequent reprintings). Despite its title, *Ethics* offers a complete metaphysical system. For Descartes's own formulation of, and arguments for, Cartesian dualism, see his *Meditations on First Philosophy* (original Latin edition, 1641/1642; many subsequent translations and reprintings). It is not easy to approach the great classics unaided. The student may, accordingly, find helpful the *Encyclopedia of Philosophy* articles on Leibniz, Spinoza, and Descartes. These three thinkers are also clearly presented in *A Critical History of Western Philosophy*, edited by D. J. O'Connor (1964). The "classic" modern work of descriptive metaphysics is P. F. Strawson's *Individuals* (1959).

Of the very large number of books devoted to aspects of the mind/body problem, we will mention a few that are especially helpful or noteworthy. Gilbert Ryle's *The Concept of Mind* (1949) is a sustained critique of Cartesianism. (It is Ryle who described Descartes' view of the human mind as the doctrine of *the ghost in the machine.*) A book that discusses both Descartes and Ryle from a point of view sympathetic to dualism is H. D. Lewis's *The Elusive Mind* (1969). The 1972/1973 Gifford Lectures by various authors, published under the title *The Development of Mind* (1973), discusses most of the main issues related to the mind/body problem.

Also recommended are Keith Campbell's *Body and Mind* (1970); Terence Penelhum's *Survival and Disembodied Existence* (1970); Norman Malcolm's *Problems of Mind: Descartes to Wittgenstein* (1971); Adam Morton's *Frames of Mind: Constraints on the Common-Sense Conception of the Mental* (1980); and D. M. Armstrong and Norman Malcolm's *Consciousness and Causality* (1984). This last book is part of a series called "Great Debates in Philosophy," with Armstrong defending and Malcolm criticizing physicalism. The best recent book on the mind/body problem is Colin McGinn's *The Problem of Consciousness: Essays toward a Resolution* (1990).

Three books that are somewhat more detailed and technical, though still useful to the beginning student, are D. M. Armstrong's *A Materialist Theory of the Mind* (1968); Edgar Wilson's *The Mental as Physical* (1979); and John Foster's *The Case for Idealism* (1982). As their titles indicate, each of these books argues for a particular position on the mind/body problem.

On theories of mind-brain identity, see *Brain and Mind: Modern Concepts of the Nature of Mind*, edited by J. R. Smythies (1965). The state-of-the-art book on brain science and philosophy is Patricia Smith Churchland's *Neurophilosophy: Toward a Unified Science of the Mind/Brain* (1986).

On free will, the student may consult the following books, listed in order of increasing difficulty: D. J. O'Connor's *Free Will* (1971); Daniel C. Dennett's *Elbow Room: The Varieties of Free Will Worth Wanting* (1984); *Essays on Freedom and Action*, edited by Ted Honderich (1973); Peter Van Inwagen's *An Essay on Free Will* (1983); and M. R. Ayers's *The Refutation of Determinism* (1968). Another book on free will that offers a comprehensive survey of the subject is R. L. Franklin's *Freewill and Determinism: A study of rival conceptions of man* (1968).

On the existence of abstract objects, Morris Kline's *Mathematics: The Loss of Certainty* (1980) contains a thorough discussion from a mathematician's point of view. A useful set of essays is provided by *Philosophy of Mathematics: Selected Readings*, edited and with an introduction by Paul Benacerraf and Hilary Putnam (1964). (See especially the essays in the section entitled *The Existence of Mathematical Objects*.) A very brief book, but one that is exceedingly illuminating, is Hilary Putnam's *Philosophy of Logic* (1971). One of the most thorough and up-to-date discussions by an author sympathetic to physicalism is provided by the two volumes of D. M. Armstrong's *Nominalism and Realism* (1978). The clearest contemporary discussion of abstract particulars is Keith Cambell's *Abstract Particulars* (1990).

The term *ontological commitment* was popularized, if not invented, by W. V. Quine. See his *Ontological Relativity and Other Essays* (1969). The term *cheap ontology* is adopted from Stephen Schiffer. The natural ontological attitude is argued for by Arthur Fine in *The Shaky Game* (1986).

For a discussion of events (and an example of *analytic metaphysics*) see Judith Jarvis Thomson's *Acts and Other Events* (1977). Another excellent book on event metaphysics that is technical but not impenetrable is Jonathan Bennett's *Events and Their Names* (1988).

The classic of "process metaphysics" is Alfred North Whitehead's *Process and Reality: An Essay in Cosmology* (1929). Although this book is intensely difficult, it has inspired several generations of disciples. On the metaphysics of time, three books can be recommended: Richard M. Gale's *The Language of Time* (1968); D. H. Mellor's *Real Time* (1981); and Paul Horwich's *Asymmetries in Time: Problems in the Philosophy of Science* (1987). On the metaphysics of space, see Graham Nerlich's *The Shape of Space* (1976).

An interesting book that looks at metaphysics from a fresh vantage point is Patrick Suppes's *Probabilistic Metaphysics* (1984). And, finally, a book by a philosopher that argues for the total abandonment of metaphysical concerns in favor of a "postmetaphysical culture" is Richard Rorty's *Contingency, Irony, and Solidarity* (1989).

Perhaps a final note of warning to the beginning student is in order: almost all contemporary works on the topics of this chapter are very difficult. However, even difficult works will yield to effort, and it is in any case useful to have a research bibliography for future reference.

CHAPTER 5

Philosophy of Mind

Philosophy of mind *comprises a heterogeneous collection of questions, problems, and issues that relate to the mental (or the psychological). Basic questions about the status of minds and the relation of the mental to the physical belong to metaphysics, and have been discussed in chapter 4. Here, we return to the question of whether it is possible, even in principle, to provide a physicalist account of all mental (or psychological) phenomena—that is, whether the mind is the sort of thing that can be studied by the physical sciences. In this chapter, we gain new insights regarding the metaphysical status of minds by looking at the characteristics of our mental lives. We begin with the language used to describe mental life (which philosophers have carefully studied), supplemented by a consideration of the work done in psychology and in the interdisciplinary study of artificial intelligence. Our picture of the mental is rounded out by psychoanalytic theorizing which, under the heading of philosophical psychology, considers such topics as the unconscious, self-deception, motivation, and rationality.*

A part of this chapter is devoted to intentionality, which many philosophers hold is the essence of the mental. Although the concept of intentionality is difficult to elucidate, the basic idea is that intentional verbs (also called mental verbs) are just those verbs capable of taking objects that do not exist. For example, a child may hope—"hope" being a typical mental verb—that Santa Claus brings her presents, even if Santa Claus does not exist.

How to analyze intentional or mental verbs is, we will discover, a controversial area. Various forms of behaviorism relate mental verbs to overt behavior, while various forms of functionalism relate mental verbs to their functions (understood in terms of organisms in interaction with environments). Other attempts to clarify mental life are neither behaviorist nor functionalist, the most important such attempt being associated with the philosopher Ludwig Wittgenstein (1889–1951).

We will also consider the status of subjectivity, of the subjective point of view, and the special character of consciousness. This will involve giving some account of the concept of experience. We will also discuss two concepts that are crucial in the understanding of our "inner" life: privacy and privileged access.

Much contemporary discussion in philosophy of mind focuses on folk psychology, which may perhaps best be described as what most of us use most of the time to explain our own and others' behavior. Such explanation is in terms of beliefs and desires. We will look at the questions: "How good is folk psychology?" "How successful is belief/desire explanation?" "Do we have any alternative to folk psychology or belief/desire explanations?" (Folk psychology, which we all use, should not be confused with "pop" psychology, which usually refers to some watered-down version of academic psychology and/or psychoanalysis.)

Finally, we look at insights and perplexities generated by two interrelated areas of contemporary research: cognitive psychology and computer science. The big questions here are: Are human minds like computers? Can computers think? Is it conceivable that a computer could be constructed that was so much like us as to be a person?

Metaphysics and the Mental

One's basic metaphysical views, whether dualist or physicalist, certainly influence one's conception of mind. Physicalists expect that more and more of our mental life will be explained in neurophysiological terms; in contrast, dualists suppose that, whatever the progress of science, it will not provide a complete explanation of the mental.

Indeed, to be a dualist is precisely to think that there is something left over which is not, even in principle, susceptible to the theoretical/explanatory/experimental/predictive approach characteristic of the physical sciences.

There are, however, two ways in which basic metaphysical views do not settle all questions concerning mind: they do not take account of what we learn from studying mental phenomena themselves, and they do not recognize that mentality is autonomous. (On the autonomy of mentality, see the discussion of anomalous monism below.)

Learning from Mental Phenomena

All of us know a great deal about mentality because we have minds. We know about experience because we have had and—for as long as we continue to be alive—will continue to have experiences. We know about consciousness because we are not only conscious but, at least sometimes, conscious that we are conscious. One might indeed wonder, then, how anything puzzling could arise in connection with this most familiar domain.

There is a sense, indeed, in which each of us is the ultimate authority about his or her own inner life. It would be, in most circumstances, impertinent for someone else to so much as attempt to tell us what we are thinking or feeling. From none of this, however, does it follow that we can provide a philosophically adequate account of the mental. For example, do we really understand why, when we intend to get up from our chair, certain bodily movements begin? Similarly, we may be aware that we notice objects in our environment that we are interested in, but how does selective attention really work? Don't we have to notice an item even to discover that it doesn't interest us, and so proceed to dismiss it? These are just some of the questions that ordinary familiarity—familiarity "from the inside," so to speak—does not help us to answer.

A little reflection will also convince us that very familar features of our mental life—for example, seeing a red apple on the table in front of us—are intimately related to certain processes (neurophysiological, optical, interpretive) that we are not usually aware of. We are aware of the apple, but not of the lenses of our eyes focusing the light reflected from its surface. Dualists and monists agree that there is more to experience than the person whose experience it is can be aware of.

Monists argue that if everything we know from science—facts about ourselves and how we function that are not directly experienced—is taken into account, our best bet is to believe that we are through-and-through physical. Not surprisingly, dualists disagree.

According to dualists (and bear in mind that *dualist* is short for *psychophysical dualist*), there are features of our mental life that cannot be physical. Arguments favoring dualism will emerge throughout this chapter. For now, consider one simple argument:

> Some mental states are essentially about:
> No physical states are about;
> ——————————————————————————————
> Therefore, some mental states are not physical states.

(Please note that "about" in the argument above is not a misplaced preposition, but rather a simple way of indicating the *aboutness*—or *contentful*, or *representational*, character—of mental states.) Students will recognize this as a variation on the basic Cartesian argument for psychophysical dualism (see p. 103). Many philosophers find such arguments quite convincing, but there is no universal agreement about what, if anything, such arguments establish. All we wish to point out here is that, if someone who comes to the study of mind with a commitment to physicalism does find this argument compelling, he or she would have to give up that commitment. Such a person would have learned something about the nature of reality in general—that is, about how to give a general answer to the question "What is there?"—from the nature of mind.

Anomalous Monism

One other important possibility should be considered at this point. A person who holds that humans are very complicated biological organisms—and many people do hold this view, more or less in the spirit of "What else *could* they be?"—need not suppose that the laws of physics, chemistry, and biology tell us anything significant about human mental life. Even if physicalism is correct, it may still turn out that mental life is autonomous, that subjectivity has its own laws, and that we do better predicting future behavior on the basis of beliefs and desires than on the basis of brain states or anything else we may learn from neurophysiology.

A few comparisons may be helpful. Everyone knows that the weather is a purely physical system composed of such "stuff" as water vapor and gas pressure. Yet there is a science of the weather which enjoys modest predictive success. That science, meteorology, is not the same as physics and chemistry put together; it has a measure of autonomy. Another example: Paintings are surely made out of chemicals and nothing but chemicals, but the reasons why paintings succeed or fail is a subject about which the science of chemistry has absolutely nothing to say. The aesthetic, or artistic, properties of paintings simply cannot be handled by chemistry. These comparisons show that considerations of what something is made out of do not settle the question of how to talk about, much less explain, its properties.

The properties of human mental life that interest us (and that are, in any case, *real* properties) have a kind of autonomy, too. People will pick up hundred-dollar bills that they see lying, unclaimed, in the gutter. That people will do so is a psychological generalization—and a very secure one, incidentally—that is quite independent of neurophysiology. The view that we are made exclusively of physical parts, but that our mental lives nevertheless evade the theoretical and explanatory efforts of the physical sciences, is called *anomalous monism*. It is monism because it is a "one-stuff" view; it is anomalous because it denies that human mental life is explained by the nomic regularities of physical science—regularities, that is, based on the laws of nature established by the physical sciences.

Philosophy of Mind and Related Disciplines

Related to the philosophy of mind are the disciplines known as philosophy of psychology and philosophical psychology. Unfortunately, these labels are not used uniformly or consistently by all writers. We can, however, sort out the terminology on the basis of dominant patterns of use.

Philosophy of Mind. Philosophy of mind is analysis of all basic concepts relating to mentality. As such, obviously, it overlaps with areas of metaphysics. Again, philosophy of mind is purely philosophical, purely conceptual, purely analytic. (One of the most important concepts belonging to philosophy of mind—the concept of intentionality—will be discussed later on in this chapter.)

Philosophy of Psychology. Philosophy of psychology refers to all reflective (or meta-level) discourse concerning the science of psychology and its results. Many contemporary philosophers think that psychology—particularly the branch known as cognitive psychology, which studies all psychological processes related to knowledge—is of direct relevance to our understanding of mental concepts. Instead of standing outside psychology and considering its methods and results as the label "philosophy of psychology" implies, these philosophers are interested in doing interdisciplinary work where the disciplines are philosophy and cognitive psychology themselves.

Philosophical Psychology. Philosophical psychology is the term usually reserved for certain somewhat more specialized topics, many of them suggested by psychoanalytic theory and practice. Although fascinating problems about mental life are raised in this area, a basic understanding of the nature of the mental can be achieved without considering them.

Characteristics of Mental Phenomena

The mental life of a human being is so complicated that, even though it is our mental life, and therefore as familiar as anything can be, we find it difficult, as philosophers, to provide a clear map of the mental and to isolate its distinctive characteristics. This section introduces some of the more important distinctions drawn in characterizing mental phenomena. It also considers *intentionality*, which many contemporary philosophers regard as the essence, or defining characteristic, of mental phenomena.

It should be kept in mind that there is no one best way to map mental phenomena. Each of these characterizations draws attention to a feature or a distinction some philosophers have found important, shedding light as it does on various aspects of a complicated, difficult-to-grasp range of phenomena.

Occurrent/Nonoccurrent Mental States

Mental phenomena that are eventlike in character and datable are said to be *occurrent*. I may suddenly realize that *p*, or think of *X*, or begin to feel pain. Other mental phenomena that are not eventlike or datable are said to be *nonoccurrent*. Beliefs are the most important examples. My belief that 11 + 13 = 24 is not something that has to occur to me, nor is it something that can be thought of as happening. (I may, of course, become conscious of my belief when I have occasion to add 11 and 13.) It is not even clear that "beginning to believe that *p*" or "ceasing to believe that *p*" are really eventlike. Sometimes the questions "When did you begin to believe that *p*?" and "When did you stop believing that *p*?" do not have correct answers. Ordinarily, though, *feeling* a desire would count as an occurrent state, whereas *having* a desire would count as a nonoccurrent state.

Dispositions

Some philosophers of mind equate nonoccurrent mental phenomena with what are called, technically, dispositions. Many non-mental properties are clearly dispositional. *Fragility*, for example, is dispositional, because something that is fragile is disposed to break in certain circumstances. Similarly, *solubility* is dispositional, because something that is soluble is disposed (or, roughly, has a tendency) to dissolve in certain specified circumstances.

Some mental verbs seem to fit the same pattern. (Mental verbs, as mentioned earlier, are verbs which, unlike verbs of physical action, are directed to objects which may or may not exist: *believe, desire, hope,* and *fear* are typical mental verbs.) My having a desire for something may amount to a tendency to seek that thing—to try to get it when I can. How hard I try or how much I am willing to pay will measure the strength of my desire. If I believe that Albany is the capital of New York state, I have, among other dispositions, a disposition to reply "Albany" when someone asks me what the capital of New York is.

Conscious/Nonconscious Mental States

Occurrent mental phenomena—becoming aware of, noticing, thinking about, realizing, seeing, feeling, and so on—seem to involve consciousness. Something occurs to me when I become, in some way, conscious of it. Alternatively, an occurrent mental state of a person, *X*, is a state of which *X* is aware. Some philosophers, accordingly, regard the distinction occurrent/nonoccurrent as merely an alternate way of expressing the distinction between conscious and nonconscious mental states. (Philosophers generally use the term *nonconscious* to cover any part of our mental life that is not conscious. The term is meant to be neutral as between various competing psychoanalytic theories of the preconscious or the unconscious.) There are, however, degrees of consciousness; it is not clear whether very low degrees of consciousness (those in which a person is said to be dimly aware of something) should be counted as occurrent.

In considering nonoccurrent beliefs and desires, the question arises as to how the person whose beliefs and desires they are comes to know about them. How do I know what I believe? How do I know what I desire? Is it possible that I have beliefs and desires of which I am absolutely unaware? These are questions that lead in the direction of the unconscious mind. The concept of the unconscious is controversial among philosophers of mind. Some deny that we have an unconscious; others deny that the concept even makes any sense. Then there are all the disagreements about what the correct analysis of this rather mysterious concept should be. One fairly straightforward approach— and one that avoids thinking of the unconscious as a place or container—is simply to define the unconscious in terms of difficulty of access. My arithmetical beliefs, though I am not usually conscious of them, are not unconscious because I can access them easily when I need them; memories of childhood traumas, on the other hand, are sometimes unconscious because they are difficult to access, difficult to bring into consciousness. Based on this analysis, being unconscious is a matter of degree.

Task Verbs/Achievement Verbs and Mental Processes

The division of mental verbs into *task verbs* and *achievement verbs* was first suggested by Gilbert Ryle. "Looking for" is a characteristic task verb: I may look for a book without finding it, or I may be successful. "Finding" is a characteristic achievement verb. All achievement verbs have success conditions built into them, which explains why I can sensibly say "I looked, unsuccessfully, for the book" but cannot sensibly say "I found, unsuccessfully, the book."

Some of Ryle's examples of achievement verbs are *spell*, *catch*, *solve*, *find*, *win*, *cure*, *deceive*, *persuade*, and *arrive*. Three other important achievement verbs are *see*, *discover*, and *know*. That these verbs are achievement verbs means not only that certain psychological processes have to be going on when a person is described in terms of one of these verbs, but also that some objective, psychology-independent requirement has to be met. Thus, whatever the character of my immediate experience, I cannot see X unless my seeing begins with light reflected from the surface of X. By the same token, I cannot discover a tenth planet, whatever my astronomical ambitions, unless there *is* a tenth planet. Finally, I cannot know that p, whatever my beliefs, unless p is true.

Intentionality and the Intentional Stance

Mental phenomena are said to be *intentional* insofar as they are about— or refer to, or function as representations or misrepresentations of—something independent of themselves. Alternatively, a mental state is intentional IFF (just in case) it has representational content. (Bear in mind that *intentionality* and *intentional* are used here as technical terms whose meanings should be distinguished from the meanings of those same words as they occur in ordinary language.)

The intentionality of the mental is closely related to the mind's ability to form *representations* (or, occasionally, misrepresentations) of the world. Thoughts and beliefs and many other "states of mind" seem, typically, to be about something; they refer to something beyond themselves. This characteristic of thoughts, beliefs, and other states of mind is sometimes called *intentional content*—"intentional" because there is no guarantee that anything in the world corresponds to that content.

Intentionality is certainly a centrally important feature of our mental life, but it is not correct to hold that all mental phenomena must be intentional in character. Tickles, itches, pains, and similar bodily sensations or feelings count as mental, since not only is a person conscious or aware of them, but also they cannot exist without someone being so conscious or aware of them. I can't have a pain of which I am totally unaware, a pain that I do not feel. But tickles, itches, pains, and the like fail to have representational content. A pain may be caused by a bodily condition, but it is not *about* that bodily condition.

Two Criteria of the Mental

Such considerations suggest that we probably employ at least two criteria of the mental. *First*, we count something as mental just in case it can exist only in consciousness. *Second*, we count something as mental just in case it is intentional. Most of the time the two criteria are convergent, but sometimes they diverge, as in the case of a pain (consciousness without intentionality) or a belief (intentionality without consciousness). If this is the correct view of the matter, we should not say that intentionality is the essence of the mental; we should claim, more modestly, that many important mental phenomena are intentional.

Aboutness

Intentionality may be such a fundamental and *sui generis* (categorically distinctive) property that it resists illuminating analysis. Still, it is useful to relate *intentional* to certain other terms that paraphrase (even if they do not define) it. One such paraphrasing term is the preposition *about*. Any mental item that has intentional content is about something. My belief that Chimborazo is a volcano in central Ecuador is about a certain volcano, Ecuador, Chimborazo, or what the name *Chimborazo* names.

Suppose, now, that *you* believe that Chimborazo is a fishing village in Sardinia. You happen to believe something wildly wrong. But what is your belief about? It is, certainly at least and probably at most, a belief about what the name *Chimborazo* names. Furthermore, the relation of "being about"—unlike such relations as "being to the left of," "being taller than," or "being the cause of"—does not require the actual existence of both *relata*. (*Relata* is the plural of *relatum*, meaning one of the items related by a relation.) No one can be taller than or to the left of Santa Claus, for example, because Santa Claus does not exist. However, the child's belief that Santa Claus will bring him presents is about Santa Claus. This is sometimes expressed as: the objects of intentional verbs can have *intentional inexistence*.

Propositional Content

Aboutness is, roughly speaking, the mental equivalent of the linguistic relation of naming, designating, or referring to. We now turn our attention to the mental equivalent of statements—or more precisely, of what statements state. What we are zeroing in on here is ordinarily expressed in English by *that p* constructions. *That p* constructions express *propositional content*. Note that different *propositional attitudes* can share exactly the same propositional content: thus, I can believe, desire, hope, or fear *that Santa Claus is coming*.

It is a good idea to make explicit something that is, in any case, fairly obvious: just as the objects of the preposition *about* need not exist, so the various "states of affairs" that propositional attitudes are attitudes toward need not obtain. (To obtain in this sense means to be the case, to be so.) Consequently, I can believe, desire, hope, or fear that Santa Claus is coming, even though it is false that Santa Claus is coming. I can, in other words, have false beliefs, unfulfilled desires, vain hopes, and groundless fears. Thinkers who emphasize intentionality are said to offer a *representational theory of mind*. This must be understood to mean, we now see, a representational and misrepresentational theory of mind.

Physical Systems and Intentional Systems

In an earlier section of this chapter (p. 124), we considered a Cartesian-style argument for psychophysical dualism based on "aboutness." That argument may be restated in terms of intentionality:

> Minds are intentional systems;
> Bodies cannot be intentional systems;
> Therefore, minds cannot be bodies.

This argument can, of course, be directly applied to humans: humans have minds so humans have something nonbodily. Although this argument (or similar arguments) has persuaded many thinkers that dualism is correct, it is far from obvious that we should accept the second premise. Why can't bodies be intentional systems? Once again, it is possible to construct an essentially anti-Cartesian argument that cuts in the opposite direction:

> Humans are physical systems;
> Humans are intentional systems;
> Therefore, some physical systems are intentional systems.

Of course, in showing that some physical systems *are* intentional systems, it is shown that it is *possible* for physical systems to be intentional systems. But not everyone accepts the anti-Cartesian argument. How should these Cartesian and anti-Cartesian arguments be comparatively evaluated, then those who think it is more evident that bodies cannot be intentional systems than that humans are physical systems will accept the Cartesian argument; those who think it is more evident that humans are physical systems than that bodies cannot be intentional systems will accept the anti-Cartesian argument. Here as elsewhere in philosophy, there may be very basic commitments (to Cartesianism, to anti-Cartesianism) that are resistant to change. Let us, however, consider one attempt to motivate change of basic commitment.

Maps

Consider maps. A map of London is certainly a physical object. It also seems to have intentional content, since it is about the city of London. Finally, it represents (or misrepresents, as the case may be) London. Doesn't this show that some physical objects are intentional? Well, not many people would conclude that it does. Indeed, the map case might be used as an argument for dualism. A dualist would say that the map, by itself, is just a physical object. What makes it a representation of London is that some person, *some mind*, connects it with London—that is, reads it or uses it in a certain way. The map example is, therefore, inconclusive.

The Intentional Stance

The "intentional stance" is a phrase used by Daniel Dennett (b. 1942). Its use can be explained as follows: Suppose we are observing the behavior of a human, a computer, or a Martian. If the *best explanation* of his or her or its behavior involves crediting him or her or it with beliefs and desires, then we should adopt the intentional stance. The intentional stance, relative to any system, is simply that which credits the system with beliefs and desires. We sometimes have the best possible reasons for crediting a certain system with beliefs and desires. Moreover, any such system (since intentionality implies mentality) should be counted a mind.

Whether we should adopt the intentional stance relative to a given system has absolutely nothing to do with what the system is made of; that is why basic stuff-obsessed metaphysics is rather beside the point. In deciding whether or not to adopt the intentional stance, the only question is whether our best explanatory theory involves ascription of beliefs and desires. The relatively abstract term *system* is used here in an effort to remain neutral about the question of what systems are made of. Soft-tissue intentional systems, like ourselves, are organisms; hard-tissue intentional systems—certain existing or future computers, perhaps—are machines. If extraterrestrials arrive on the scene and attempt to communicate with us, we will—or at least should—count them as intentional systems or minds, no matter what they turn out to be made of. (Note that this assumes that the communication is rich enough to allow crediting the extraterrestrials with thoughts and feelings. There are degrees of communication—for example, between my dog and myself—that correspond to degrees of mentality.)

How to Analyze Mental Verbs

Contemporary philosophers of mind have devoted a great deal of effort to providing analyses of mental verbs. This analysis is not superfluous. Although we all have beliefs and desires, and can correctly employ the corresponding mental verbs, it is by no means an easy matter to provide an account of what it means to believe or to desire. In this section, we will consider the main accounts of mental verbs offered by contemporary philosophers.

Behaviorism

Behaviorism is the view that, for any mental verb, it is possible to construct an analysis of the following form:

$$X \text{ mental verbs}^* \text{ IFF } X \underline{\hspace{3cm}},$$

where the blank is filled in with a description of *overt*, or publicly observable, behavior. An example might be: X believes that it is going to rain soon IFF when X goes out, X wears a raincoat and takes an umbrella. Most contemporary philosophers regard this extreme form of behaviorism as a bankrupt intellectual project.

This is not to say, however, that studying behavior will shed no light on mental life. Indeed, one may reject behaviorism as a view of what mental life consists in, while nevertheless recommending *methodological behaviorism* for scientific psychology. (Methodologi-

---

*   e.g., believes, desires, hopes, fears that *p*

cal behaviorism is the view that only overt behavior should be taken account of in developing the science of psychology.) In the science of psychology, the alternative to exclusive reliance on public behavior is admitting *introspection* or *introspective reports. Introspection* is sometimes defined as the mind's observation of itself—a kind of looking inward that allows a person to "see" what no one else can see. The trouble with introspection as a basis for science, however, is precisely this privacy. Ordinarily, what is seen by one person can be seen by others. This allows for double-checking, and provides us with a solid "intersubjective" basis for scientific work. By defintion, this is not possible with introspection.

Logical Behaviorism

Unlike extreme forms of behaviorism, which go so far as to deny that humans have consciousness, logical behaviorism is a view about the meaning of mental terms. A pain may be an inner or subjective experience, but once a person learns to use the word *pain*, he or she comes to associate the word with public criteria. Much of the appeal of logical behaviorism comes from the idea that we learn to use the words of a public language by learning to follow rules or apply criteria in a way that is open to criticism by members of our linguistic community. Language is essentially public or social. So-called private language is logically impossible, as is private ostensive definition.

Private Ostensive Definition

Ostention means pointing, so *ostensive* means "pointing-based." People sometimes feel they can provide a meaning for a word like *pain* by saying something along the lines of: "By *pain* I mean what I am feeling now." This won't work, however, for two reasons. *First*, other people will not know what you mean, since they cannnot see, or feel, or otherwise experience, what you are trying to name. *Second*, private ostensive definition accounts do not explain how you know that what you are now feeling is what other people call pain. We can ostensively define *red* by pointing to a red color chip, but this is public ostensive definition. (Incidentally, this shows that *red* must name a color in the world—that is, a color possessed by objects—and not a characteristic of private or inner experience.)

Functionalism

The term *functionalism* is used in philosophy in a number of distinct, though not completely unrelated, ways. In philosophy of mind, functionalism is the view that mental states are to be identified by their causal functions which, with other mental states, eventuate in behavior. Unlike behaviorism, which tries to identify a given mental state with patterns of behavior, functionalism takes mental states to be *causes* of behavior.

Functionalist accounts of mental life have focused mainly on beliefs and desires. A particular belief may be a brain state, but what makes it the belief that it is is its particular function in guiding the actions of the person whose belief it is. It is obvious to common sense (and rightly emphasized by functionalists) that our beliefs guide us when we behave or act, but that what makes us act is our beliefs *plus* our desires. Thus, believing it is about to rain, I take an umbrella because I desire to stay dry. My beliefs as a whole provide me with a map by which I steer. (The larger my percentage of *true* beliefs, the more accurate my map.) My desires, on the other hand, determine where I want to go. It should be added that desires are not independent of beliefs: a person desires what he or she believes is good or worthwhile or desirable. Even Satan couldn't desire evil without saying, "Evil: Be thou my Good!"

Functionalism and Dispositions

Functionalist accounts of mental verbs are also dispositional. My belief that it is raining or is about to rain disposes me to take an umbrella. I won't, of course, take an umbrella unless I go out. My going out, then, is one of the circumstances triggering the disposition. Also, a disposition to do one thing (such as take my umbrella if I go out) may be overridden by another disposition entailed by some other belief—perhaps, the belief that I look silly carrying an umbrella. What I do here will depend on whether my desire to stay dry is or isn't stronger than my desire not to look silly.

Functionalism and the Intentional Stance

It should also be noted that the intentional-stance view is a form of functionalism. In explaining actions on the basis of beliefs and desires, we are considering how those beliefs and desires function jointly in the production of actions. Again, intentional-stance explanations abstract from questions about what intentional systems are made of. In exactly the same way (and motivated by exactly the same theoretical/explanatory considerations), functionalism is indifferent to how functions are realized. An organism made of cells, a computer made of chips, a Martian made of we-know-not-what can all be in precisely the same functional state. For example, a human chess player and a computer chess player can be in exactly the same functional state—that is, about to make the same move to accomplish the same strategic purpose within the parameters of the game of chess—even though the physical descriptions of the contestants will be vastly different.

Wittgensteinian Approaches

The philosopher Wittgenstein's views on the mental, though they bore certain affinities with behaviorism, logical behaviorism, and functionalism, cannot be identified with any of these positions. In the first place, Wittgenstein did not offer his own theory on the nature of the mental. His purpose was to criticize what he regarded as *false pictures* of our mental life that had captivated previous thinkers. Many of these pictures arose because of basic mistakes that people, both philosophers and nonphilosophers, were inclined to make about how language works.

Perhaps the most common of these mistakes—and one that Wittgenstein thought especially misleading in philosophy of mind—is the tendency to think that every noun names. Words like *meaning* and *understanding*, because they do not name external or physical processes, are taken to name internal mental processes. This leads us to suppose that there is always a secret inner process of thinking running parallel to speaking. Wittgenstein asked us to take seriously the possibility that, at least sometimes, words such as *meaning* and *understanding* do not name anything.

Note that it doesn't follow that these words are meaningless, or that they should be eliminated from our vocabulary. An example will help make this point clear. It is perfectly sensible to say "I did it for *X*'s sake," but it would be crazy to look for a "sake," or to ask what *X*'s sake consists of. We understand *X*'s sake, not through locating some thing-like or entity-like item, but by considering stretches of *X*'s life in relation to *X*'s welfare and happiness. In a similar way, Wittgenstein suggested that, instead of looking within, we ought to look at all the circumstances that surround our use of language in deciding whether something is said *and meant*, or heard *and understood*. It is not its inner accompaniment, but rather the wider context into which it fits that makes a given sentence meaningful.

Finally Wittgenstein denounced the "craving for unity" and the "craving for generality" that lead us to suppose that *meaning*, *understanding*, and similar psychological terms express the same simple and uniform essences every time they are used.

Subjectivity

In addition to their attempts to provide an account of mental life along physicalist lines, their efforts to understand intentionality, and their technical analyses of mental verbs, many contemporary philosophers of mind have shown a renewed interest in inner life as it is lived from the inside—in experience, that is, in subjectivity.

Subjectivity and Objectivity

When I say "It is raining," although I may be relying on my own experience of the world, and although I am certainly using a bit of language (which must be counted a collective human invention), what I am saying is nevertheless true—true independently of me, my experience, my mind, my language-based expressive abilities. There were presumably days, long before the arrival of the first human beings, when it rained. Though no one was around to have experiences of the weather or to say things about the weather, it is nonetheless true that it was, on those primal rainy days, raining.

A truth such as that expressed in the sentence "It is raining," which is totally mind-independent and experience-independent, is said to be an *objective truth*. The question naturally arises, particularly for those committed to a scientific picture of the world, whether all of reality can be described using objective, and nothing but objective, truths. Many contemporary philosophers find this doubtful, including some who would count themselves physicalists.

Consider colors. We know that colors have something to do with the selective absorption and reflection of light waves of various amplitudes. We also know that our seeing colors involves a lot of complicated neurophysiology. In addition, there also seems to be *our experience of colors*. Think humans away again by imagining what it was like in the prehuman world. We can safely assume that there were still light waves of various amplitudes bouncing around; they, after all, don't depend on us. But just as surely there was no such thing as "our experience of color"; that is something that does, very obviously, depend on us. From such considerations as these arises the concept of a person as a center of experience, of conscious awareness, and what depends on persons as such centers of experience or conscious awareness is said to be *subjective*. (Sometimes *subjective* means illusory or unreal or deceptive or even biased, but none of those meanings is relevant here.)

The Objectivity of the Subjective

Calling objective truths *facts*, let us consider some facts about X. X has brown hair, weighs 150 pounds, lives on Elm Street. X was born in Hannibal, Missouri. These are all clearly mind-independent truths, or facts, as we are here using the latter term. Now, consider some other facts about X. X once had the frightening experience of turning over in a canoe in the middle of the Mississippi. X often dreams of his dead brother. X is, at this very moment, noticing a shade of blue—X thinks it may be called *cerulean*—in an early Renaissance painting he is looking at.

It is clear that these things depend on X having a mind. A fishing pole in the ill-starred canoe may also have tumbled into the Mississippi and got wet along with X, but it didn't—as of course it couldn't—have a "frightening experience." Nevertheless, it is objectively true of X that he had and is having these experiences. What makes them objectively true, or *facts*, is that they are independent of my mind, or of the mind of any observer or third party. And, of course, they *become* independently true of X's mind as well. X may eventually forget his experience of turning over in the canoe, and even come to deny quite sincerely that he ever did such a thing. It will nevertheless still be true, in an entirely mind-independent way, that X once had that experience.

It would seem to follow from all this that any objectively correct and absolutely complete list of what there is in the universe would have to include, in addition to such things as galaxies and electrons, animal organisms and nervous tissue, the various experiences, including dream experiences, of X. This may all seem too obvious to be worth mentioning; however, some physicalists have denied it.

Veridical/Nonveridical Experiences

In considering the ontological status of experiences, we must be careful to avoid a mistake that is sometimes made. People sometimes say that dreams are not real, but this is not correct: X's dreams of his brother, for example, are real. More, they are parts of his complete biography. What the dreams are dreams *of* is, of course, not real. X may dream of sitting down and eating dinner with his brother, but he doesn't really do so.

We can perhaps clarify the situation by adopting the following technical terms. Experiences divide into the *veridical* and the *nonveridical*. An experience is veridical IFF it is of what it appears to be of to the person whose experience it is. An experience is nonveridical IFF it is *not* of what it appears to be of to the person whose experience it is. Experiences are real, whether they are veridical or nonveridical. A visual experience of a mouse that begins, in the ordinary way, with light reflected from the surface of the mouse is veridical. On the other hand, a person—perhaps under the influence of a hallucinogenic drug—may have an experience *qualitatively identical* (or identical from the inside) with the mouse-provoked experience, with no mouse at all involved. Such an experience is nonveridical.

A mistake that is almost the opposite of saying (falsely) that dreams are unreal is to say: "It's real in a dream." Dreams are real, but things are not real in dreams. One way of diagnosing the mistake is to see that the phrase "in a dream" is a *pseudolocative*—that is, a phrase that seems to specify the location where something happens or takes place, but really doesn't. Contrast pseudolocatives such as "in a dream," "in Greek mythology," and "in *David Copperfield*" with such real locatives as "in my apartment," "in New Jersey," and "in Chicago."

The difference between real locatives and pseudolocatives may be sharpened by considering the following pair of arguments:

I kissed her in New Jersey;
Therefore, I kissed her.

I kissed her in a dream;
Therefore, I kissed her.

It is obvious that the first argument is valid, and that the second argument is invalid. If further convincing is necessary, ask yourself whether you would rather find a sack of money in New Jersey or in a dream.

Privacy and Privileged Access

Are experiences private? In one sense, certainly, experiences can be public. X's experience of turning over in the canoe might have been witnessed by many others (and might have been, on that account, embarrassing as well as frightening). But what did the witnesses really witness? Strictly speaking, all they saw was X turn over in the canoe. They didn't *see* X's experience. They might even have seen that X was frightened, but they didn't see X's experience of being frightened. Because X's actual experience—what the situation was like for X from the inside—was hidden from the spectators, there was the possibility (whether or not X took advantage of it) of X's pretending not to be frightened. It is our capacity to hide our feelings that allows us to be insincere.

Though some philosophers of mind deny that thoughts and experiences and other mental phenomena are private, our description of X's case supports the idea that experiences are private. And so are thoughts: you may be able to guess what I am thinking, but I can mislead you. You have no direct access to my thoughts. The description of X's case also supports the idea that X, at least sometimes, has *privileged access* to his inner life. X can know—although this doesn't mean that X always *does* know—how frightened he was. I know what I am thinking, as I look at your new hat, in a way I hope you don't perceive. Even if fear, in the canoe case, and strong disapproval, in the hat case, are likely to betray themselves through signs observable by others, most thoughts and feelings in most circumstances cannot be guessed on the basis of external indicators.

The kind of privacy under discussion should not be confused with the possibility of a *private language*. True, you can't see my experiences, or otherwise experience them in the direct and first-hand way that I do. However, there is no way that I can talk about my experiences, even to myself, without using descriptions that belong to a shared public language.

The kind of privileged access under discussion should not be confused with *incorrigible access*. It is sometimes held that a person cannot make any mistakes about the character of his or her inner life. However, even though he or she knows it intimately, mistakes of many kinds are still possible. This is obviously true for beliefs and desires, and it is also true of conscious states or states of awareness. X is feeling frightened, but he may not realize just how frightened he was until he is safe on land.

Folk Psychology

Earlier, in our consideration of the social sciences, we touched on *folk psychology*. You will recall our observation that every human being, at a surprisingly early age, learns to explain and predict the behavior of other people. We are not only able to explain (often, though not always) what people are up to, but we can also (again, often though not always) make very good, "educated" guesses about what they are *going* to do. The rough-and-ready—and, for the most part, tacit and unformulated—theory on the basis of which we so explain and predict is what is now generally called folk psychology.

Although folk psychology is probably very complicated, it is based on a few simple ideas. One is that people have beliefs. Another is that people have desires. Yet another—and perhaps the most crucial of all—is the assumption that people are rational. Now, *rational* can mean a number of things. What it means here, though, can be specified along the following lines: to say that X is rational means that, if X desires O, and believes that A-ing is the best available way to get O, X will A. (In reality things are much more complicated than this, of course: X will have a number of desires of different strengths, as well as different opportunities and different costs associated with each.) This kind of rationality is what is sometimes called *means/end* rationality. Note that it says nothing about the rationality of X's beliefs, or about the worthwhileness of X's desires.

Two problems with this formulation of means/end rationality have been much discussed in the literature on rationality. *First*, is it really true that people are rational in this sense? Folk psychology does not need to claim that absolutely everyone is rational in the means/end sense, only that most people are. And we are, as folk psychologists ourselves, aware of people who are consistently irrational. They stand out as exceptions to the general norm. *Second*, for the large majority of people who are rational, is this an adequate formulation of rationality? Qualified thinkers disagree about this. A minor problem is that people have lots of desires that may conflict: *A*-ing may indeed get me *O*, but may also involve me in something I desire to avoid. More difficult is the question of whether a person's commitment to morality should be counted as just another desire.

There is also a problem which arises with respect to patience: on the one hand, the human tendency to postpone and procrastinate, and on the other, the human ability to wait for better opportunities. Given the active state of research in folk psychology and rationality theory, it is probably premature to attempt a definitive evaluation of these issues. We should bear in mind, however, that for the explanatory and predictive purposes of everyday life, folk psychology has no real competitor.

Cognitive Psychology and Computer Science

Philosophy of mind, as a branch of philosophy, ought to be purely conceptual or analytic. And indeed, it is still true that most of what philosophers of mind do can be described as conceptual analysis. Nevertheless, the concepts of interest at present to philosophers thinking about mind often originate in work done by cognitive psychologists and computer scientists. There is, after all, no reason why philosophers should restrict their attention to common-sense concepts, or to concepts belonging to the philosophical tradition itself.

Cognitive Psychology

Cognitive psychology is the study of human organisms as information-processing systems. (It may also be defined as the study of humans as intentional or representational systems.) Until recently, most psychology was behaviorist, and psychological research was based on a fairly simple stimulus/response model of *mentation* (mental functioning). Cognitive psychology arose in an attempt to overcome the many shortcomings of stimulus/response psychology.

We can better understand the nature of both the behaviorist and the cognitive approaches to human psychology by considering the following diagram:

THE ORGANISM

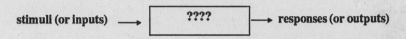

stimuli (or inputs) ⟶ | ???? | ⟶ responses (or outputs)

Behaviorist, or stimulus/response, psychology tends to assume that there is always a relatively simple relation between inputs and outputs. Responses of the organism to various stimuli—the blinking response, for example—are thought of as being "hard-wired" into the nervous system of the organism in question, and unaffected by thought or experience. However, most human responses are not like this. Cognitive psychology, accordingly, has stressed the necessity of replacing the question marks in the diagram above with a *model of mind*. To be of value, such a model must adequately explain the very complicated relation between inputs and outputs, and in particular the detailed knowledge of the environment that the outputs reflect.

Models of Mind

At present, cognitive psychologists are constructing an abstract and partly speculative model of mind. They are thinking in terms of the representational and computational functions of the mind (that is, what the mind must do), rather than in terms of the actual neurophysiological realizations of mental functions. Moreover, they admit that any model, given the level of present knowledge, embodies some guesswork— some "best bet now" kind of thinking.

Cognitive Penetrability/Cognitive Impenetrability

Some input-output relations, such as the blinking reflex, do not involve belief, cognitive content, information, or a representation/ misrepresentation of reality. These functions, which are often crucial for survival in humans and certain other animals, are said to be *cognitively impenetrable*. By contrast, those input-output relations that depend on representations of reality and/or the manipulation of information are said to be *cognitively penetrable*. Any model of mind must, accordingly, have room for both cognitively penetrable and cognitively impenetrable functions.

Minds and Brains

Cognitive psychology attempts to construct a model of mind that will explain human intellectual abilities. It is a purely abstract or functional model—that is, as a psychological model it does not try to say what sort of physical system would be needed to perform the postulated functions. In fact, all (or very nearly all) cognitive psychologists believe that the functions they describe in abstract terms are performed in the brain. It is, therefore, generally conceded that any psychological model of mind must be compatible with everything we know about how the brain—that complex chunk of soft-cell hardware—actually works.

Computer Science

Much speculation on human mental life has been inspired by the development of more and more sophisticated computers. Computers are, of course, very different from human beings in respect to the stuff they are made of: the cells in our brains are not very much like the chips in computers. However, since cognitive psychology characterizes mental processes in functional terms, there is no reason why some of our thinking cannot be the same as that of a computer—for example, in having the same informational content. This does not mean either that computers think or that humans think like computers. It simply means that we cannot rule out functional similarities on the grounds of essential differences in material construction.

Computational Thought

Whatever the final fate of the idea that computers can think, it is a useful research strategy in cognitive psychology to assume that human mental processes are computational in character. We often speak in terms of great "leaps of thought" and "sudden insights," and we are inclined to think of geniuses in all fields in terms of "creativity" and "imagination." And this is entirely appropriate. However, psychologists studying our mental life have as their job the explanation of how such leaps of thought, sudden insights, creativity, and imagination are possible. A science of mind that aims to be explanatorily complete cannot tolerate ultimate mysteries.

One obvious strategy is to break down big leaps and other spectacular mental feats into lots of little steps. High-level mental accomplishments may arise when many subsystems or mental modules work together. This approach to explaining higher-order mental functions is sometimes referred to as the *modularity thesis*. Given certain inputs each mental module computes an output, following a simple mechanical rule or algorithm.

Artificial Intelligence

Can computer scientists and engineers actually construct a machine that thinks? Is artificial intelligence (often abbreviated AI) a real possibility? In considering these questions, two extremes should be avoided. AI enthusiasts often exaggerate the progress made toward *machine simulation* of human mental functioning. Computers are very far from being a competitive threat to humans—though they are getting very good at playing chess. On the other hand, it is probably foolish to rule out all possibility of computers thinking. After all, *thinking* covers a lot of ground, a lot of different tasks. And, finally, AI is still in its early stages: predicting the future of science and engineering, here as elsewhere, is something that philosophers are no better equipped to do than anybody else.

Philosophical Psychology

Although the "hot" areas in philosophy of mind (with "hot" being defined in terms of the funding available for research, prestige of investigators, and general consensus as to where the most interesting problems cluster) are inspired by cognitive psychology, computer science, and AI, there is a hardy perennial among subject matters that takes its problems from everyday life, literature, and psychoanalysis. *Philosophical psychology* has attempted to clarify such concepts as emotion, desire, sexual desire, self-deception, and motive. It turns out that such familiar concepts, when thought about with analytical clarity, are revealed to be puzzling and sometimes inconsistent— and these are areas where cognitive psychology, computer science, and AI have not been helpful.

Other animals may have minds, but human beings are alone capable of asking questions about the nature of mind. (If there are extraterrestrials with minds like ours—or better—they, too, can ask questions about mind.) We have seen that some questions about mind are basically metaphysical. What is the ontological status of mind? How does our conception of mind fit in with everything we know about the physical world? How we think about these questions will in part depend on our basic metaphysical views (monism, dualism), but any metaphysics must be one that has a place for the kind of mind we know we have.

What kind of mind do we have? What is the nature of the mental? Not all philosophers, thinking about mind, agree that there is a single essence or nature of mind—a single relatively small core of defining properties or necessary features. Here, as elsewhere, we encounter the possibility that an important concept may be a "family-resemblance" concept.

Nevertheless, much of what is most important in human mental life can be captured by thinking of ourselves as intentional systems. Many of our states of mind, whatever they may be made of, certainly refer to or represent a world beyond themselves. An intentional system is one whose behavior can be best explained by ascribing to it both beliefs and desires. Here again, we encounter the Cartesian concern about whether or not physical systems (which is what physicalists say we are) can be intentional systems.

We constantly use what is called folk psychology to explain and predict the behavior of ourselves and other people. Although folk-psychological explanations are rough-and-ready and only imperfectly successful, there is at present no alternative to this belief/desire approach.

Not surprisingly, philosophy of mind has been inspired by certain developments in psychology. Philosophers of mind once spent a great deal of time criticizing "naive behaviorist" or "stimulus/response" models of the mental; now they welcome the new and improved models of mind put forward by cognitive psychologists. As we have seen, models of mind are abstract and functional in character. A functionalist approach is not, as such, concerned with how "functional states" are realized physically. It is possible that a human, a computer, and an extraterrestrial may all be in the same functional state. Philosophers of mind have, accordingly, looked as much to computer science as to brain science for clues to the nature of the mental.

Recommended Reading

Many of the main terms and topics in philosophy of mind are treated, in their alphabetical place, in the *Encyclopedia of Philosophy*. See, in particular, the articles on behaviorism and intentionality. See also the article on behaviorism in *The Handbook of Western Philosophy*.

Of the many books intended for the beginning student, the following are particularly helpful: *The Philosophy of Mind*, edited by V.C. Chappell (1962); *Philosophy of Mind*, edited by Stuart Hampshire (1966); Alan R. White's *The Philosophy of Mind* (1967); Jerome A. Shaffer's *Philosophy of Mind* (1968); Norman Malcolm's *Problems of Mind: Descartes to Wittgenstein* (1971); C. H. Whiteley's *Mind in Action: An Essay in Philosophical Psychology* (1973); *The Philosophy of Mind*, edited by Jonathan Glover (1976); Colin McGinn's *The Character of Mind* (1983); Joseph Margolis's *Philosophy of Psychology* (1984); *The Philosophy of Mind: An Introduction*, by Peter Smith and O. R. Jones (1986); Paul M. Churchland's *Matter and Consciousness: A Contemporary Introduction to the Philosophy of Mind* (revised edition, 1988); Jenny Teichman's *Philosophy and the Mind* (1988); and Gregory McCulloch's *The Game of the Name: Introducing Logic, Language, and Mind* (1989).

Although Gilbert Ryle's *The Concept of Mind* (1949) was not intended for the beginning student, its lucid prose style makes it accessible to anyone.

Jonathan Miller's *States of Mind* (1983) consists of interviews conducted by Mr. Miller with leading philosophers of mind, computer scientists, cognitive psychologists, and other interested parties. This book is so much fun to read, and provides one with a good idea of so many important views at so little cost, that it almost seems like cheating.

One of the clearest and most insightful writers on the whole range of topics in philosophy of mind (but with particular emphasis on intentionality) is Daniel C. Dennett. All three of his books in this area are worth reading: *Content and Consciousness* (1969); *Brainstorms: Philosophical Essays on Mind and Psychology* (1978); and *The Intentional Stance* (1987).

A very clear presentation of Wittgenstein's views on mind is provided by George Pitcher's *The Philosophy of Wittgenstein* (1964); see especially the chapters entitled "Mind and its Place in Language" and "Sensations and Talk of Them." For an original, contemporary treatment, broadly Wittgensteinian in sympathy, see Arthur W. Collins's *The Nature of Mental Things* (1987).

A number of other books worth consulting, some of them quite specialized and all more or less difficult, are Sir Russell Brain's *The Nature of Experience* (1959); Gilbert Harman's *Thought* (1973); T. E. Wilkerson's *Minds, Brains and People* (1974); David Pears's *Questions in the Philosophy of Mind* (1975); Raziel Abelson's *Persons: A Study in Philosophical Psychology* (1977); Brian Loar's *Mind and Meaning* (1981); *Thought and Object: Essays on Intentionality*, edited by Andrew Woodfield (1982); Lynne Rudder Baker's *Saving Belief: A Critique of Physicalism* (1987); Fred Dretske's *Explaining Behavior: Reasons in a World of Causes* (1988); Jay L. Garfield's *Belief in Psychology: A Study in the Ontology of Mind* (1988); *Mindwaves: Thoughts on Intelligence, Identity and Consciousness*, edited by Colin Blakemore and Susan Greenfield (1989); Michael Lockwood's *Mind, Brain and the Quantum: The Compound 'I'* (1989); and D. W. Hamlyn's *In and Out of the Black Box: On the Philosophy of Cognition* (1990).

On subjectivity and the subjective point of view, two books by Colin McGinn are recommended: *The Subjective View: Secondary Qualities and Indexical Thoughts* (1983), and *Mental Content* (1989). Another philosopher who writes on many topics in philosophy of mind, but with particular emphasis on subjectivity, is Thomas Nagel. His *Mortal Questions* (1979) contains the contemporary classic "What is it like to be a bat?" See also his more recent *The View from Nowhere* (1986). For a completely different approach to consciousness, see Donald R. Griffin's *The Question of Animal Awareness: Evolutionary Continuity of Mental Experience* (1976).

The following books are among the best at the interface of philosophy of mind and cognitive psychology: Jerry A. Fodor's *Representations: Philosophical Essays on the Foundations of Cognitive Science* (1981); Jerry A. Fodor's *The Modularity of Mind* (1983); Philip N. Johnson-Laird's *Mental Models* (1983); Owen J. Flanagan, Jr.'s *The Science of the Mind* (1984); Anthony J. Sanford's *The Mind of Man: Models of Human Understanding* (1987); and Jerry A. Fodor's *Psychosemantics: The Problem of Meaning in the Philosophy of Mind* (1988). Worthy of special note is a three-volume series edited by Daniel N. Osherson and Howard Lasnik under the general title of *An Invitation to Cognitive Science*: vol.1: *Language*; vol. 2: *Visual Cognition and Action*; vol. 3: *Thinking* (1990).

Among the best of the books that relate philosophy of mind to computer science and AI, we particularly recommend Keith Gunderson's *Mentality and Machines* (1971); Hubert L. Dreyfus's *What Computers Can't Do: The Limits of Artificial Intelligence (revised edition, 1979); Mind Design: Philosophy, Psychology, Artificial Intelligence*, edited by John Haugeland (1981); Zenon W. Pylyshyn's *Computation and Cognition: Toward a Foundation for Cognitive Science*

(1986); and Philip N. Johnson-Laird's *The Computer and The Mind: An Introduction to Cognitive Science* (1988).

On folk psychology, see Stephen P. Stich's *From Folk Psychology to Cognitive Science: The Case Against Belief* (1983), and Paul M. Churchland's *A Neurocomputational Perspective: The Nature of Mind and the Structure of Science* (1989).

Many of the most important books in the area of philosophical psychology have been published over the years in a series entitled *Studies in Philosophical Psychology*, edited by R. F. Holland. Among many excellent titles the following are especially recommended: Peter Geach's *Mental Acts: Their Content and Their Objects* (1957); D. W. Hamlyn's *The Psychology of Perception* (1957); R. S. Peter's *The Concept of Motivation* (1958); A. C. MacIntyre's *The Unconscious: A Conceptual Study* (1958); Norman Malcolm's *Dreaming* (1959); D. M. Armstrong's *Bodily Sensations* (1962); Peter Alexander's *Sensationalism and Scientific Explanation* (1963); Anthony Kenny's *Action, Emotion and Will* (1963); Jonathan Bennett's *Rationality: An Essay Toward an Analysis* (1964); Herbert Fingarette's *Self-Deception* (1969); and M. O'C. Drury's *The Danger of Words* (1973).

CHAPTER 6

Philosophy of Language

Philosophers have always been interested in language, but not until the twentieth century has language become a central philosophical topic. It has become widely accepted that the best way to solve (or dissolve) problems in all areas of philosophy is to pay close attention to the language in which those problems are formulated. This heightened awareness of language and the increased reliance on its analysis among philosophers of our own time is referred to as the linguistic turn.

There are many reasons why language has become increasingly important for philosophy. First, our concepts and thoughts, although expressed in a multitude of different languages (and sometimes expressed without the use of any language), are in the vast majority of cases closely tied to language. Language is now seen as a great reservoir of categories and concepts, without which sophisticated thinking would be impossible. This is largely because a common older view of language as a mere instrument for the expression of thought is no longer accepted. If philosophy is defined as the analysis of concepts, it turns out that it can do this best by paying close attention to how concept-expressive words are used. Second, language-using behavior is the most complex and subtle displayed by humans and, accordingly, provides us with many clues not only about how the mind works, but also about rationality, rule-following, and other basic philosophical topics. Third, the science of language, called linguistics, offers much material for philosophical reflection. Here, as in philosophy of mind, stimulation comes from developments in science. Indeed, it is sometimes difficult to say of some highly interdisciplinary work whether it belongs to philosophy or to linguistics.

As we shall see, the philosophical study of language can be approached in many different ways. One useful classification of approaches divides the study of language into syntactics, which studies the relation of linguistic signs to each other; semantics, which studies the relation of linguistic signs to reality; and pragmatics, which studies the relation of linguistic signs to their human users.

The single most important concept in the philosophy of language is the concept of meaning. We shall consider various kinds of meaning, as well as the principal theories of meaning that philosophers have formulated. In doing so, we will have to distinguish the sense of meaning at work in a sentence like "Those clouds mean rain" from the sense of meaning at work in a sentence like "Bachelor means unmarried adult man who is not a priest." We must also distinguish meaning as reference from meaning as sense. Reference is involved when I say, "I meant Bob Smith"; sense is involved when I say, "The German sentence 'Es regnet' means 'It is raining'." Finally, we will distinguish between what a person means, called speaker's meaning, from what sentences that he or she uses standardly mean, called sentence meaning.

The Nature of Language

Everybody knows what language is. *Language*, to most people, refers to one of the world's natural languages, one or more of which most people speak every day. Most people are also aware that some languages—Latin, for example—once spoken by many people are no longer in day-to-day use, surviving primarily in written form as the object of scholarly interest. Both philosophers and linguists, beginning with this familiar conception of language, have introduced a number of analytical distinctions and a corresponding terminology. The more important of these are discussed in the following sections.

Natural Languages/Artificial Languages

Both philosophers and linguists distinguish natural from artificial languages. We shall examine each in turn.

Natural Languages

English, French, Spanish, and Chinese are a few examples of natural languages. Natural languages are spoken by relatively large groups of people. They evolve slowly, and the changes that they undergo are rarely "designed in" by individuals or groups. Some of the earliest scientific studies of languages were concerned with the slow— and surprisingly regular—changes in sound patterns within a given language, or among historically related languages. Such studies—that is, studies of certain changes over a period of time—belong to *diachronic linguistics*. It is also possible to study language at a given moment, abstracting from all questions of development or change. Such studies belong to *synchronic linguistics*. Synchronic linguistics focuses on language as a system or structure of interrelated items—for example, individual words—that cannot be understood in isolation.

Artificial Languages

Artificial languages, such as computer languages, are devised by individuals or committees of individuals for particular purposes, and have "designed in" characteristics thought to promote those purposes. In fact, the relation between linguistic signs, such as words, and their meanings is almost always a matter of convention. There is no reason, for instance, that the word *dog* should mean domestic canine; what makes *dog* mean what it does is that speakers of English observe, and expect each other to honor, the convention that associates *dog* with dogs.

Even more important, there is more than one way to cut up the world and each natural language does so somewhat differently. This double conventionality of all linguistic signs is sometimes referred to as *L'arbitraire du signe* (Fr.:"the arbitrariness of the sign"), a phrase made popular by one of the founders of modern linguistics, Ferdinand de Saussure (1857–1913). The one possible exception to the arbitrary character of linguistic signs is *onomatopoeia*, the imitation by certain words—for example, *boom* and *bow-wow*—of the sounds that they name. Inventors of an artificial language can be understood as introducing a set of words or other symbols with a set of explicit conventions guaranteeing each word or symbol a single clearcut meaning.

Ordinary Language

Ordinary language describes the language spoken by most people most of the time—in other words, the language of everyday life. It is distinguished from *specialist languages*, which contain technical terms like *semantic ascent* and *radioimmunoassay*.

Many twentieth-century philosophers have held that ordinary language, in the sense just clarified, not only gives us access to all philosophically important concepts, but also provides us with the most subtle medium in which to think about and discuss those concepts. Other philosophers have been reformist in spirit. Inspired by logic and mathematics, they have sought to construct formal, or "ideal," languages that avoid what they regard as the shortcomings of ordinary language: ambiguity, vagueness, and vacuity. Although such philosophers cannot realistically expect the wholesale adoption of their proposed reforms, they can at least adopt them themselves, and use them in their articles and books.

Overcoming Ambiguity

Many words in ordinary language are *ambiguous*—that is, they mean two or more quite separate things. One way to overcome ambiguity is to apply the device of *subscription*. Consider, for example, the word *reason*, which can mean *cause*, *motive*, or *justification*, or have any one of several other less common meanings. If context does not *disambiguate*—that is, render a potentially ambiguous linguistic item unambiguous—we can always write "$reason_c$," "$reason_m$," and "$reason_j$," being careful to make our readers aware of the code involved.

Overcoming Vagueness

Many words in ordinary language are *vague*—that is, there are instances where it is hard to say whether or not they apply. For such vague terms, when precision is necessary we can *stipulate* (or explicitly announce) how we are going to use the term. A stipulative definition of *old*, for example, might read: "By *old*, I mean having reached one's 67th birthday." No one can argue that this is not indeed what *old* means, since stipulative definitions do not claim to report how people use certain words, but rather aim to establish usage for a given purpose in a given context. It does not follow, however, that a stipulation cannot be pointless or silly.

Getting Rid of Vacuous Terms

Philosophers who think that ordinary language is in need of reform have also worried about *vacuous*, or empty, terms—terms that appear namelike but that actually name nothing. Consider the pair of proper names, *George Washington* and *Zeus*. As proper names, both purport to pick out some individual. *George Washington* does; *Zeus* does not. Nothing stands to *Zeus* in the way that a certain man, George Washington, stands to *George Washington*.

A mistake sometimes made by beginning students of language is to claim that *Zeus* is the name of a certain idea or concept. *Zeus* names a god, but a god who does not exist. *The concept of Zeus* names a certain idea or concept—an idea or concept that does exist.

Consider the pair of common nouns, *horse* and *unicorn*. As common nouns, both purport to apply indifferently to any member of a certain class. However, the class of horses has members, because there are horses, whereas the class of unicorns has no members, because there are no unicorns. Again, it is a mistake to suppose that *unicorn* names a certain idea or concept. In fact, *unicorn* names a kind of animal, a kind that does not exist. And, of course, *the concept of unicorn* names a certain concept—a concept that does exist.

Terms such as *Zeus*, which do not name (as other terms in their category name), and *unicorn*, which do not apply to individuals (as other terms in their category apply to individuals), are called vacuous terms, or empty terms.

Feasibility of Getting Rid of Vacuous Terms. Philosophers as well as other language specialists have sometimes imagined an ideal language free of vacuous terms. Is this a feasible goal? And, if we could do it, would it be worthwhile? Experts do not agree about how these questions should be answered. Still, a plausible (and widely accepted) answer would run as follows: We could build as many of our "current ontological commitments" into language as we can establish independently of language. We know we don't believe in Zeus, Santa Claus, witches, and phlogiston, so we could get rid of those four terms. But this would be pointless, and probably harmful. It is pointless because the existence of vacuous terms in the language does no harm so long as we remember that not every noun names. Language may help us think, by providing us with an enormous inventory of concepts and categories, but it does not do our thinking for us: each of us has to decide whether to say "Zeus exists" or "Zeus does not exist."

Everything humans take seriously, and are committed to, finds its way into language, where it remains long after beliefs lapse and commitments are canceled. Language is not, directly, an inventory of what exists, but rather an inventory—in part archeological and historical—of what humans have thought worth talking about and worth saying. This cumulative, historical/memorial character of language is, finally, the reason it would be positively harmful to try to purify language of terms that do not accord with current convictions. Language helps us trace histories and express them. We want to be able to say that people once believed in witches, but that most people now do not; or that science, at one stage, tried to explain combustion with phlogiston; or that alchemists tried to change lead into gold by employing something they referred to as the "philosopher's stone."

Form

Most people can distinguish the *form*, or pattern, a sentence has from its content. They recognize that the sentences "All Swedes are Protestants" and "All ravens are black" have a common form or pattern, even though they have different contents—the first being about the religion of the Swedes, the second about the color of ravens. There are many ways of isolating and analyzing linguistic form. It should be noted, though, that linguists take a somewhat different approach to the study of form in language than do philosophers.

Linguists' Approach to Form

Grammar and Syntax. Linguists studying particular languages try to develop classifications of word and sentence forms that can be used to describe interesting relations among those forms. The result of their efforts (for a particular language, *L*) is sometimes referred to as a *grammar of L*, *syntax of L*, or *grammar and syntax of L*. This apparent terminological confusion can be explained as follows: *Grammar*, narrowly defined, means a classification of parts of speech and types of sentences; *syntax*, narrowly defined, means a specification of combination rules that specify permissible combinations of words from various grammatical categories. Finally, besides their use in accordance with these strict definitions, *grammar* and *syntax* are often used interchangeably.

Comparativism. The first order of business for a linguist is to develop a grammar-and-syntax for a particular language. After this has been done for a number of languages, linguists can make comparisons. Comparative study has shown that many, though not all, syntactical/grammatical features can be found in ranges of languages, particularly those which have evolved from a common ancestor.

Example of Grammatical/Syntactical Form. Consider the pair of sentences "John loves Mary" and "John fears Mary." Both have the form *s Rs o*, where *s* stands for the subject, *o* for the object, and *R* for any one of a certain class of verbs. What makes this specification of form interesting is that it can be used to define an operation, known as *passive transformation*: given as input *s Rs o*, we can, at will, derive as output *o is R-ed by s*. For our example sentences, passive transformation produces the *passive transforms*: "Mary is loved by John" and "Mary is feared by John."

Philosophers' Approach to Form

Logical Grammar, Logical Syntax. Philosophers are much less interested than linguists in language-specific features. Of more interest to philosophers are those aspects of grammatical/syntactical form that play a role in correct or incorrect reasoning, inference, and argument. For example, sentences of the form "All *S* are *P*" play a role in arguments known as syllogisms.

Logical Form. This leads to another feature of the philosopher's approach: arguments are often stated in some standardized form involving sentences having a certain form. Accordingly, ordinary language sentences are often *regimented* or, as it is sometimes put, *translated into standard form.* Thus, in order to fit the standard mold the sentence "All dogs bark" might become "All dogs are barkers."

We should remember, however, that there is no such thing as *the* form of a given sentence. We indicate form in a variety of ways, depending on our purposes. Aspects of form unimportant in understanding some reasoning processes may be crucial in understanding others. Also, precisely which forms we find it convenient to isolate will depend on the logical system we are using. "All *S* are *P*" is the right isolate for the traditional logic of terms, whereas "For every *x*, if *Sx*, then Px" is the right isolate for modern quantificational logic. ("Sx" is the standard way of writing "x is S.")

Language Acquisition and Innateness

Language Acquisition

Humans are not born speaking their native languages. Moreover, the language they eventually come to speak will depend on the language spoken by the people around them. These facts have suggested a basically empirical explanation of language acquisition: that is, we learn our native language by experience. We imitate those around us who also positively and negatively "reinforce" our efforts by providing rewards—for example, smiles—and punishments (frowns), as appropriate. However natural, this empirical (experience/imitation) model of language acquisition has recently come in for serious criticism.

Criticisms of the Experience/Imitation Model

A set of interrelated criticisms has been raised—most forcefully by Noam Chomsky—against the experience/imitation view of language acquisition. These criticisms can be summarized as follows: (1) The number of sample sentences the child hears is too small. (2) Items in the child's collection of sample sentences are imperfect. The child hears sentences that contain many small performance mistakes—for example, pauses, repetitions, slips of the tongue. (3) Language-using ability does not seem to be a function of general intelligence; for example, many mentally subnormal children learn to speak their native languages.

Linguistic Competence and Linguistic Creativity

These arguments against the experience/imitation model are based on a conception of language-using ability as *linguistic competence*. Linguistic competence is not merely the ability to reproduce sentences that the speaker has heard, but to produce (and understand) many novel sentences. Linguistic competence is an open-ended ability to generate sentences that other speakers will recognize as well-formed, and will be able to understand. This absolutely nonparrotlike character of linguistic competence is referred to as *linguistic creativity*.

Innateness

How is linguistic competence, including linguistic creativity, to be explained? Not all theorists, whether philosophers or linguists, agree about the correct answer to this question. There are still those who think that "learning from experience" can explain language acquisition. Others, following Chomsky, have suggested that there is a *universal grammar* built into our nervous system that is merely "customized" to our particular native language by early language-relevant experiences. If this view is correct, we should expect the empirical study of languages to isolate an *abstract grammar* common to all languages. Such an abstract grammar would, if found, be the innate core shared by all natural languages.

In any case, deciding how much of any skill or competence, linguistic or otherwise, is innate (or inborn) and how much is learned from experience depends partly on empirical research. To that extent, such a decision cannot be made on the basis of a global philosophical preference for—or aversion to—empiricism.

Syntactics

Syntactics is traditionally defined as the study of the relation of linguistic signs to each other. A linguistic sign is called, in more ordinary English, a *word*. Nonspecialists tend to take the concept of *word* for granted, but in linguistic theory it is not easy to say what should be counted a single word. Nor is it easy, in practice, to construct word lists for languages that are being studied from scratch.

Let us assume that linguists have specified all the words for a given language. The next step is to classify the words by grammatical category. For many languages, these will be such familiar categories as *noun*, *verb*, *adjective*, and so on. The whole thrust of grammatical classification, however, is for purposes of syntax, that specifies which grammatical categories of words can be combined. The syntax of a language, *L*, is the *set of combination rules for L*. Our implicit grasp of syntax allows us to identify a word-string like "The were up is at apple" as *syntactically incorrect*. Presumably, we can reject this sentence without even thinking about meaning. That is, it is not rejected on grounds of meaninglessness. Note that there are meaningless sentences that are, from point of view of syntax, perfectly correct: "Some lazy numbers lurk furiously on sticks of even-numbered slime" is an example.

The Independence of Syntax

One important—and controversial—question in the philosophy of linguistics is whether it is possible to isolate a completely independent syntactical level. Can we really make judgments about syntactical correctness without considering the meanings of the words whose combinations we are examining? Again, this is not a question about which there is consensus.

Syntax and Formal Approaches

Emphasis on syntax is closely related to those research programs—in, variously, logic, linguistics, and computer science—that attempt to discover how much computation (or, in ordinary English, "thinking") can be done without reference to meaning. If rules for symbol manipulation based on symbol-shape or other purely formal characteristics can be formulated, such rules can have the form of *algorithms*—that is, rules that can be followed to a uniquely correct result without the application of human judgment. It is obvious that even a pocket calculator achieves this much, for a range of arithmetical calculations. It is the shapes of the input signals that determine the shapes of the output signals, with no reference whatsoever to what the input signals (presumably, numerals) mean, or to the vexed question of what numbers *are*. Current research concerning *machine translation* of natural languages also involves the attempt to use purely formal/syntactical features of linguistic items.

Semantics

Semantics is traditionally defined as the study of the relation of linguistic signs to the world ("world" being understood to include every sort of extralinguistic reality). A semantic theory will tell us: (1) how many fundamental semantic relations there are, and (2) how each should be characterized. There is, for better or worse, more than one semantic theory in the field, but any semantic theory will have something that corresponds to (or performs the semantic role of) denotation, description, and truth.

Denotation

To denote is to name. This is what proper names do (when they are not vacuous). Other linguistic items, such as pronouns, on occasion may also name. "Socrates" denotes, or names, Socrates. We can also say that "Socrates" refers to or designates Socrates. Denotation, reference, and designation all function, in the literature, as equivalents of *naming*. Denoting expressions are also called *individual terms*.

How Names Work

Despite our familiarity with names and naming, it proves difficult to give an adequate account of just how names work. What is it, exactly, that I understand when I understand the name "Socrates"? Certainly, it must be more than just knowing that "Socrates" names Socrates. One suggestion is that I must, additionally, know *who* Socrates is. Perhaps it is enough to know that he was an ancient Greek philosopher, a teacher of Plato, and the person who said "All I know is that I know nothing." Though a plausible suggestion, this raises the following problem. If these associated descriptions guide us in determining who the *referent* or *designatum* (object named by a name) is, it is natural to think that the referent or designatum is whoever the associated descriptions apply to. This, too, might seem plausible, but suppose some (or even all) of my information about Socrates is wrong. Suppose some other individual, and not Socrates, was the teacher of Plato. Wouldn't "Socrates" name her?

This result does not seem acceptable. Again, although we think of Shakespeare as the writer of a set of famous plays, if it were to turn out that they were really written by Francis Bacon, it does not seem correct to hold that "Shakespeare" really all along named Bacon.

Rigid Designation

Another suggestion—associated with Saul Kripke (b. 1940)—is that proper names (and possibly certain other linguistic items) are *rigid designators*. A linguistic item is a rigid designator IFF it picks out the same individual in all possible worlds. Since philosophers often speak of "possible worlds," it is perhaps worth saying a few words about what "possible world" means. A possible world is a "could-have-been" world. Although in the actual or real world, Socrates did teach Plato, he might not have. There is a possible world, or could-have-been world, where Socrates did not teach Plato. To say the actual world is not the only possible world is, accordingly, a colorful and figurative way of saying that things might have been different.

This can now be applied to the name "Socrates." "Socrates" still names Socrates in the possible worlds where various things we know about Socrates are false. In fact, the unique individual picked out by the name "Socrates" might even have been named something else; however, he could not have *been* someone else. This is why there is no possible world in which Socrates fails to be Socrates, even though there is a possible world in which Socrates fails to be named "Socrates."

Baptism

If the name "Socrates" is not hooked to Socrates via descriptions that apply to Socrates, how is it hooked? One suggestion is referred to as the *baptism theory* of names (or the *causal theory* of reference). "Socrates" gets hooked to Socrates via an initial naming ceremony—a baptism—which has some appropriate person saying, "I hereby name this little kid [a particular human being who is being held or pointed to or looked at] *Socrates*." The name is then passed along, in a chainlike way, to later users. This is called the causal theory of reference because later uses of the name have earlier uses among their causes, and so constitute a causal chain that can be traced all the way back to the intitial baptism.

Sentences with Vacuous Names

Certain names, though grammatically classified as proper names, fail to name individuals. Whatever the history of such names, their use cannot be traced back to an initial baptism. Names that fail to name are said to be *vacuous* (or *empty*). Two separate problems arise when vacuous terms occur in sentences:

(1) Suppose I say, "Zeus is the father of the gods." Have I said something false? If so, then the sentence "Zeus is *not* the father of the gods" should be true. But if Zeus does not exist, there is not even anyone *not* to be father of the gods. Perhaps what we should say is that, since both sentences—"Zeus is the father of the gods" and "Zeus is not the

father of the gods"—*presuppose* the existence of Zeus, if this *presupposition* is incorrect, both sentences are neither true nor false. Note that this solution involves distinguishing, at least for some statements, what is stated from what is presupposed—a distinction accepted by some, but not all, philosophers of language.

(2) Many vacuous names have a certain status as parts of well-known myths or fictions. "Zeus" is one example; "Oliver Twist" and "Holden Caulfield" are examples from well-known novels. We want to be able to say that the sentence "Oliver Twist was for a while a pickpocket" is true, while the sentence "Oliver Twist was for a while a lens-grinder" is false. But, as the discussion of presupposition has made us aware, there is no person for either the true sentence or the false sentence to be about. The solution, then, is to treat both sentences as elliptical. What they mean, spelled out in full, might be expressed as follows: "According to Dickens's *Oliver Twist*, Oliver Twist was for a while a pickpocket" (a true statement about a real novel); and "According to Dickens's *Oliver Twist*, Oliver Twist was for a while a lens-grinder" (a false statement about a real novel).

Description

The second major semantic relation may be referred to as *description*, or *predication*. It is fundamentally different from denotation/reference/designation. Descriptions do not name individuals; rather, they *apply to*, or *are true of*, individuals. There is a connection between a name and a particular individual, but a description applies to *any* individual who happens to satisfy the description. Thus, *red* applies to all red things. I can understand a descriptive expression—for example, "honest politician"—even though I do not know whether it applies to any individuals.

Intension/Extension

All descriptive terms have *intensions* and *extensions*. The *intension* of a term consists of all properties that are part of its definition. For *red*, this would simply be the property of being red; for *unicorn*, it might be being equine, lion-tailed, and one-horned.

The *extension* of a term consists of all individuals, past, present, and future, to which the term applies. The extension of the term *red*, then, is simply all red things. The extension of the term *unicorn* has no members, or is empty; its extension, borrowing a mathematical term, is the *null set*. Two terms—for example, *featherless biped* and *rational animal*—with different intensions may have the same extension. This may also be expressed as: two terms with different intensions may be extensionally equivalent.

Definite Descriptions

Descriptive terms or phrases introduced by the definite article are referred to as *definite descriptions*. Some semantic theories list definite descriptions under the category of names or referring expressions. It is certainly true that such definite descriptions as "the man who is standing by the bar" serve to pick out individuals in much the same way names do. We would probably regard a certain individual as having been picked out by that definite description even if that individual turns out to be, in fact, a woman leaning against the bar.

On the other hand, in using definite descriptions speakers certainly commonly intend the definite description to pick out whatever/whomever the description applies to. This is the case with the definite description in the following sentence: "The person who discovered the cure for polio deserves a lot of credit." Some *uses* of definite descriptions are namelike; other uses are more purely descriptive. It is, of course, part of even the descriptive use of definite descriptions that they should apply to at most one individual. If there is not a unique person who discovered the cure for polio, *the person who discovered the cure for polio* will apply to—and will pick out—nothing. (Occasionally, definite descriptions are used to describe, and possibly pick out, a unique group—e.g., "the people who discovered the cure for polio.")

Truth

The third major semantic relation is truth. Descriptions are said to be "true of" individuals. This, however, is a special use of *true*, and should not be confused with *is true*, which applies to whole statements. Statements are indeed just those sentences which are, as wholes, *semantically evaluable*—that is, just those sentences for which the question of truth and falsity arises.

In general, semantic relations relate linguistic items to extralinguistic reality. How does this work for truth? In semantic theory, an attempt is made to understand truth in terms of the schema:

$$\text{``}p\text{''} \text{ IFF } p.$$

A particular instance might be "It is raining" is true IFF it is raining. This may seem trivial, but it is certainly built into our concept of truth. A somewhat less trivial version can be given along the following lines: a sentence of the form "a is P" (where a names an individual, and P is a description or predicate) is true IFF the individual picked out by a *satisfies* the predicate P:a is said to satisfy P just in case P applies to a. This formulation, which connects the three semantic categories of denotation, description, and truth, also captures what everyone should be prepared to admit, no matter what theory of truth he or she subscribes to. (For the various theories of truth, see the appropriate sections in chapter 2.)

Pragmatics

Pragmatics is traditionally defined as the relation of linguistic signs to their users. Language is, on any account, not primarily something stored away in dictionaries and grammar books, but rather something in constant use by human beings. The easiest way of indicating the topics that make up pragmatics is to say that they include whatever topics linguists and philosophers of language cannot deal with in either syntactics or semantics. Indeed, in many discussions of language, "That's just a matter of pragmatics" is used to dismiss topics or problems from serious consideration.

A few sample topics in pragmatics are given in the next three sections.

Speech Acts

Traditional grammar-and-syntax classifies sentences into a few broad categories: indicative, interrogative, imperative, and exclamative. This hardly suffices to capture all the functions sentences perform, however. Unlike syntax or semantics, which look —primarily—at type sentences, pragmatics considers the token sentence as it is uttered (or written) in a linguistic performance. In saying a sentence, a speaker is doing something. The speaker is performing a *speech act*, also called an *illocutionary act*. There are a great many different speech acts. A declarative sentence may be used to promise, warn, advise, kid, insult, apologize, welcome, and so on. For example, although the sentence "I promise to come to your party" is grammatically declarative, it is not ordinarily used to state a fact about the speaker, but rather to create an obligation that the speaker would not otherwise be under.

Conversational Implicature

A token sentence is always interpreted in the context and/or circumstances of its utterance. In making such interpretations, we are guided by folk psychology, by our understanding of "conversational standards," and by whatever general knowledge of the world seems helpful. An example should make clear what is meant by conversational standards. Suppose I ask a guest, "Would you like some coffee?" The guest replies, "Coffee will keep me awake." I interpret this as a rejection of my offer. Why? Because I assume my guest is honoring a conversational standard of relevance.

What my guest says does not, by strict logical standards, imply that she does not want coffee, but it does imply this according to the standards of conversational implicature. If someone says "I have three children," I take this to mean that he has exactly three children. If I later discover that he has five children (and, accordingly, at least three children), I will feel that I have been misled. The speaker may have logic on his side, but conversational implicature and general standards of conversational helpfulness are on mine.

The Dictionary/Encyclopedia Distinction

Linguists and philosophers of language generally attempt to distinguish between what a person knows about words that is part and parcel of his knowing a language (this is called *linguistic information*, *semantic information*, or *lexical information*), and anything else a speaker may know. Ideally, dictionaries should contain only that information about words that is a part of linguistic competence—that is, only linguistic/semantic/lexical information. Everything else belongs in encyclopedias—that is, in various inventories of general knowledge.

Any use of "encyclopedic" knowledge in interpreting linguistic items belongs to pragmatics. It should be added that not all theorists of language regard the dictionary/encyclopedia distinction as adequate or clear. Even in practice, dictionary-makers characteristically provide what, by some standards, would count as encyclopedic information. *Dog* is "domestic carnivore, *Canis familiaris*, bred in a great many varieties" according to *The Random House Dictionary of the English Language*; but is "bred in a great many varieties" hard-core linguistic information? Those who argue against a sharp line between dictionaries and encyclopedias—and, accordingly, between semantics and pragmatics—think this question has no clear-cut answer.

The Use/Mention Distinction

Although we use words mainly to talk about extralinguistic reality, it is sometimes necessary or desirable to talk about words themselves. Words are said to be *used* when they are employed to talk about extralinguistic reality; for example, the word *Boston* is used in the sentence "Boston is a populous city." Words are said to be *mentioned* when they are themselves under discussion; thus, the word *Boston* is mentioned in the sentence " 'Boston' has six letters," which is obviously about the word and not about the city. By convention, quotation marks are used to create the names of words, phrases, and sentences. In linguistics, italicizing or underlining is also used to create the names of linguistic items. For example, the sentence "It is raining" is about the weather, whereas the sentence "*It is raining* is a declarative sentence" is not about the weather, but about the italicized sentence.

Meaning

Meaning is a term that is overloaded with meaning. The classic discussion of meaning, *The Meaning of Meaning* by Ogden and Richards, runs to some 482 pages. Here, we will simply present some of the basic kinds of meaning in terms of a few fundamental contrasts, then go on to describe briefly the main theories advanced to explain meaning.

Varieties of Meaning

Natural Signs/Conventional Signs

Certain phenomena are signs of other phenomena. Black clouds are a sign of rain. (This is also put: Black clouds mean rain.) The relation between black clouds and rain is part of the causal order of nature, and all humans can do is notice it. Symptoms, in the ordinary medical sense, are always *natural signs*. *Conventional signs*, in contrast, derive their meaning from human conventions. A convention is an agreeement that has force in some human community, either because people have slowly come to accept and respect it or through an explicit understanding (sometimes having the force of law). The system of traffic lights and road signs is a good example of a convention which, though it may have a basis in tradition, has now the force of law.

Nonlinguistic Signs/Linguistic Signs

All conventional signs, such as traffic lights, that are not part of a natural language are classified as *nonlinguistic signs*. *Linguistic signs*, then, are all those conventional signs that are part of some natural language: words, phrases, and sentences. Linguists also speak of the minimal units of language, the smallest linguistic signs, as *morphemes*. So the single word *acceptable* contains two morphemes: *accept* and *able*. Nonlinguistic signs have nonlinguistic meaning of various sorts, while linguistic signs have linguistic meaning of various sorts.

Cognitive Meaning/Noncognitive Meaning

Cognitive meaning is defined as the kind of meaning that allows certain declarative sentences to be true or false. Alternatively, cognitive meaning may be defined as truth-value-relevant meaning. It is cognitive meaning that is referred to in the maxim "Questions of meaning are prior to questions of truth"—a maxim that means that, ordinarily, we must know what the cognitive meaning of a sentence is before we can begin to consider what truth-value it has.

Some declarative sentences do not have the right kind of meaning for truth appraisal (semantic evaluation). These are said to lack cognitive meaning, though they will ordinarily have various kinds of *non-cognitive meanings*. "Some green numbers are lazy" does not have the right kind of meaning for truth appraisal—in other words, it does not have cognitive meaning. "Some green numbers are lazy" does have noncognitive linguistic meaning, and it may—in terms of triggering images—have psychological meaning for some people.

Meaning as Sense/Meaning as Reference

The classic example used to explain these two aspects of meaning was provided by Gottlob Frege (1848–1925). "The morning star" and "the evening star" have distinct senses. There is no ideal word for sense. It sometimes overlaps with *intension*, and is sometimes what we mean by *meaning*. In any case, the sense of "the morning star" is "heavenly body seen by earthlings in the morning," and the sense of "the evening star" is "heavenly body seen by earthlings in the evening." It turns out that, though distinct in sense, the two expressions have the same reference: they both refer to the planet Venus. Frege, incidentally, developed the sense/reference distinction to explain why "The morning star is the evening star" is informative, while "The morning star is the morning star" is not informative.

Speaker's Meaning/Word Meaning-Sentence Meaning

In the best of circumstances, what I mean in using a word is the same as what the word means; and what I mean to say in using a sentence is the same as what the sentence says. But what I mean (my communicative intent) is in principle distinct from—and may in practice be different from—the standard meanings of the linguistic items that I select. I may be looking for a word to indicate the high point of an event, and choose *climacteric* or *climatic*, in which case the word I choose (meaning what it means) will not say what I mean.

Again, I may think the sentence "Mary is no older than Harry" means that Mary and Harry are the same age. If speaker's meaning and word meaning or sentence meaning are different, there is the likelihood of misunderstanding, of misinterpretation. This is not inevitable, however, since most people have some capacity (using folk psychology and situational clues) to figure out what the speaker really meant, even if that is not what he or she actually said. The study of speaker's meaning and how it is determined, as opposed to word or sentence meaning, belongs to pragmatics.

Theories of Meaning

Even within the category of linguistic meaning, there are various kinds of meaning. One reason there are so many different theories of meaning is that theorists have been looking at—and working out theories for—different kinds of linguistic meaning. Theories of meaning are also influenced by rival conceptions of human psychology. The main theories of meaning are described briefly in the following paragraphs.

Intention-Based Semantics

Intention-based semantics—developed by H. P. Grice (1913–1988)—attempts to explain speaker's meaning (also sometimes called *utterer's meaning*) as a form of intentional action. Again, the aim of intention-based semantics is to explain semantics in purely psychological terms—specifically, in terms of intentions and beliefs. In all central cases of communication, a person who utters a sentence intends (and has grounds for expecting) to induce a belief, *p*, in another person. Furthermore, the speaker intends the other person to believe that *p* just because the other person recognizes the speaker's communicative intention. Thus, I utter "Today is Tuesday" intending and expecting to induce the belief that it is Tuesday in those who hear my utterance. Those who hear me realize that my uttering "Today is Tuesday" is an intentional communicative action with a standard relation to a certain belief about the day of the week.

Intention-based semantics makes the meaning of an uttered sentence a function of the belief it usually (or in normal circumstances) induces. How much is really explained by this theory will, accordingly, depend on whether *contents of beliefs* can be characterized without reintroducing semantic, or language-based, categories.

Functionalist Theories

A number of family-resemblant theories, with overlaps and inter-relations, have been presented as functionalisms. These can be divided into three main groups.

> (1) Theories that hold that the meaning of such linguistic items as words and phrases must be understood in terms of the functions these items play in the linguistic system, or language, as a whole.

(2) Theories that hold that the linguistic behavior of humans viewed as organisms in environments must be understood in terms of how that behavior contributes to well-being and survival.

(3) Theories that hold that brain-states, characterized functionally, may be the ultimate metaphysical carriers of the psychological and the linguistic.

Conceptual Role Theory

Conceptual role theory attempts to explain what conceptual mastery consists in. What does it mean to say, for example, that someone has mastered the concept of a dog? It is just to know the role played by the word *dog* if one speaks English, by the word *chien* if one speaks French, by the word *Hund* if one speaks German, and so on. Although the explanation of possessing a concept, in conceptual role theory, is explained in terms of understanding the role of a word, the role of that word may be the same as the role of other words in other languages. This gives concepts a certain independence of particular languages. (It should be noted that conceptual role theory is a form of functionalism.)

Behaviorism

Behaviorism, in philosophy of language, is simply an application of psychological behaviorism. To say that a person understands a sentence, S (or knows what S means), should translate into a series of statements about the overt, publicly observable behavior of the person in question. It is doubtless true that we can often use behavioral clues in deciding whether a person understands a sentence (or anything else, for that matter), but this does not mean that the understanding *is identical with* the behavior.

Since linguistic behavior is probably the most complicated behavior of which humans are capable, it is not likely that it can be understood in terms of (necessarily simpler) nonlinguistic behavior. (This is not to deny that we can often helpfully relate different linguistic behaviors. For example, the truth sentence "S believes that p" is related to a tendency S has to answer the question "Do you believe that p?" with "Yes.")

Mentalese Theories

Many cognitive psychologists and some philosophers of language believe that humans possess a *language of thought*. This is taken seriously and literally. There are, they say, internal symbols that have the properties of intentionality and systematicity. These internal symbols make up the language of thought, or—to express it more informally,—*mentalese*. The language of thought is not acquired; in fact, it explains how we are able to acquire the natural language we speak.

Proponents of mentalese regard themselves as putting forward an empirically testable theory of human language-using capacities. They also emphasize the *nonmiraculous* character of their hypothesis. The language of thought is physically realized in our brains and central nervous systems. To say that the language of thought is *innate* is, accordingly, to say that much more is hard-wired into our nervous systems from the start than empiricists have ever imagined.

Truth-Conditional Semantics

To understand a sentence, *S*, according to *truth-conditional semantics*, is just to know the conditions in which *S* would be true. This seems to many thinkers the most obvious and natural theory of meaning, at least for declarative sentences. I understand the sentence "It is raining" because I know the sort of weather that would make that sentence true and the sort of weather that would make that sentence false. Furthermore, not only can I give an abstract description of truth-making and false-making weather, I can recognize each when it is going on. I can therefore *decide*, on any given occasion, which truth-value "It is raining" has.

Not all sentences are as easily "decidable" as "It is raining." Consider the sentence "There is no largest prime number." I can, of course, say what its truth condition is: it is true just in case there is no largest prime number. This is, however, only an abstract description of the truth condition and is, suspiciously, expressed in the very same words as the sentence itself. It is currently a controversial point whether we are entitled to say we understand sentences whose truth conditions we can only specify in the language of the sentences themselves, and whose satisfaction we cannot decide.

Assertibility Theories

To understand a sentence, *S*, according to an *assertibility theory*, is just to know the conditions in which *S* may be asserted. "May be asserted" here is understood to mean "is warrantedly assertible" or "is justifiably assertible" or "is assertible without criticism." (See also the discussion of the assertibility theory of truth in chapter 2.)

For some sentences, the truth-conditional account and the assertibility account will overlap. I will be criticized for asserting that "It is raining" in just those conditions that, according to the truth-conditional theory, make my assertion false; for other sentences, the two accounts diverge. The classic example—introduced by Michael Dummett (b. 1925)—is "Jones was brave" said of Jones, now dead, who never faced danger. According to the truth-conditional view (also called the *classical* view), this sentence must be either true or false, even if we cannot decide which. However, since this sentence does not have determinate assertibility conditions, it will, according to assertibility theory, turn out to be neither true nor false.

Verificationism

Verificationism, also known as the *verifiability criterion of empirical meaningfulness*, is closely related to assertibility views. What it says is that to understand any nonanalytic sentence is to know what would count as verifying it—or, in other words, what would count as *definitive evidence* for its truth. Because of problems having to do with the verification of such universal generalizations as "All crows are black" (which everyone counts as empirically meaningful), many writers in sympathy with verificationism have substituted *falsifiability* for *verifiability*. I understand the meaning of "All crows are black" because I know what would count as *definitive evidence* for its falsity.

There may be sentences, composed of quite familiar words, such as "A city will be built here someday" and "Prayer works," which do not satisfy the falsifiability criterion. One reason why the sentences just mentioned cannnot be falsified is their openendedness to the future. Thus, a given prayer hasn't worked yet, but it might eventually. Similarly for the sentence about the city being built.

Use Theories

The view that "meaning is use," though often associated with Wittgenstein, was not put forward by that philosopher as a general theory of meaning. However, many thinkers, starting from Wittgenstein, have thought that something like a general theory of meaning could be based on Wittgenstein's slogan. According to these theorists, the only way of understanding sentences is to observe how they are used in their real-life environments. Obviously, this requires careful description of superficially similar, but nevertheless distinctive, uses of linguistic items. Wittgenstein did say that to understand a language is to understand a form of life. This seems to suggest that those who wish to study language must do something for their own "tribes" very much like what ethnographers/anthropologists do for the tribes they study. This involves, at the very least, making overall sense of the total set of practices, linguistic and nonlinguistic, composing a form of life.

No-Theory Theories

Wittgenstein's own view seemed to be that a philosophical theory of meaning was both impossible and unnecessary. Nothing is hidden behind our linguistic practices that could serve to explain them the way microphysical reality lies behind and explains macrophysical reality. What we need, according to Wittgenstein, are clear descriptions of linguistic phenomena—reminders of what everyone really knows. This leads back, of course, to the idea of philosophy as ethnography, as careful and detailed description—and this is connected to another idea. We need these clear descriptions of what everyone knows when we are gripped by some false picture of how things must be. Wittgenstein conceived of the detailed descriptions as a therapeutic antidote to the false pictures.

One contemporary philosopher—Stephen Schiffer (b. 1940)—has presented a very succinct no-theory theory of meaning: there is no meaning (though, of course, we can for convenience talk about what I mean, what you mean, what words and sentences mean), so there is nothing for a theory of meaning to be about.

We have seen that language-using behavior (linguistic behavior), despite its great familiarity, gives rise to a number of philosophical problems. Some of these problems are suggested by linguistics, the science of linguistic phenomena. Indeed, much interesting work on language is interdisciplinary.

Linguistic phenomena are complex and many-sided. Syntactics studies the relation of linguistic signs (words, phrases, sentences) to each other. Every natural language has its own syntax—that is, a set of rules indicating how words from various grammatical categories may be combined. Syntactics also includes all those formal features of a language that can be studied independently of meaning.

Semantics studies the relation of linguistic signs to the world, to extralinguistic reality. We have seen that there are three main semantic relations: the relation between names and the items they name, the relation between descriptions and the items they apply to, and the relation between statements (that is, sentences possessing truth-values) and whatever makes statements true or false. Finally, pragmatics studies all those features of language related to its actual use by speakers and writers.

There are many kinds of meaning that have nothing to do with language and its conventions. But even within language, meaning is not a homogeneous phenomenon. We must, for example, distinguish what people mean, in using language, from what the words and sentences they use mean. We have also seen that meaning as sense must be distinguished from meaning as reference. One of the most important kinds of meaning is cognitive meaning— that aspect of the meaning of a statement that is relevant in deciding its truth-value. The two sentences "It is cold and it is sunny" and "It is cold but it is sunny," while having slightly different total meanings (the "but" indicates surprise and/or contrast), have exactly the same cognitive meaning.

Finally, we surveyed the most important theories of meaning still of interest to philosophers. How do we explain what is going on when we understand the meaning of a word, phrase, or sentence? What does grasp of meaning consist in? These are the questions that the various theories of meaning try to answer.

Recommended Reading

Although much work on language has been done since its publication, *The Encyclopedia of Philosophy* contains useful surveys that are not outdated. There are many brief discussions of various topics and terms connected with language, but the most useful surveys, for orientation purposes, are "Language, Language, Philosophy of," and "Artificial and Natural Languages." In *The Handbook of Western Philosophy*, the articles "Theories of Meaning from 'Reference' to 'Use' " and "Theories of Meaning: After Use Theory" are obviously relevant.

Almost all discussions of topics in the philosophy of language, even those pretending to be elementary, are difficult and dense. A good basic textbook in linguistics is John Lyons's *Introduction to Theoretical Linguistics* (1968). Another book by a linguist from which the philosophical student can learn a lot is Zellig Harris's *Language and Information* (1988). The linguist who has had the most impact on philosophy is certainly Noam Chomsky. Of his many books, the philosophy student might want to look at *Cartesian Linguistics* (1966) and *Reflections on Language* (1975).

Four more books by linguists should be mentioned. Zeno Vendler's *Linguistics in Philosophy* (1967) aims to show how linguistics can be used to solve philosophical problems. George Lakoff's *Women, Fire, and Dangerous Things: What Categories Reveal about the Mind* (1987) challenges many of the standard assumptions of linguists and philosophers of language, in particular the assumption that a sharp line can be drawn between semantics and pragmatics. *The Vastness of Natural Languages* by D. Terence Langendoen and Paul M. Postal (1985) is a technical book that emphasizes the analogies between linguistic and mathematical systems. Finally, James D. McCawley's *Adverbs, Vowels, and Other Objects of Wonder* (1979) is a lively collection of essays—some very technical, some accessible—on a broad range of linguistic topics.

Three books that are relatively easy to read, and whose titles suggest the areas covered, are Ian Hacking's *Why Does Language Matter to Philosophy?* (1975); Simon Blackburn's *Spreading the Word: Groundings in the Philosophy of Language* (1984); and *Relevance: Communication and Cognition* (1986) by Dan Sperber and Deirdre Wilson. It is from the last book that the "Coffee will keep me awake" example in the discussion of conversational relevance (p. 165) was borrowed.

The clearest recent survey, covering all the topics in this chapter, is Robert M. Martin's *The Meaning of Language* (1987).

Six anthologies of articles in the series *Oxford Readings in Philosophy* have articles at various levels of penetrability relating to philosophy of language. They are *Philosophical Logic*, edited by P. F. Strawson (1967), which includes Dummett's article "Truth," whence the "Jones was brave" example derives; *The Theory of Meaning*, edited by G. H. R. Parkinson (1968); *Reference and Modality*, edited by Leonard Linsky (1971); *Semantic Syntax*, edited by Peter A. M. Seuren (1974); *The Philosophy of Linguistics*, edited by Jerrold J. Katz (1985); and *Propositions and Attitudes*, edited by Nathan Salmon and Scott Soames (1988). Another useful anthology is *Reference, Truth and Reality: Essays on the Philosophy of Language*, edited by Mark Platts (1980).

A number of useful books deal either with special topics or approach the study of language from a particular, often controversial, point of view. (The student should bear in mind that these books were written for specialists, and are for the most part very difficult.) They include Willard Van Orman Quine's *Word and Object* (1960); L. Jonathan Cohen's *The Diversity of Meaning* (1962); David Harrah's *Communication: A Logical Model* (1963); Jerrold J. Katz's *The Philosophy of Language* (1966); Leonard Linsky's *Referring* (1957); David K. Lewis's *Convention: A Philosophical Study* (1969); John R. Searle's *Speech Acts: An Essay in the Philosophy of Language* (1969); Jerrold J. Katz's *The Underlying Reality of Language and its Philosophical Import* (1971); Charles Landesman's *Discourse and its Presuppositions* (1972); Jay F. Rosenberg's *Linguistic Representation* (1974); Jerry A. Fodor's *The Language of Thought* (1975); Ruth Garrett Millikan's *Language, Thought, and Other Biological Categories: New Foundations for Realism* (1984); Norbert Hornstein's *Logic as Grammar: An Approach to Meaning in Natural Language* (1984); J. N. Hattiangadi's *How is Language Possible?* (1987); Sybil Wolfram's *Philosophical Logic: An Introduction* (1989); and Mark Richard's *Propositional Attitudes: An Essay on Thoughts and How We Ascribe Them* (1990).

Stephen R. Schiffer's *Meaning* (1972) gives a particularly clear and persuasive presentation of a Gricean, or intention-based, semantics. Schiffer's later (1987) book, *Remnants of Meaning*, tells us why the theory of meaning his earlier book presented cannot work, and offers a no-theory theory of meaning.

CHAPTER 7

Ethics: Social and Political Philosophy

Ethics, as a reflective philosophical endeavor, attempts to make theoretical sense out of our classification of actions into the basic categories of the morally permissible, the morally impermissible, and the morally obligatory. Humans do, persistently, evaluate their own and other people's actions from a moral point of view. What exactly are they doing when they do this? Can our moral evaluations be defended in some systematic way, or are they, at bottom, cultural prejudices? We shall see that philosophers, in attempting to deal with these questions, have put forward a number of theories about the nature of morality. These second-order, or meta-ethical, theories are of three fundamental kinds: (1) cognitivist theories, which hold that ethical judgments are true or false, that there are moral truths and possible knowledge of those truths; (2) imperativist theories, which hold that ethical judgments are really rules, and so are neither true or false; and (3) emotivist theories, which hold that ethical judgments are really exclamations of feeling.

The most important difference in the ways in which philosophers think about moral evaluation depends on whether or not they think that the consequences of an action are relevant in determining its moral

*status. Those who say consequences are irrelevant are called deon-
tologists; those who say consequences are the main thing are called
consequentialists. Needless to say, deontologists and consequentialists
differ greatly about what should count as a good moral argument.*

*Almost all human beings live in social groups; additionally, most
human beings live in states—that is, in political units that exercise a
certain legal power over individuals. One of the themes of the second
half of this chapter is, accordingly, how personal morality is affected
by its social and political context.*

Ethics

Etymology

In contemporary English, the words *moral* and *ethical* are often
used almost as synonyms. *Ethics* and *ethical* derive from the Greek
ethos, meaning usage, character, personal disposition. *Morality* and
moral derive from the Latin *mores*, meaning customs, manners,
character.

Two other etymologies should be noted: *society* and *social* derive
from the Latin *socius*, meaning companion or ally; *politics* and *political*
derive from the Greek *polis*, meaning city. Since such Greek cities as
Athens and Sparta were independent, sovereign, political units, *polis* is
sometimes translated city-state. It is this usage that influences our use
of *political* and related terms.

First-Order and Second-Order Problems

Deliberation

People are led to act for a variety of reasons—reasons that are not
only complicated but of very different kinds. What people want, desire,
or feel they need—their short-term plans and projects as well as their
long-term ambitions and goals—all influence their choice of actions.
Of course, many actions are so routine or habitual that they call for little
or no prior thought; in other cases, however, there is much thinking
about what to do prior to action. Such thinking is called *deliberation,*

and actions that proceed from it are done *deliberately* or with *deliberation*.

Assume that a certain range of actions is under consideration because the agent thinks that the performance of actions in that range will satisfy a desire. (*Agent* is the preferred term in ethics for the person acting.) There are three kinds of questions that may arise: technical, prudential, and moral.

Technical Questions

Technical questions are questions about the best or most efficient way to do something. Someone committed to murder will still have to think about the best way—shooting, stabbing, poisoning, whatever—to carry out his plan. Less dramatically, many of the practical tasks and projects of everyday life give rise to technical questions.

Prudential Questions

Prudential questions are questions about how an action under consideration will affect the agent's long-term, all-around self-interest or well-being. Many actions that satisfy a desire of the moment or further a particular project are nevertheless rejected for reasons of prudence. Prudence requires the ability to project, and be moved by, the future consequences of present actions; and people seem, in fact, to differ considerably in the degree to which they possess this ability. Although prudential considerations are distinct from moral considerations (being essentially self-centered), criminologists and other students of human behavior estimate that 70 or 80 percent of immoral, antisocial, or "other-person-hurting" behavior is also imprudent. "Enlightened self-interest" would, accordingly, eliminate most of this objectionable behavior.

Moral Questions

Some actions that are technically feasible and even prudent may nevertheless be rejected on moral grounds. A person may be considering a certain act, but finally decide against it, saying, "I can't do that; that would be wrong!"

Unfortunately, this does not stop everyone. For "morally conscientious" people (that is, people who worry about morality), however, actions that are obviously immoral are not even considered—are not perceived, that is, as real options. For example, most of us do not spend time wondering whether we should or should not commit murder to further some end; murder is so fundamentally "ruled out" that we don't even think seriously of it. There are, however, many cases where it is far less clear whether a given course of action is or is not morally acceptable. In such cases, we have to do a lot of hard thinking, after which there is still no guarantee that we will come to a clearcut, obviously correct decision.

The Moral Point of View

In asking the question, "But would it be wrong?" we are looking at an action from "the moral point of view." This way of looking at actions is *sui generis* (that is, in its own distinctive category), and cannot really be explained in terms of anything more fundamental. The few defective human beings who have no idea what we are talking about when we talk about morality will probably never arrive at a conception of morality in any case. Many people commit morally unacceptable acts and there are many disagreements about morality, but few people can be said to completely lack a conception of morality. Almost everyone, in other words, knows what it is like to look at an action from the moral point of view.

We should add that not all philosophers agree that morality is *sui generis*. Various attempts have been made to derive morality from considerations of self-interest, prudence, or economic rationality.

"Right" and "Wrong"

In ordinary English, we frequently talk about morality in terms of "right" and "wrong"; however, we should remember that we really divide actions into three categories, not two. Actions are *permissible*, or OK to perform; *impermissible*, or not OK to perform; and *obligatory*, or not OK not to perform. We should also remember that the term *wrong* is ambiguous, since it can mean technically wrong, aesthetically wrong, wrong as a matter of etiquette, prudentially wrong, legally wrong, or morally wrong. All of these are separate senses of wrong, although this does not mean that there cannot be relations among them. For example, the fact that an action is legally wrong will often mean that it is also imprudent, or prudentially wrong.

First-Order Moral Problems

As they arise in deliberation, moral questions are practical; they are questions the agent is asking about what to do *in the immediate future*. And, more often than not, the agent can answer such questions, and proceed to act with an untroubled conscience. Sometimes, however, problems resist solution. Then the agent has a serious *first-order moral problem*. Whether or not a particular agent is led to reflect in a more general way about the nature of morality, humans have, collectively, been led from consideration of practical and more or less pressing problems to reflection on the general intellectual framework within which the practical problems should be situated.

Second-Order Moral Problems

Second-order moral problems, also called *meta-ethical* problems, are philosophical problems about the nature of morality. Such problems give rise to philosophical theories about morality, or rival views about how moral sentences should be analyzed. In the next section, we will consider the three major theories about the nature of morality: cognitivism, imperativism, and emotivism.

Theories of Morality

Cognitivism

Cognitivism is the view that moral sentences—sentences such as "Stealing is wrong" and "Premarital sex is morally permissible"—have truth-values, or, in other words, are either true or false. This can also be expressed as: moral sentences are genuine statements. A cognitivist, then, holds that there is such a thing as moral knowledge, that people attain when they have justified true beliefs about morality. (See the discussion of knowledge in chapter 2.) It follows that moral questions such as "Is stealing wrong?" and "Is premarital sex morally permissible?" are objective questions—that is, questions that have correct and incorrect answers.

In contemporary discussions, cognitivism is also called *moral realism*. When cognitivism (or moral realism) is stated, many non-philosophers find the view appealing; however, it is also true that nonphilosophers often say things that are incompatible with cognitivism. "Morality is a matter of opinion" or "Morality is just a matter of what people in your tribe think is OK or not OK" cannot be said by the consistent cognitivist.

The Argument from Arguments

One argument for cognitivism is called *the argument from arguments*. People offer arguments that have moral sentences as premises and conclusions. It is generally assumed that we can, for example, argue in favor of the claim that stealing is morally wrong. But logic teaches us that the components of arguments must be genuine statements; therefore, moral sentences are genuine statements.

The Correspondence Problem

The major difficulty for cognitivists concerns explaining what moral sentences correspond to when they are true. Suppose you are a cognitivist, and think the sentence "Stealing is wrong" is true. What makes that sentence true? Where do we look to see that it is true? The difficulty is providing something for "Stealing is wrong" that is equivalent to what we can all readily provide for an ordinary nonmoral statement like "It is raining." If someone asks what makes the latter statement true, we say "Local weather"; if we are asked where to look, we say "Out the window."

Are Moral Sentences Analytic?

The weather comparison may seem irrelevant. Where do we look, after all, to see what makes "All bachelors are unmarried" true? Well, we certainly don't have to take surveys of bachelors, or acquire any other information about the world. We consider the definition of *bachelor* and the definition of *unmarried*, and discover, when we think it through, that "All bachelors are unmarried" is necessarily true because it is analytically true (or true "by definition"). Perhaps this is a better model for moral sentences.

Unfortunately, it is hard to see how sentences like "Stealing is wrong" could be true by definition. We can, of course, make them true by definition by defining *stealing* as wrongful taking. Our moral sentence then becomes "Wrongful taking is wrong," which is analytically true but not particularly helpful. All this definition accomplishes is to force a person who, as things are, wonders whether stealing is wrong, to wonder whether any takings are wrongful takings.

Imperativism

Imperativism is the view that moral sentences are *disguised imperatives*. Though grammatically declarative, moral sentences function as *rules*. We should say, at the outset, that it is not an objection to imperativism that it claims sentences in one grammatical category do not have the usual function sentences in that category have. Not all sentences in a given grammatical category need have the same function, and, in any case, grammatical declaratives are, in any view, used in a wide variety of ways. It is possible, accordingly, that "Stealing is wrong" amounts to "Don't steal!" and that "Premarital sex is morally permissible" amounts to "Don't have a rule 'Don't have premarital sex!'!"

Arguments for Imperativism

A number of considerations, rather than a single argument, motivate the adoption of imperativism. *First*, imperativism seems a possible alternative for those who think that cognitivism is defeated by the correspondence problem. *Second*, everyone wants moral sentences to be action-guiding, and rules are directly action-guiding. *Third*, imperativism actually explains what moral arguments are about. Instead of picturing moral arguments as about whether certain classes of actions have mysterious properties of "moral rightness" or "moral wrongness," we are really arguing about what rules groups of humans should live by—which rules it is a good idea to have.

Proponents of imperativism admit that this approach does not solve all our moral problems, but go on to claim that it does give us something fairly nonmysterious to think about. And it does have the advantage of making moral discussion in some ways similar to legislative discussion about which laws it would be a good idea to have.

Although a rule such as "Don't steal!" has no truth-value, imperativists can easily deal with the argument from arguments. The components of arguments are such statements as "It is a good idea to have the rule 'Don't steal!' " It is not always easy to decide about what rules it would be a good idea to have, not always easy to get people to agree about this, and not always easy to decide what considerations are relevant. Still, it is possible to imagine fairly compelling arguments. For example, even without an excessive commitment to private property, it seems fairly obvious that people cannot function very well—and will in general be severely inconvenienced—unless the things they use stay put. A pen, a pair of glasses, a car need to be where you expect them to be when you need them. These sorts of very ordinary considerations suffice to show that it is a good idea to have a rule against stealing.

Emotivism

Emotivism is the view that moral sentences are disguised exclamatives. A moral sentence such as "Stealing is wrong" expresses negative emotions about stealing. "Stealing is wrong," according to the emotivist, amounts to something like "Stealing, *phooey!*" or "Stealing, *ugh!*" Historically, emotivism has probably been the least popular of the three major views about moral sentences, though this does not by itself demonstrate that emotivism is incorrect.

Reason and Emotion

Many people reject emotivism because they think it makes us too irrational. This reaction may be correct. We do argue rationally about morality, and—unlike cognitivism and imperativism—emotivism has a very difficult time explaining how moral argument is possible. It should be remembered, however, that—as many contemporary debates show—moral questions are capable of generating very strong feelings. People often make up bad arguments for moral positions that they have been led to by primitive feelings. When people introduce categories like "the disgusting" into moral discussion, we can be fairly sure that strong emotions rather than sound arguments are at work. And none of this is an argument for emotivism.

Feelings and Cognitive Assessment

There is indeed an additional argument against emotivism. Emotivism claims that feelings (or emotions) explain our moral judgments; in other words, our moral judgments turn out to be disguised expressions of those feelings. Against this, it is argued that feelings (or emotions) are ordinarily the consequence of cognitive assessments—of things that we believe to be true. I feel upset because I believe something has gone wrong; I feel pleased because I believe something good has happened. If this is how feelings come in, then we need to discover what it is about stealing that triggers the strong feeling of disapproval, often called *disapprobation*. Emotivists tell us that stealing is wrong because people respond negatively to stealing; but people may respond negatively to stealing because of something *true of* stealing that their *cognitive assessment* of stealing reveals.

It should be added that people, both philosophers and non-philosophers, argue about what feelings people *ought* to have. Suppose you feel upset by the idea of premarital sex. Instead of using your feeling as the basis for a moral assessment of premarital sex, perhaps you could ask yourself whether you ought to feel upset. If you then discover that there is no reason to feel upset, your negative feeling may disappear. On the other hand, if you discover that there are reasons to feel upset, then it is these reasons, and not your feeling, that are relevant in judging that premarital sex is immoral.

Deontological vs. Consequentialist Approaches

The three basic theories of morality are very general theories about how such moral sentences as "Stealing is wrong" function; as such, these theories leave many other aspects of our thinking about morality unexplored. The most important of these aspects concerns the relevance of consequences in assessing the morality of actions. About this, there are two main views: (1) the *deontological* view, in which moral obligation or duty is primary; and (2) various *consequentialist* views that maintain that our obligations to perform or refrain from performing various actions depend on the consequences the actions in question have.

Deontological Approaches

Approaches that emphasize the primary or underived character of "duty" or "moral obligation" are referred to as *deontological* (deriving from the Greek *deon*, meaning binding, right, proper). According to deontologists, such sentences as "Stealing is wrong" and "Premarital sex is morally permissible" are genuine statements—statements understood to be about duties. On their account, "Stealing is wrong" means

"Humans have a duty not to steal" and "Premarital sex is morally permissible" means "There is no duty to refrain from premarital sex."

Problems about Duties

There are two problems about duties. The *first problem* concerns their metaphysical status. What is it exactly that duties are supposed to be? From the list *rocks, electrons, tables, chairs, duties,* we can probably say what each thing is—except for duties. This is not satisfactory. We might, of course, try saying that a duty is a thing we ought to do, but things we ought to do are very different from the ordinary things that exist around us. For what I ought to do is not something that exists and can be seen outside of me, but something I should (but might not) do. The logical gap between any descriptions of reality and any claims about what ought to be done is generally referred to as the *is/ought problem.*

The *second problem* concerns how we discover what our duties are. It may seem obvious that we should refrain from stealing, but how do we know this? What do we say to a person who challenges us? Furthermore, how do we find out our duties in more controversial cases? After all, people—including both philosophers and nonphilosophers—disagree about such issues as whether we have a duty to refrain from premarital sex. Attempts to settle this sort of disagreement will be considered in the following sections on religion, intuition/conscience/moral sense, and reason.

Religion

Many people, including some distinguished philosophers, look to religion to provide a basis for morality. For example, the Ten Commandments may be regarded as a specification of our duties. This works well enough for people with religious commitments. There are, however, two serious problems facing the attempt to base morality on religion. *First,* there are many different religions, and there are people who are nonreligious. And while it may be perfectly reasonable for a person within a particular religious denomination to consult recognized texts and authorities relative to that religion, no one would claim that this is something that *any* reasonable person would do. It is perfectly reasonable for a Catholic, for example, to consult Catholic religious authorities and texts recognized by those authorities, but it would be unreasonable for Catholics to insist—which in fact they do not—that everyone should do the same.

Second, suppose that God has forbidden murder by issuing the commandment "Thou shalt not kill!" and that we agree that this is how we know we have a duty not to kill. This still leaves the following question: Does God forbid murder because it is wrong, or is murder wrong because God forbids it? Choosing the first alternative pictures God *recognizing* the wrongness of murder and issuing a command for the guidance of humans. This makes the wrongness of murder logically independent of God and His commandments, but does not answer the question of what makes murder wrong.

Choosing the second alternative does answer the question of what makes murder wrong: it is God's forbidding it that makes it wrong. But not everyone can accept this, for it seems to entail that being kind or "honoring thy father and mother" might have been wrong if God had forbidden those instead of what He did forbid. It is indeed hard to understand how forbidding something could make it really wrong if it wasn't really wrong already. This problem, first discussed by Plato in the dialogue *Euthyphro*, is known as the *Euthyphro problem*.

Intuition/Conscience/Moral Sense

Many philosophers at various times have held that human beings have distinctive "intuitions" about duty or moral obligation. This is also sometimes put by saying that "conscience," or our "moral sense," tells us what our duties are. It is a matter of psychological fact that people often make spontaneous judgments about morality that strike them as obviously correct; but this does not mean that intuition, conscience, or moral sense can function as a source of knowledge. If I ask you how you know it is raining, you may with full justification (and perhaps even with justified impatience) reply that you *see* that it is. But then, any sighted person can see this. I can, if I feel the need, immediately confirm your observation with an observation of my own.

This explains, in part, why there is complete *convergence* (that is, movement toward agreement) about all matters that can be settled by simple sensory observation. None of this applies to intuition/conscience/moral sense, however. When I ask you how you know that stealing is wrong, and you reply that you have an intuition that it is (or that your conscience tells you that it is, or that this is what is revealed to your moral sense), this really amounts to the answer "I just know!"

That is why intuition/conscience/moral sense are no help in settling moral disagreements.

Reason

The most famous attempt to base a deontological ethics on reason was made by Immanuel Kant (1724–1804), and added the term *Kantianism* to the permanent vocabulary of philosophy. As a rational being, Kant said, he accepts the following principle: "I should never act in such a way that I could not also will that my maxim [my rule of action] should be a universal law." Suppose, he asks, he finds himself in a situation in which it would be advantageous to make a promise with no intention of keeping it: "Could I say to myself that everyone may make a false promise when he is in a difficulty from which he cannot otherwise escape? I immediately see that I could will the lie but not the universal law to lie."

This is often referred to as the *universalizability criterion*. Kant recognized that even rational beings will have powerful inclinations to act contrary to the moral law, but will nevertheless be capable of acting out of respect for it. A rational being will come to regard the moral law as a law he imposes on himself (the condition of *autonomy*), rather than a law someone else imposes on him (the condition of *heteronomy*). Kantianism is still a powerful force in ethical thinking.

Kant's Categorical Imperative. Kant's basic principle—which he regarded as the absolutely binding foundation of all morality—is called the *categorical imperative*. The categorical imperative can be stated as follows: so act that you can will the maxim of your action to be a universal law binding on the will of every rational person. (*Categorical* here means unconditional. The contrast is with conditional rules, which take the form: if you want such and such, you must do so and so; for example, if you want to succeed in business you must dress neatly.)

Criticisms of Kant. All forms of consequentialist thinking involve an implicit criticism of Kant: Kant simply ignored consequences. In addition, two other problems are raised in connection with Kant. *First*, the categorical imperative is a purely formal principle. It tells us that our maxims or principles have to be universal in form, but it doesn't tell us what they should actually be. *Second*, Kant held that moral rules are absolutely binding in all circumstances. Many ethicists argue, however, that such rules as "Don't lie!" and "Don't break a promise" have legitimate exceptions. For example, the Dutch family sheltering Anne

Frank from the Nazis was entitled to tell lies to Gestapo agents in order to save her life.

Consequentialist Approaches

All forms of *consequentialism* hold that the only satisfactory way to think about morality is to think about consequences. This can be done in a variety of ways. For example, we can think about the consequences of a particular act; we can think about the consequences of adopting a certain general rule. And these considerations are not unrelated. If certain kinds of acts have bad consequences, a rule against those acts (if it can be made effective) should have good consequences.

One of the major appeals of consequentialism is that it gives us something nonmysterious to think about and discuss. Of course, since the consequences of actions at the time it is most urgent to think about them are still future, we cannot be consequentialists unless we are willing to venture predictions. It is also true that the consequences of individual actions as well as the consequences of having certain rules can not only be very complex, but also mixed: partly good and partly bad. For these reasons, consequentialism should not be thought of as a shortcut method for making moral judgments.

Utilitarianism

The most common form of consequentialism, called *utilitarianism*, is associated with Jeremy Bentham (1748–1832), James Mill (1773–1836), and the latter's son, John Stuart Mill (1806–1873). The younger Mill defined utilitarianism as the view that "holds that actions are right in proportion as they tend to promote happiness, wrong as they tend to produce the reverse of happiness." He added that by happiness he meant pleasure and the absence of pain, and by unhappiness, pain and the privation of pleasure. In deciding the moral status of an action, we try to predict as accurately as we can all its future consequences. Of these consequences, those which either produce pleasure or pain or diminish pleasure or pain are directly relevant. We then perform a kind of calculation or weighing up, and are morally permitted to perform the action if pleasure and pain-reduction reckoned together outweigh the combination of pain and pleasure-reduction. (Bentham described this as the *felicific calculus*, from *felix*, Latin for happy.)

Because the earlier utilitarians were mostly economists, they called the positive effects of actions *utilities* and the negative effects *disutilities*. (Units of utility are still often referred to as *utiles* in contemporary discussion.) We should explicitly note that utilitarianism and other forms of consequentialism are directed to the classification of actions; the praiseworthiness or blameworthiness of agents is a separate, and less fundamental, matter.

In working out his felicific calculus, Bentham held that the only thing that mattered was *quantity* of pleasure and pain. In contrast, J. S. Mill introduced the idea of *quality*, and spoke of higher and lower pleasures. That is why Mill was able to say, famously, that it is better to be a Socrates unsatisfied than a pig satisfied.

The Greatest Happiness Principle

In deciding moral permissibility or impermissibility, the agent must consider consequences—not only as they affect him, but as they affect anyone else they touch. One of the great strengths of utilitarianism as a progressive moral vision is its commitment to the idea that everyone counts the same. My pleasures and pains are no more important (though no less important) than those of any other human being. I may enjoy playing my radio on a crowded bus, but doing so may be ruled out because of other people's displeasure. (We should add that *pleasure* is meant to include a broad range of positive states, some more physical, some more intellectual; and that *pain*, in a similar way, includes everything negative, from the mildly annoying to the intensely physically painful.) For utilitarians, ownership of pleasures and pains is morally irrelevant: what counts is the greatest happiness of the greatest number of people.

Act Utilitarianism

John Stuart Mill's definition of utilitarianism, quoted above, formulates what came to be known as *act utilitarianism*. This is the view that we think about actions one by one, considering the expected consequences of each action. One objection to this is that it takes too long: by the time the utilitarian calculation is complete, the opportunity for action is past.

There are also counterexamples of the following sort. Suppose that, by killing one innocent person, I can save 100 innocent people who would otherwise die. (You can consider this as a purely hypothetical example; if you bring in possible real-world consequences, such as setting a precedent or lowering respect for life generally, it gets much more complicated.) Am I allowed to kill the innocent person? Some utilitarians have had the courage of their convictions to answer yes. Loss of life is bad (it represents an enormous disutility, certainly), but loss of 100 lives is a hundred times as bad. (It represents an enormous loss of utility x 100.) However, many utilitarians—and almost everyone else—have found this case troubling.

Rule Utilitarianism

Instead of focusing on individual acts and their consequences, *rule utilitarianism* considers the consequences of adopting certain rules. When we begin to think about morality, we find ourselves in a social group that promotes obedience to a large number of rules. (In modern societies, some of these rules will also have "official" status as laws.) Are these rules, including the laws of the land, worth having? Should we try to obey them ourselves, encourage others to obey them, and teach our children to respect them? There is also the question of whether our lives might be improved by adopting rules not currently honored.

Rule utilitarianism provides a general theoretical framework for considering all these questions. Within this framework, moral discussion is like idealized legislative discussion. True, the discussions of actual legislators involve the elements of political compromise and special interest, but—at their best— legislators consider a single question: All things considered, would the lives of all citizens be improved by the passage of this law? The rule utilitarian asks the same question about actual or potential moral rules.

Rule utilitarianism is not open to the same objections as act utilitarianism. A society may have to think long and hard about which moral rules its members should follow, but the agent in a situation calling for immediate action simply applies the rules already adopted to the situation at hand. And, if it is thought, on rule-utilitarian grounds, that a moral rule is worth having, presumably that rule should be uniformly followed. For example, we don't kill innocent people to produce stocks of transplantable organs, even if in a given case this would maximize utility, because we have a moral rule against murder. In our society, we also have a law against murder, although it is our moral conviction that murder is wrong that is the more fundamental.

Absolute or Defeasible Rules. There remains, however, the question of whether rules should (or could) be followed uniformly—that is, with no exceptions ever being made. People who hold that rules should be followed without exception have a conception of rules as *absolute*. Many religious people, for example, regarding moral precepts as expressions of God's will, conceive of rules in this absolute way. (So does Kantianism.) Since consequences are always irrelevant, the bad consequences of obeying a rule in a particular case cannot be used to justify an exception.

Even for "absolutists," however, the situation is less clearcut. Consider the rule, "Thou shalt not kill." A relatively small number of pacifists take this to rule out killing in war, capital punishment, and even killing in self-defense. But many other people, who think of themselves as honoring that rule absolutely, take it to mean "Thou shalt not kill the innocent." This amounts to "Thou shalt not kill *unless* the person to be killed is an enemy combatant, is guilty of a capital crime, or is trying to kill you."

Those who think of moral rules as human inventions for regulating (at best, imperfectly) our own conduct in complex circumstances are not surprised that no sentence-long formulations are entirely satisfactory; it is better, perhaps, to think of rules as *defeasible*. The concept of defeasibility can be explained as follows: Adopted moral rules have a strong *presumption* in their favor, and they hold unless that presumption is "defeated" by an explicit argument to the contrary. Note that since the presumption is in favor of the rule, the "burden of proof" rests on those who wish to defeat the presumption. For example, there is a rule against lying. No special justification is needed for obeying that rule. However, there may be circumstances in which it is permissible to lie. This has to be argued.

It is sometimes urged against the view of rules as defeasible that, if people are taught this view, they will invent reasons for not honoring moral rules whenever that is convenient. But this is not a good argument against defeasibility. Whether moral rules are regarded as absolute or defeasible, it is always possible to see one's own conduct in a good light. Those who wish to see rules as absolute while making exceptions simply bury the exceptions in the content of the rule, or else they self-deceptively ignore their own disobedience. The correct understanding of rules should not be mixed up with questions about how to foster moral conscientiousness or rule-compliance.

Defeasibility and Rule vs. Act Utilitarianism. Some thinkers have argued that, if rules are regarded as defeasible, rule utilitarianism cannot be distinguished from act utilitarianism. It would then turn out that all the counterexamples to act utilitarianism also work against rule utilitarianism. This seems to follow only if the presumptive force that rules are accorded by a defeasibility-sensitive rule utilitarianism is equated with complete lack of force. In other words, acknowledging that a rule like "Don't lie" is defeasible (despite its being a very good rule to have adopted) doesn't return us to the situation of the act utilitarian, who must figure out what to do from scratch in each new action-requiring situation. In most situations, we can and should follow the rules having presumptive force, since in most situations there is nothing that defeats or cancels that presumptive force.

Facts and Values. One of the advantages of rule utilitarianism (which, remember, is a form of imperativism) is that it establishes a framework for moral discussion in which facts may have a decisive significance. In discussing an actual or potential moral rule, we are always entitled to ask what in fact are the consequences of keeping or adopting that rule. Suppose we can find out something about the connection (or lack of connection) between premarital sexual experiences and human unhappiness. This is relevant to a discussion of whether we ought to promote a rule against premarital sex. Critics of rule utilitarianism often point out that we must still evaluate outcomes or measure them against our standard of values. While this is true, the evaluation of outcomes is often unproblematical. For example, whether or not something causes physical pain is a factual, or empirical, question. That pain is a bad thing, a disutility, and intrinsically regrettable (so that the less we have of it, the better) is a value judgment. Fortunately, this and similar (fundamental) value judgments are shared by many people in our society. Naturalism in ethics is the view that all moral questions can be settled by facts alone. Utilitarianism, though it makes facts important, is not a form of naturalism.

Utilitarian Puzzles

One reason philosophers discuss utilitarianism as much as they do is that it gives rise to a number of interesting puzzles. The basic utilitarian principle is to maximize utility, which, as we have seen, Mill defines in terms of pleasure and pain. Pleasures and pains are mental, or subjective, states, which has led Robert Nozick (b. 1938) to pose the following question: Suppose you could connect yourself to an "experience machine," directly wired to your brain, that is programmed to provide you with a lifelong succession of intense and varied pleasures. Most people say that they would not want to be connected to such a machine; Nozick asks why not. That the experience machine has no appeal suggests a belief that utility should be measured not in terms of subjective states, but rather in terms of what objectively satisfies desires. But people have a great many kinds of desire. Is there some common measure of desire satisfaction? If not, it may turn out that utilitarian calculation (Bentham's "felicific calculus") cannot be carried out.

One further problem might be mentioned. Suppose my desires just happen to be stronger than yours. Does that mean that I should get more of what satisfies them than you get of what satisfies yours?

Relativism

Anthropological Awareness

Every human is born into a social group from which he or she picks up an enormous collection of rules, norms, and values. Anthropologists refer to these basic social groups as *tribes*, and to the process of becoming a member in good standing of one's tribal group as *enculturation*. In the course of enculturation, we absorb all kinds of values. We learn to say, in agreement with our neighbors, "That's nice!"; "That's good!"; "That's bad!"; "That's terrible!"; "That's disgusting!"; "That's pleasant!"; "That's irritating!"; and so on. There may be (or may once have been) tribes with no idea of the existence of other tribes with different forms of life. ("Form of life" [*Lebensform*] was introduced by the philosopher Wittgenstein, and is now commonly used by both philosophers and social scientists to refer to a tribe's total culture.) Most people in the modern world, however, are acutely aware of the existence of other peoples who follow different rules, who honor different values. Anthropologists have also learned that even forms of life very different from our own can be appreciated in their own terms;

that is, they cannot be dismissed as "primitive," "barbarian," or "irrational." And all of this constitutes *anthropological awareness*.

The Relativist Position

Does anything philosophically interesting follow from anthropological awareness? Some philosophers answer: Nothing special. We start from where we are and—using reason, argument, and criticism—we progress toward rationally defensible rules and values. Other philosophers hold that, even if we are capable of using reason, of arguing, and of criticizing, we still cannot produce a defense of our rules and values that is so totally objective, impartial, and nonarbitrary that anyone, from any culture, will have to accept it.

This view, called *cultural* (or *moral*, or *ethical*) *relativism* is most often pictured as a very bad thing. Quite often, philosophers argue: "*X*'s view leads to relativism; therefore, *X*'s view should be rejected." People have even said, "Don't respect other people's values, because that leads to relativism"; or "Don't be tolerant of human differences, because that leads to relativism"; or "Don't study anthropology, because that leads to relativism."

Evaluation of Relativism

The major claim of relativism is that we can argue with people in a rational way only if we share certain common premises; when we run out of common premises, rational argument comes to an end. This is a logical truth that rests upon the structure of arguments, and as such it cannot be grounds for worry or regret. All arguments, all rational proofs, on any topics whatsoever, have the same basic structure: a conclusion is shown to follow from certain premises. Conclusions are, accordingly, always premise-relative. This is the trivial truth that relativism dramatizes in various upsetting ways: our arguments persuade only those who accept the premises from which we begin.

We can, of course, often derive the premises of one argument from other arguments. But this cannot go on forever, not only because we don't have infinite time and because infinite arguments would be humanly incomprehensible, but because we soon reach a point where we can't think of anything more basic to support our basic premises. When I argue about morality, for example, I use as a premise (or assumption), "Physical pain is a bad thing" (which doesn't mean, incidentally, that it is not sometimes a necessary evil). Anyone who doesn't accept this premise—and whether he or she is from my own or some other tribe doesn't really matter—will not find my arguments compelling. There is no point in worrying about this, since it is built into the nature of argument, of rational persuasion. However, this still leaves a great deal for argument to accomplish, since we have certainly not thought through everything that does follow from commonly accepted premises.

Social and Political Philosophy

Individual and Society

One can scarcely think about ethics without thinking about the relations between humans; such rules as "Don't break promises," "Don't lie," and "Don't steal" all assume a world of other people. Moral behavior is often characterized as other-regarding (as opposed to selfish) behavior, and ethical theories like utilitarianism emphasize the fact that all human beings, insofar as they are affected by an act, must count equally in the determination of its moral status.

We can concede all this and still picture the moral agent in an exaggeratedly *individualistic* way. We do this when we think of the agent as an isolated ego, calculating his own advantage, his behavior imperfectly constrained by moral rules that are only grudgingly obeyed. In fact, humans are members of many "societies" to which they are tied by love, affection, loyalty. Clearly, the most important of these, at least at the beginning of a human life, is the family. It is doubtful whether abstract morality—our sense of what morality as such requires—would work at all were it not for our intimate, concrete, affection-suffused relations with others.

Communitarianism

Reacting against an excessively individualistic view of humans as isolated and essentially competitive egos, held in check by a purely external morality, some thinkers—both professional philosophers and others—have envisioned communities in which humans would be united by affection, and in which moral rules would be unnecessary. Such utopian communities have even occasionally been put into practice, and their histories provide interesting insights into radically alternative human arrangements. What they have not provided, however, is a model for large-scale societies like our own. Almost all societies in our own time are composed of enormous aggregates of people, almost all of whom are—and are destined to remain—perfect strangers to each other. They are also people (at least, in countries like the United States) of different origins, religions, life-styles, tastes, and preferences. Some social utopians and some social conservatives dream of homogenizing all these people, but that is not a real-world possibility. We accordingly look to law and morality to provide a framework that allows this irreducible plurality of people to live together in a relatively frictionless and mutually respectful way.

Society and State

A minority of tribes, anthropologists report, seem to be societies without being states—that is, they seem to be groups of people living together without a centralized power in charge of making laws, settling disagreements, providing public services, or doing anything else that the state is normally expected to do. Such tribes are called *acephalous* (literally, headless) tribes. When anthropologists first encountered such acephalous tribes, they insisted on seeing the chief or headperson and only reluctantly accepted the fact that there was no such person or even concept.

Even without the inspiration of these anthropological societies without states, however, we might well ask, simply as part of the general philosophical exercise of taking nothing for granted, why there are states. Why do we tolerate enormous concentrations of power in the hands of a few people? Why do we pay taxes? Why do we obey the law? Why do we—at least some of us, sometimes—feel patriotic? (Before we proceed, note that philosophers here distinguish questions that have to do with the actual origin of states and their subsequent development from questions that have to do with the justification of the state and its power.)

Justification

The task of justifying the state can be taken up at a number of levels. At the most concrete level, a philosopher may say something in defense of "the government," where this means the particular people in power, their particular policies, and their particular approach to governing. One level up, a philosopher may attempt to justify a particular *kind* of state, such as the form of electoral democracy that we have in the United States. At the most abstract level, finally, a philosopher may attempt to justify the very idea of having a state. It should be added that philosophers have also been active as *anti-justifiers*—that is, variously, as critics of particular governments or administrations, as radical critics of certain kinds of states, and as opponents of all forms of state organization and power. Philosophers in this last group, known as *anarchists*, hold that the state is not even a necessary evil.

The State as Benefactor

One argument for states goes back at least as far as Plato's dialogue, *Crito*. Here, Socrates is presented arguing a case for staying in jail and accepting his capital punishment. (He had been found guilty of impiety after a fair and legal trial.) Socrates argues that by accepting all the advantages of citizenship in Athens over a long period of time, he has tacitly agreed to obey the laws of Athens even when they operate to his personal disadvantage. Socrates expresses his gratitude for the benefits he has derived from the state. At the very least, the state as protector against external enemies and keeper of the domestic peace provides the environment necessary for all particular associations of citizens, for family life, for education, and for every form of work.

The State of Nature

The characteristically modern justification of state power was most vividly argued by Thomas Hobbes (1588–1679). Hobbes invites us to consider what human life would be like without a state to make and enforce laws. He calls this condition the "state of nature," where life would be—in Hobbes's famous phrase—"solitary, poor, nasty, brutish, and short." Hobbes did not present the state of nature as an actual historical condition, but as a purely conceptual or hypothetical alternative to life organized under state power. Thus, any rational person living in a state who wonders why he surrenders some of his own rights and powers to the central authority need only consider the alternative. Such a person will then realize that, were he to find himself in a state of nature, he would soon try to exit from it, to live gratefully under the dominion of a state.

The Social Contract

Humans, according to Hobbes, exit the hypothetical state of nature by mutual agreement to live under a common power. It is as if humans had signed a "social contract" to obey the laws of the land and to live together in peace. Hobbes himself thought that the state of nature was so bad that humans should (and, if they were clear-headed, would) agree to live under a strong central power if this were (as he indeed argued it was) a necessary condition of domestic tranquility. Later philosophers, however, have had other ideas about just what sort of contract a rational being could be expected to accept.

The Veil of Ignorance

Perhaps the most influential contemporary social-contract theory is to be found in John Rawls's *A Theory of Justice*. Rawls (b. 1921) pictures the just society as that which would be chosen by rational beings who are constrained to decide on institutions and laws "behind a veil of ignorance"—that is, without knowing what their actual social positions will be. It might be thought that such beings would opt for a condition of absolute equality as their safest bet. However, Rawls argues persuasively that the ignorant original contractors would opt for (and count as "fair") a social system in which inequalities of wealth existed so long as those inequalities made the least advantaged better off than under any alternative distribution. A case can be made, along Rawlsian lines, that competitive capitalism is a fair system, even though some people are immensely better off than others, since the least advantaged would be even worse off in a more equal (but less economically efficient) arrangement. This is, of course, a purely abstract argument that is not meant to suggest that any actual society satisfies Rawlsian conditions of fairness.

Marxism

Indeed, there is a whole spectrum of criticism, inspired by Karl Marx (1818–1883), which claims that liberal, Western-style democracies, though representing themselves as serving the interests of all citizens, in reality only serve the interests of a particular class: the major owners of capital. One of the most interesting concepts in the Marxist approach is that of ideology: a massive, systematic, and mainly unconscious falsification of social reality, which disguises narrow class interest as general welfare.

Laws

Sovereignty and Legitimacy

States (sometimes also called *nation states*) like the United States and Great Britain are said to have *sovereignty*,—that is, supreme and independent power of government within certain territorial boundaries. Anarchists hold that such states merely have a monopoly of power within a geographical area, and function according to the principle that "might makes right." However, most philosophers hold that at least some sovereign states have legitimacy—that is, that they govern lawfully (or by right, or with a certain moral authority). Consider the mugger who issues an order backed by a threat. His victim may comply, out of fear or prudence, but is not morally obligated to do so. An anarchist might say that it is not really different when a citizen obeys the law. The vast majority of philosophers, however, hold that the mugger example precisely contrasts with the exercise of legitimate power by the state.

Theories of Legitimacy

Though most political philosophers acknowledge that states may be legitimate, not all agree on an explanation of legitimacy. Classically, the two main theories have been "top-down" and "bottom-up." *Top-down* theories hold that legitimacy comes from God. The sovereign power (originally, the king) rules on earth as the representative of God, and issues laws that are in accord with "natural law" (or God's universal law for man). *Bottom-up* theories, by comparison, hold that legitimacy comes from the people governed: without the consent of the governed, a state is illegitimate. The representatives make laws on behalf of the people. Opinion divides as to how an ideal representative (e.g., a member of parliament or a senator) should function. One view is that a representative is elected for his or her good judgment, and hence should exercise that judgment in voting for those laws that he or she thinks best; the other view is that the representative is elected to speak for his or her constituents, and should vote for those laws that *they* think best.

Morality and Legality

Comparing morality and legality sheds light on both. Questions about *morality* do not have to specify a "where" and a "when": lying does not stop being wrong at some national border; breaking promises wasn't morally permissible until a certain date. People's views about morality may depend on where and in what period they live, but what their views are about is not supposed to vary.

Questions about *legality*, in contrast, do have to specify time and place. What is legal and illegal depends on the legislative acts of those who have the power to make laws for a given territory. Of course, there is more to it than that. Custom may come to have the force of law, for example. Also, what the law really says may emerge only as the decisions of judges accumulate, and—in the North American and similar systems—even a law passed by a compctcnt lcgislative assembly may be declared unconstitutional. However, it is still obvious that something may be illegal in one country and legal in another. It is also obvious that laws change: new laws may bc passcd; old laws may be rescinded.

Most citizens of modern states have too much knowledge of the actual legislative process to think that their laws are necessarily optimal. Consequently, there are two bad arguments that they will not make. *First*, they will not argue, "It's not illegal so it can't be immoral"; *second*, they will not argue, "It's not legal so it can't be moral." We realize that morality is only imperfectly reflected in actual laws. Pressure to change laws sometimes comes from people who believe that something immoral is not currently illegal, and that it should be. Pressure also sometimes comes from people who believe that something moral is currently illegal, and that it shouldn't be. It is natural, of course, that citizens should want their moral views reflected in the law. On the other hand, it would be folly to try to enact as law all of our moral commitments. Most of us think we have a moral obligation not to be unkind, for example, but it would not be appropriate (or feasible) to make unkindness illegal.

What Should States Do?

There is widespread contemporary disagreement about the appropriate uses of state power. At one extreme, people defend a conception of the *minimal state*. The police power of the minimal state both insures domestic peace and settles otherwise irreconcilable disputes between citizens. It probably also provides some other services that cannot be provided, either efficiently or at all, by private parties. There is, of course, considerable dispute about just what services fall into the category of the necessarily public. For example, schools presumably could all be private (and some philosophers have argued that they should be).

No large-scale modern state actually functions as a minimal state. Of course, nothing follows about how states should function from the facts about how they do function. Actual states may be doing too much or too little, or too much in one area and too little in another. It is true, however, that almost all social thinkers assign the state some welfare functions in addition to minimal protection functions. For example, few critics of excessive state involvement in welfare think the state should cease to concern itself with the welfare of children; even people who are unhappy with what they see as the distended scope of government regulation do not think that the state should repeal child-labor laws. Basically, varying conceptions of how much the state should do reflect two disagreements—the first about rights and obligations, the second about which values are most important.

Rights and Obligations

Rights and obligations are correlative: if I have a right, one or more others must have an obligation. I have a right, for example, to exclude people from my property. This is a right *against everyone*—that is, everyone has an obligation to keep out. Similarly, if you owe me $20, I have a right to that $20 when the loan is due , and you (and not others) have an obligation to pay me.

These unproblematical considerations are applied, in political philosophy, in diametrically opposed ways. Some argue as follows: People have a right to decent housing. However, no private parties have an obligation to provide decent housing. Therefore, the state (that is, the public authority) has an obligation to provide decent housing. Others argue: No one has an obligation to provide decent housing; therefore, no one has a right to decent housing. It is obvious that different people, depending on which of these arguments they find more compelling, will have very different views of what the state should do.

Natural Rights

Whether or not people have a right to decent housing, many political thinkers hold that all humans, no matter what state they live in, have certain basic human rights (traditionally called *natural rights*) that the state and its laws must respect. This idea is embodied in the founding documents of the United States, for example. The American Declaration of Independence states: "We hold these truths to be self-evident, that all men are created equal; that they are endowed by their Creator with certain inalienable rights; that among these are life, liberty, and the pursuit of happiness; that, to secure these rights, governments are instituted among men." Just which rights humans have, however, and how the possession of rights is to be interpreted concretely, remain controversial questions in the theory of rights. According to the contemporary rights theorist Ronald Dworkin (b. 1931), an individual, X, has a right when collective goals, however important, are not sufficient reasons for limiting X's freedom or imposing losses on X.

Values

Some philosophers claim that certain of our basic values, even if not strictly incompatible, are in a certain tension, so that social arrangements that realize more of one value will necessarily realize less of some other. One pair of values in possible tension consists of *fairness* and *economic efficiency*; another, of *equality* and *freedom*. Social and political philosophers disagree about whether these values are indeed in tension, and even those who agree they are in tension tend to disagree about which values are more important for a society to achieve.

Almost all human beings—it would probably be fair to say all normal human beings—judge their own as well as other people's actions from the moral point of view. This point of view, as we have seen, is sui generis: *it cannot be reduced to anything else.*

Although nothing is more familiar than moral judgment, the exact basis for such judgment is not easy to state; indeed, philosophers even disagree about how basic moral sentences function. We have seen that there are three main views about that. (1) Cognitivism is the view that moral sentences express genuine statements. This makes morality objective. (2) Imperativism is the view that moral sentences are really rules. To argue about morality is, accordingly, to argue about which rules humans should live by. (3) Emotivism is the view that moral sentences are disguised exclamatives that simply express positive or negative emotions, or feelings of approbation or disapprobation. Given this view, it is hard to see how rational argument about morality is possible.

Another major difference in moral theory is that between deontologists, who think consequences are irrelevant to the moral status of actions; and consequentialists, who think that consequences determine moral status. Utilitarianism is the most influential form of consequentialism. In utilitarian theory, consequences are measured against the yardstick of pleasure and pain. These qualities, however, must be understood in a general and inclusive way. Pleasures are all those positive states that make a contribution to well-being, welfare, or human flourishing; pains are all those negative states that lessen or detract from the same.

The actions about which we make moral judgments are the actions of humans who live in various social groups such as the family, to which they are bound by love, affection, and loyalty. It is also the case that the humans whose actions are of interest to us in ethics are also citizens of the state, and subject to its laws. Human behavior is motivated by both short-term and long-term needs and desires, and by a great variety of projects, plans, and goals. Behavior is constrained by two imperfectly overlapping sets of rules: morality and the law. Ultimately, the kind of life that humans live—what is ruled out and what is made obligatory—is shaped by both sorts of constraints working in complement.

Recommended Reading

In *The Encyclopedia of Philosophy* the student may wish to consult the articles on "Religion and Morality"; "Kant, Immanuel"; "Ethics, History of"; "Ethics, Problems of"; "Responsibility, Moral and Legal"; and "Moral Sense." See also "Philosophy of Law, History of" and "Philosophy of Law, Problems of." *The*

Handbook of Western Philosophy has useful articles under the following titles: "The Nature of Moral Philosophy"; "Teleological Theories of Morality"; "Morality and Universal Law"; "Utilitarianism, Emotivism and Prescriptivism"; "Political Obligation: Some Sceptical Views"; "Defenders of the State"; "The Philosophy of Rights"; and "The Limits of the State."

Of the many textbooks and anthologies intended for the beginning student, the following are especially worthwhile: Richard B. Brandt's *Ethical Theory* (1959); *Theories of Ethics*, edited by Philippa Foot (1967); *Ethics*, edited by Judith J. Thomson and Gerald Dworkin (1968); *Moral Concepts*, edited by Joel Feinberg (1969); Gilbert Harman's *The Nature of Morality: An Introduction to Ethics* (1977); J. L. Mackie's *Ethics: Inventing Right and Wrong* (1977); Robert G. Olson's *Ethics: A Short Introduction* (1978); *Divine Commands and Morality*, edited by Paul Helm (1981); Robert Spaemann's *Basic Moral Concepts* (1989); and Mary Midgley's *Can't We Make Moral Judgements?* (1991).

Books on a more advanced level that may still be useful to the beginning student include R. M. Hare's *The Language of Morals* (1952); David P. Gauthier's *Practical Reasoning: The Structure and Foundations of Prudential and Moral Arguments and Their Exemplification in Discourse* (1963); Kurt Baier's *The Moral Point of View: A Rational Basis of Ethics* (1965); Robert G. Olson's *The Morality of Self-Interest* (1965); Russell Grice's *The Grounds of Moral Judgement* (1967); Julius Kovesi's *Moral Notions* (1967); J. N. Findlay's *Axiological Ethics* (1970); Charles Fried's *An Anatomy of Values: Problems of Personal and Social Choice* (1970); Philippa Foot's *Virtues and Vices* (1978); Stuart Hampshire's *Morality and Conflict* (1983); Virginia Held's *Rights and Goods: Justifying Social Action* (1984); *Morality and Objectivity*, edited by Ted Honderich (1985); Bernard Williams's *Ethics and the Limits of Philosophy* (1985); David Gauthier's *Morals by Agreement* (1987); Amartya Sen's *On Ethics and Economics* (1987); David Wiggins', *Needs, Values, Truth*, (1987); Harry G. Frankfurt's *The Importance of What We Care About: Philosophical Essays* (1988); James Griffin's *Well-Being, Its Meaning, Measurement and Moral Importance* (1988); Russell Hardin's *Morality Within the Limits of Reason* (1988); *Essays on Moral Realism*, edited by Geoffrey Sayre-McCord (1988); and David O. Brink's *Moral Realism and the Foundations of Ethics* (1989).

Most books on ethics include sections on utilitarianism. The following are a few of the many books devoted to the subject: J. J. C. Smart and Bernard Williams's *Utilitarianism: For and Against* (1973); Donald H. Regan's *Utilitarianism and Co-operation* (1980); *The Limits of Utilitarianism*, edited by Harlin B. Miller and William H. Williams (1982); *Utilitarianism and Beyond*, edited by Amartya Sen and Bernard Williams (1983); and *Utility and Rights*, edited by R. G. Frey (1984). In a class by themselves are John Rawls's

A Theory of Justice (1971) and Robert Nozick's *Anarchy, State, and Utopia* (1974), the latter being an answer to Rawls. It is in Nozick's book that the experience machine is discussed.

A few other noteworthy books in the area of social and political philosophy are *Political Philosophy*, edited by Anthony Quinton (1967); Joel Feinberg's *Social Philosophy* (1973); A. John Simmons's *Moral Principles and Political Obligation* (1979); Joel Feinberg's *Rights, Justice, and the Bounds of Liberty: Essays in Social Philosophy* (1980); John Dunn's *Rethinking Modern Political Theory* (1985); John Gray's *Liberalism* (1986); David McLellan's *Ideology* (1986); Robert Nisbet's *Conservatism* (1986); Zygmunt Bauman's *Freedom* (1988); and Robert E. Goodin's *Reasons for Welfare: The Political Theory of the Welfare State* (1988).

Worthy of special mention is Robert A. Dahl's *Democracy and Its Critics* (1989). Although Dahl is a political scientist and not a philosopher, his book turns out to be a good introduction to the philosophical problems related to democracy and to political theory generally.

There is an enormous subfield known as philosophy of law. The following books all have sections devoted either to sovereignty and legitimacy, or to the relations between legality and morality: Martin P. Golding's *Philosophy of Law* (1975); *The Philosophy of Law*, edited by R. M. Dworkin (1977); Joseph Raz's *The Authority of Law: Essays on Law and Morality* (1983); and Joel Feinberg's *Harm to Others: Limits of the Criminal Law* (1984). Ronald Dworkin is perhaps the leading contemporary philosopher of law, and in any case a very readable one. His three main books are *Taking Rights Seriously* (1977), *A Matter of Principle* (1985), and *Law's Empire* (1986).

Although our discussion in this chapter dealt with general theoretical questions, philosophers have in fact addressed practical questions. Indeed, there is a subfield of ethics known variously as practical ethics or applied ethics. Representative books in this area include *The Problem of Abortion*, edited by Joel Feinberg (1973); Peter Singer's *Animal Liberation: A New Ethics for Our Treatment of Animals* (1975); *Ethics and the Environment*, edited by Donald Scherer and Thomas Attic (1983); *Business Ethics: Readings and Cases in Corporate Morality*, edited by W. Michael Hoffman and Jennifer Mills Moore (1984); James Rachels's *The End of Life: Euthanasia and Morality* (1986); and Douglas P. Lackey's *The Ethics of War and Peace* (1989). Another useful collection that contains philosophical reflections on such things as the right to work, drug testing on humans, surrogacy, and genetic engineering is *Moral Philosophy and Contemporary Problems*, edited by J. D. G. Evans (1988).

CHAPTER 8

Philosophy of Religion

Religion in its many varieties has always inspired philosophical reflection. Even today, many people turn to philosophy for answers to questions suggested by their religious beliefs. Philosophy relies on "unaided" human reason; it proceeds by analysis and argument. In contrast, most religions rely on some authoritative document—the Bible, for example—that is regarded as divinely inspired. This privileged source of not otherwise accesssible truths is called revelation. Philosophy in general advises epistemological caution, recommending belief only where there is sufficient evidence. In contrast, religion relies on faith—belief which, by definition, goes beyond what available evidence could make reasonable. So our first question is how we should think about reason and faith, reason and revelation.

Our next question will concern the meaningfulness of religious language—that is, whether religious language has cognitive meaning. For those who have grown up using religious language, it may seem surprising that philosophers have raised this question, but the question has an obvious basis. The language we use in everyday life presumably evolved to allow us to talk about the things around us; it has, for the most part, obvious cognitive significance. Can this

207

language, then, be used, meaningfully, to talk about the super-natural—to talk about God?

Those who think that the sentence "God exists" is a genuine statement (that is, a real statement capable of being either true or false) divide into theists, who hold that it is true; atheists, who hold that it is false; and agnostics, who do not know whether it is true or false. We shall, in considering these basic options, look at the following questions: How is God to be conceived? What is the nature of God? Are there any reasons, apart from religious faith itself, to believe in the existence of God? Can reason establish that there is a God? (This is sometimes put: Can we prove the existence of God?) We shall look at the major attempts of philosophers to do so.

Three other important topics will be discussed: (1) the problem of evil—the question of how evil can exist if there is indeed an all-powerful and all-good God; (2) the immortality of the soul—the question of whether humans have an immortal soul, a spiritual part that survives the death of the body; and (3) the nature and possibility of religious experience (which in its most intense form is called mystical experience).

Reason and Faith

Reason

The word *reason* is used to cover a broad range of human intellectual abilities. Most relevant here, though, is our capacity to form beliefs for good *reasons*—that is, on the basis of evidence. Not only is it descriptively true of humans that they are capable of rational belief formation, but this sort of belief formation is generally regarded as normative. This is to say that in belief formation we generally regard evidence-sensitivity as a norm or standard to be followed, departures from which are criticizable or blameworthy. It is in most circumstances considered a defect in rationality to come to believe that p without good reasons for thinking that p is true. And even if p does happen to be true, we would never say that a person who came to believe that p by a defective route knows that p. (Perfectly reasonable people may have hunches that p, but they don't believe that p, and act on the basis of p, unless they find good evidence that *p*, independent of their hunches or "gut" feelings.)

Faith

There are a great many different religions, as well as various points of view within each one. A philosopher who is making very general comments, therefore, cannot pretend to be able to define concepts to everyone's satisfaction. Moreover, philosophy does not presume to take the place of the detailed study of the various religions. It is nevertheless possible to pick out concepts from their more concrete contexts, and to define them in generally acceptable ways. In this spirit, then, we define *faith* as a set of beliefs at least some of which are not supported by evidence (or at least go beyond the available evidence). For many religious people, faith is not something that a person could come to have by sifting through evidence; rather, faith is viewed as "a gift of God," as something essentially supernatural in character.

Faith as Irrational Belief Formation

Does the person who has religious faith violate norms of rational belief formation? Is faith, in fact, a form of irrational belief formation? Given a definition of faith as a set of beliefs, some of which are not supported by evidence, it is hard to see how faith can fail to violate norms of rational belief formation. Interestingly, not all religious people react the same way to the suggestion that faith is irrational. There is what might be called the "So what?" response, and also what might be called the "It-isn't-really-true!" response.

The "So What?" Response

Many religious people are happy to admit that faith is irrational; all they claim is that the beliefs constituting their faith are true. These are not beliefs that one could have arrived at by "natural reason" or by "unaided human reason," however. So? So much the worse for rational belief formation. This was the attitude of Tertullian (*c*.160-*c*.220), the early church father who said *Credo quia absurdum* ("I believe because it is absurd"). If you believe that your faith provides you with those beliefs necessary for eternal salvation, then, you may not worry much about rationality. You will admit, perhaps, that you cannot persuade someone who is not lucky enough to share your faith to accept the truths of faith by purely rational means.

Certainty. In ordinary life, how certain we are about something will normally depend on our assessment of the available evidence. Religious people generally regard faith as making all the beliefs in the set of beliefs constituting that faith as *absolutely certain*. It is for this reason that religious people will claim, not merely to believe, but *to know* the truths of their faith. It therefore turns out that *to know*, *knowledge*, and related words and phrases are all ambiguous: *knowledge*, for example, can mean either "justified true belief" or "maximally certain belief." Note that these are obviously related, since—apart from the special case of faith—being maximally certain is a consequence of being justified.

The "It-Isn't-Really-True!" Response

Many religious people do not accept the idea that faith is irrational. There are three main ways in which such a charge of irrationality can be evaded or qualified.

(1) The religious person may claim that, although we should generally follow norms of rational belief formation, we need not and indeed should not when it comes to faith. Faith is thus viewed as *nonrational*, or possibly even *superrational*, rather than irrational.

(2) The religious person may point out that many things, in every area of life, are taken "on faith" or believed "on trust." We all accept things from authorities that we could not ourselves derive from "available evidence." All this, it is claimed, is natural, inevitable, and perfectly reasonable. (Note that this leads to the further question of whether we have, in picking our authorities, acted rationally or not.)

(3) The religious person may hold that many important components of faith are rational by normal standards. It is rational to believe in God. It is rational to believe in a supernatural realm. It is rational to believe that God would provide a revelation for our guidance, and it is rational to believe that the Bible is that revelation. This can all be true even if some of the things the Bible tells us (and which we believe because we believe the Bible is God's word) go beyond anything that reason could establish. This is a view that sees reason and faith as cooperative, or complementary, rather than antagonistic. Thus, reason leads us to faith, and faith takes us further than reason could.

Natural Theology/Dogmatic Theology

Theology is the study of God, His attributes, and His relation to the world. (The word derives from the Greek, *theos*, god, and *logos*, word or discourse.) Anything that can be established by unaided human reason—that is, by reason working independently of any revelation—is called *natural theology*. To put it another way, natural theology is that part (if any) of theology that can be established by natural reason. Anything that requires acceptance of the revelation-based dogmas of a particular religion is referred to as *dogmatic theology*. (A dogma, it should be recalled, is a belief that is mandatory for members of a particular religion.)

Not all interested parties draw the boundary lines between natural and dogmatic theology in the same place, since there is considerable disagreement about how much reason alone can establish. One extreme position, known as *fideism* (from *fides*, Latin for faith), holds that reason by itself can establish nothing about God—in other words, that there is no such thing as natural theology. Historically, most religious people have not been fideists, however.

An illustration of how the lines between natural and dogmatic theology are commonly drawn runs as follows: the proposition "God exists" belongs to natural theology, whereas the proposition "God is *triune*" (that is, a trinity of Father, Son, and Holy Ghost) belongs to dogmatic theology.

The Meaningfulness of Religious Language

Familiarity and Intelligibility

Most of us are familiar with ghost stories. If we were to read, "The ghost came into the room and moved the furniture around," we would not draw a cognitive blank: we could make sense of this sentence. Similarly, most of us are familiar with stories involving time travel. Here, if we were to read, "They got into the time travel machine and traveled back in time to 1968," we could make sense of those words, too—might even feel that we understood what was being narrated.

Our two sample sentences are of such a familiar kind that we do not, as a matter of psychological fact, worry about their intelligibility.

(Something is *intelligible* if we can understand it, give a coherent account of it, make sense of it, figure out what is going on.) Nevertheless, a few relatively obvious questions may convince us that our grasp of what is going on is much less secure than we are likely, unreflectively, to think. For example, how does the ghost (which is not physical) come to have a spatial location? How can the ghost—which can, after all, pass through walls and other solid objects—*move* anything? (We seem to be crediting the ghost with an inconsistent physics!) Turning to the other sentence, a little reflection suggests the following questions: When does the time travel take place? Should we assign time travel a certain velocity—something on the order of three years backwards per minute? Will someone who was born in 1970 go out of existence as the journey proceeds in the direction of 1968? Obviously, psychological familiarity is not enough to answer these questions.

The point of these examples is not to suggest that religion is like ghost stories or time-travel yarns—that is, something intellectually disreputable. Rather, the point is purely general. Psychological familiarity does not guarantee intelligibility. Religious language may be intelligible, but this is not guaranteed by its eminent familiarity.

Cognitive Meaning and Truth

Philosophers who discuss the intelligibility of religious language have concentrated on one type of meaning: cognitive meaning. This is because cognitive meaning is the type of meaning most closely connected to truth and falsity. Religious language, on any account, must be credited with a complex range of *performative* and/or *ritual* uses. And religious language certainly possesses great psychological meaning, where *psychological meaning* is defined in terms of the power to trigger thoughts, feelings, and images. However, this still leaves open the question of whether or not religious language can be used to make truth-claims—that is, to say anything true or false.

Meaning Prior to Truth

Outside philosophy, people tend to assume cognitive meaningfulness and to worry exclusively about truth. "God exists" is assumed to be cognitively meaningful without discussion; what is discussed is whether it should be believed. In fact, however, *questions of meaning are prior to questions of truth*: you cannot really consider whether a sentence is true unless you know what it means. Once stated, this is obvious, but it is nevertheless too often forgotten in practice.

Cognitive Meaning and Belief

A somewhat more subtle point (and one frequently missed) is that it is impossible to believe what you don't understand. Suppose your physics teacher, from whom you have every reason to take things on trust, tells you that $E = mc^2$. And suppose, further, that you really have no idea whatsoever what it means to say that energy equals mass times the speed of light squared. Then, you do not come to believe that $E=mc^2$; you have no belief about what energy is. What you do believe is that your teacher's sentence—"$E = mc^2$"—is true.

Ordinarily, we don't notice the difference between believing that a sentence, p, is true and believing that p. This is because, understanding as we do what the sentence means, we pass without effort from sentence to sentence *content*. We can barely feel the difference between believing that the sentence "It is raining" is true and believing that it is raining. Nevertheless, where intelligibility is a problem, this difference is crucial.

Intelligibility and the Concept of God

Why is the intelligibility of religious language an issue for some philosophers? We shall discuss this in terms of the single sentence, "God exists." This will illustrate the sort of things that worry some philosophers, but it should not be regarded as taking the place of more detailed discussion of the full range of religious language. Although some writers treat *God* as a proper name, most interpret the sentence "God exists" as "There is at least one and at most one divine being." Can we form a conception of this divine being? Can we work out an intelligible concept of God? In seeking to answer these questions, we must be guided by what religious believers say about the nature of God. They will not all say quite the same thing, but there is enough consensus to support a general analysis.

God as a Person

Most religious people believe that God is a person. Here is an intitial problem. Our idea of a person was presumably developed to apply to persons like ourselves. We know what it is like to be a human person. Can we take our concept of person and apply it to a being like God, who is so different? This is the general problem of taking concepts developed in one area (or for one sort of object) and seeing how far they can be stretched without loss of meaning (unintelligibility). But the problem is even more acute here because of certain other properties that God is standardly said to possess. Not only is God supposed to be a person; He is supposed to be perfect, immaterial, and infinite.

The Concept of a Perfect Person. What can we make of the concept of a perfect person? One response might be that, since *person* implies "like us" and *perfect* implies "not like us," the two halves of the idea of a perfect person cancel each other out and we are left with no cognitive content. In this view, "perfect person" is clearly unintelligible. (A less extreme view might be that "perfect person" is not clearly intelligible.)

The Concept of an Immaterial Person. For some, the logic of this pair of concepts will be similar to that of perfect person, but there is one important difference. Many people conceive of human persons as essentially immaterial—as identical, that is, with that soul that survives the death of the body. If we can make sense of the human soul as capable of independent existence, then there is no reason in principle why we cannot make sense of God as an immaterial person. (Though *soul* is certainly a popular word that is used effortlessly by vast numbers of people, not all philosophers think it possible to make sense of souls.)

The Concept of an Infinite Person. Is it possible to extrapolate from the kind of persons we are—conspicuously finite, limited, other-person-needing, desirous, ignorant, etc., etc.,—to the kind of person God is supposed to be? Some philosophers have suggested that infinity is beyond comprehension by our finite minds. Others have suggested that, since we can understand infinity in mathematics, there is no reason why we cannot understand God's infinity. Whatever, it should be mentioned that not all parties to the discussion hold that God's infinity is anything like mathematical infinity. And, in any case, our understanding even of mathematical infinity may not be all that secure.

Evaluation of the Intelligibility Problem

Some philosophers have made the extreme claim that "perfect person," "immaterial person," and "infinite person" are each, like "square circle," internally contradictory. Some have even interpreted this as a disproof of God's existence, on the grounds that an inconsistent concept cannot be instantiated. (In other words, there can't be anything that the concept of God specifies, since the total specification is inconsistent.) It is open to the religious person to reply that this inconsistency shows, at most, that a given *conceptualization* (or way of conceiving) of God is incorrect. Instead of making the extreme claim that what is said about God is inconsistent or contradictory, it is more plausible to maintain that the phrases used of God (and the associated concepts) are not obviously and clearly intelligible. They require stretching language in ways that may jeopardize cognitive meaningfulness, and in any case require an effort to think about what lies at the edges of what we can understand.

This is not something that the religious person wishes to deny; on the contrary, the religious person stresses that it is indeed hard for humans to understand God. A complete understanding of God, given what God is supposed to be, *should* be beyond the grasp of finite minds like ours. But the alternative to "not understanding completely" is not "not understanding at all."

The Nature of God

Two Approaches

What concept of God is the philosopher supposed to analyze? There are two ways of answering this question, ways that exactly parallel the distinction between descriptive and revisionary metaphysics.

The Descriptive Approach

Those who take the descriptive approach see their task as analyzing the standard concept of God as this actually occurs in the thought of religious believers. In general, when Western philosophers speak of the standard concept of God, they have in mind the concept of God derived from the Judaeo-Christian tradition.

The Revisionary Approach

Those who take the revisionary approach see their task as constructing an adequate concept of God, and one that may differ in major or minor ways from the traditional concept.

Concept Instantiation

In thinking about the nature of God, we must bear in mind several elementary truths about concepts and their instances.

(1) We may have a concept (this involves having a word in our language and/or an idea in our heads) that does not correspond to anything real. We have the concept of a unicorn, for example, but there are no unicorns. The concept of a unicorn tells us that anything that is a unicorn has to be (among other characteristics) one-horned and equine. No actual animal fits that specification, however. There are no instances of the concept *unicorn*, or—to put it in technical terms—the concept *unicorn* is not *instantiated*.

Of course, most of our concepts are instantiated. The concept *chair*, for instance, is instantiated, because there are things in the real world that correspond to that concept—things that have all the properties that the concept *chair* specifies chairs must have. The concept *chair* is instantiated, to put it most simply, because there are chairs.

(2) It is generally acknowledged that some concepts cannot be instantiated. These are internally inconsistent concepts like "square circle." We don't have to look around the world to see whether or not there are square circles. They are "ruled out" because they are logically impossible. (We are using here the obvious principle that *what cannot exist does not exist*. Although a few thinkers have suggested that the concept of God is internally inconsistent, this view is not generally accepted.)

(3) Some thinkers have claimed that there are certain concepts that must be instantiated. God, it is suggested, is such a concept. However, that there could be a concept that must be—or is *necessarily*—instantiated is not generally accepted. There is, however, one argument for the existence of God, known as the *ontological argument*, that is based on this idea.

The Divine Attributes

We have already mentioned some features of the traditional (or "standard," or most widely accepted) concept of God. God is, in the first place, conceived to be a person. Religious practices, such as worshiping and praying, and religious attitudes like love and gratitude, make sense only if God is personal. Note, however, that although God is regarded as personal, He is not thought of as similar to human persons. God is immaterial, infinite, and perfect. Perfection can be taken to include all the *divine attributes* (or "properties of God"). These include omniscience, omnipotence, immutability, eternality, and omnibenevolence. We will comment on each of these in terms of the way God is "standardly" conceived.

Omniscience

God is said to be *omniscient*, or all-knowing. God's omniscience can be formulated as follows: if *p*, then God knows that *p*. In other words, if something is true, then God knows it. There are two problems connected with omniscience that should be noted.

(1) It is not clear whether *knowledge* applied to God could mean the same thing that it means when applied to humans. In our case, when we know something, it seems always pertinent to inquire how we came to know—how we found out, what evidence we relied on. In fact, this is built into the concept of human knowledge. But in God's case, it is very doubtful that any of this applies: God just knows. God knows miraculously. God knows in a way that lies entirely beyond our understanding.

(2) The question is sometimes raised whether God's omniscience is compatible with free human action. This is the question of whether or not "divine foreknowledge" is compatible with human choice. If God knew from all eternity that, for example, Adam was going to eat the forbidden apple, then it might seem to have been settled as to what Adam would do long before he made his fateful choice in the Garden of Eden. But if something is settled prior to choice, there really isn't any choice at all. Other thinkers have suggested that this way of looking at the matter is the reverse of correct. Thus, Adam didn't eat the apple because God knew that Adam was going to eat the apple; rather, God knew that Adam was going to eat the apple because this is what Adam—acting on his own choice—finally did.

Several somewhat surprising features of omniscience should also be mentioned. Because God is omniscient, He cannot learn anything or discover anything. Nor can God respect anyone's "right to privacy." Also, not only is God imagined as knowing all the truths expressible in actual natural languages, He is presumed to know every truth that any possible language could express; and, beyond that, if there are any inexpressible truths, God knows these, too.

Omnipotence

God is said to be *omnipotent*, or all-powerful. This is also often expressed by saying that God can do anything. Most thinkers interpret this to mean that God can do anything that can be done—anything, that is, that is logically possible. On the other hand, a minority of thinkers have held that God can do anything without qualification. These later thinkers go so far as to say that God could make $2 + 2 = 5$. (Associated with this view is a riddle that goes back to the Middle Ages: *Question*: Could God make a stone so heavy He couldn't lift it? *Answer*: Yes, and He could lift it.)

Whatever human beings accomplish, they accomplish by some definite means, planned or unplanned. What God does, though, He presumably does in an absolutely miraculous way. This is how we must understand God's creation of the world. The standard conception is that God created the world *ex nihilo* ("from nothing"). Moreover, God created the world in a way that humans cannot begin to understand.

Immutability

God is said to be *immutable*, or unchanging. This is an attribute that is particularly hard to reconcile with the conception of God as a person who is capable of acting—capable, for example, of answering our prayers. It is sometimes said that the concept of strict immutability, which derives from Greek philosophy, is foreign to the Biblical idea of God. This is not a question, however, about which philosophy can take a stand.

Eternality

God is said to be *eternal*. This attribute is sometimes understood in terms of *omnitemporality*. To say that God is omnitemporal means that at any moment of time, t, God exists at t. Further, it doesn't matter whether the moment is past, present, or future. The more common view, however, is that mere temporal limitlessness (or temporal infinity) does not capture the essence of God's eternality. Eternity has to be conceived, according to this view, as having nothing to do with time. Perhaps if time and change are closely connected, then God's changelessness (or immutability) places Him outside time. In any case, religious people believe not only that God, unlike even the oldest things around us—unlike even the universe itself—did not *begin to be*, but also that He, unlike even the longest lasting things around us and unlike—in all probability—the universe itself, will not *cease to be*.

Contingent beings like ourselves come into and go out of existence, willy-nilly. But if there is a necessary being—and God is the main candidate for such a being, a being who cannot *not* be—there will, of course, never be a time when such a being does not exist. This conception of a necessary being whose essence, or nature, involves existence can be found in the writings of the medieval Arabic philosopher, Avicenna (980–1037), and was later used by Gottfried Leibnitz (1646–1716) in an important proof of God's existence.

Omnibenevolence

God is said to be *omnibenevolent* or all-good. This is the attribute of God most closely connected to religious worship and love. God is conceived to be the sum of all positive values, perfectly and infinitely good, and good in all His actions and effects.

Positions on God's Existence

There are three basic positions one can take about the existence of God—that is, about whether or not the standard concept of God is instantiated. These positions are theism, atheism, and agnosticism.

Theism

A *theist* is a person who believes that the standard concept of God is instantiated. In other words, a theist holds that there really is a being who has all the properties or attributes specified in the traditional conception of God. Put most simply, a theist is a person who thinks the statement "God exists" is true. Theists can be divided into *religious theists*, whose primary basis for belief in God is faith, and *natural theists*, whose primary basis for belief in God is rational evidence, or proof.

Atheism

An *atheist* is a person who believes that the standard concept of God is uninstantiated. An atheist holds, alternatively, that nothing has all the properties or attributes specified in the traditional conception of God. Put most simply, an atheist is a person who thinks the statement "God exists" is false. There is, of course, no such thing as a religious atheist. All atheists must suppose, rightly or wrongly, that human reason provides a decisive justification for disbelief in God.

Agnosticism

An *agnostic* is a person who does not know whether the statement "God exists" is true or false. To put it another way, an agnostic does not know whether the concept of God is instantiated or not. (The word *agnosticism* derives from the Greek negative prefix, *a*, and *gnosis*, one of the Greek words for knowledge.)

Proofs for the Existence of God

We have considered both the traditional concept of God and the attributes God is said to possess. We will now examine the more important proofs for God's existence that have been advanced, beginning with some observations about what a proof is.

Proof/Disproof

To offer a *proof* for a statement, *p*, is to offer a valid argument with *p* as its conclusion; to offer a *disproof* of *p* is to offer a valid argument with not-*p* as its conclusion. What can be derived as a conclusion always depends on the premises one starts from. When people ask, "Can the existence of God be proven?" and expect a simple yes-or-no answer, they are forgetting this basic feature of all arguments (or proofs), whatever their subject matter. In practice, what we look for is an argument for a desired conclusion that begins with premises that those we are trying to persuade are likely to accept. That is why an argument such as

> It says in the Bible that God exists;
> Everything the Bible says is true;
> Therefore, God exists,

while it is a *valid* argument (meaning that if its premises are both true, its conclusion is true), has almost no persuasive power. People who think that everything the Bible says is true, think that because they believe the Bible to be inspired by God. Consequently, they *already* believe that God exists, and don't need any further convincing by this argument. On the other hand, people who do not believe in God (and so might have their beliefs changed by this argument) are not likely to accept its second premise.

A final general remark about proof and disproof is in order. Failure to find a proof in no case constitutes disproof; failure to find a disproof in no case constitutes proof. A theist cannot fairly say that the fact (assuming for the moment that it is one) that atheists have not come up with convincing disproofs "proves" that God exists; an atheist cannot fairly say that the fact (assuming for the moment that it is one) that theists have not come up with convincing proofs "proves" that God does not exist.

Arguments for God's Existence

Philosophers have devised many proofs for the existence of God. In philosophy, we evaluate these proofs by the same standards of logic and rationality that we apply to any other arguments. We shall consider next the three kinds of arguments for God's existence that have been most commonly offered: the cosmological argument, the ontological argument, and the teleological argument.

The Cosmological Argument

The label *cosmological argument* really applies to a family of related arguments, all of which begin with observed (or otherwise obvious) features of the universe, or *cosmos*, and try to show that the only way of explaining these features is by postulating the existence of God. Motion, cause and effect, and contingency are the features most commonly used in this type of argument. Here, in condensed form, are three samples of cosmological argument:

Things move;
They don't move themselves;
Their movers don't move themselves;
This series of movers cannot be infinite;
Therefore, there must be a first unmoved mover, whom we call God.

Most things are effects;
Their causes are in turn effects;
The cause/effect series cannot be infinite;
Therefore, there must be a first uncaused cause, whom we call God.

Contingent beings need to be explained;
Their explainers need in turn to be explained;
This explanation series cannot be infinite;
Therefore, there must be an unexplained explainer, whom we call God.

These arguments have generated many thousands of pages of commentary, friendly and unfriendly, supportive and critical. It is probably safe to say that few contemporary philosophers accept these arguments (though that does not by itself, of course, "prove" that the arguments are no good). Perhaps the main reason why these arguments are generally less persuasive today than they once were is that it no longer seems so obvious that the universe itself must be finite. Why can't the system of motions constituting the universe itself be infinite in time? Why can't cause-and-effect series be infinitely long? Why can't some contingent beings explain other contingent beings in an open-ended, or nonterminating, way? According to some contemporary thinkers, there is no reason why not. However, this still leaves open the question of whether even an infinite universe, with no temporal starting point, requires an explanation for its existence.

The Ontological Argument
There have been many versions of the *ontological argument*. An argument for God's existence is ontological IFF it tries to show that

God's actual existence follows from the concept or idea of God. The sample version here is similar to that given by St. Anselm (1033–1109):

> The concept of God is of a being no greater than
>   which can be conceived;
> But a being which exists is greater than a being
>   which is merely conceived;
> If God did not exist, God would not be a being no greater than
>   which can be conceived;
> Therefore, God exists.

Like the family of cosmological arguments, the various versions of the ontological argument have provoked extensive discussion. Again, most contemporary philosophers do not accept any form of the ontological argument, though one contemporary philosopher, Alvin Plantinga (b. 1932), has produced a very sophisticated version that he thinks should persuade fair-minded thinkers.

What most philosophers find unacceptable, or at best puzzling, about the ontological argument can be put as follows: It certainly makes sense to define God as "the greatest conceivable being." But what this definition rules out is not the nonexistence of God, but rather the existence of any being greater than God. Now, the concept of anything will specify the set of properties that the things that instantiate that concept must possess; but existence is not a property, and so cannot be built into any concept. (This is usually put by saying that existence is not a predicate.)

This criticism of the ontological argument can also be explained in terms of "necessary beings." God is defined as a necessary being, and necessary beings have to exist; so it looks like God has to exist. So, what is wrong with this line of reasoning? The problem is that all it shows is that, if there *were* a necessary being, that being would have to exist. It does not show that there *is* a necessary being—a being that cannot not exist.

The Teleological Argument

The *teleological argument,* also known as the *argument from design*, is based on the idea that many natural objects, such as animal organisms, seem designed. Their parts—such organs as eyes and ears, for example—are well fitted to serve functions that help the organism to flourish, or at least to survive, in its particular environment. The teleological argument says that the only way to explain the natural teleology (or natural purposiveness) that we observe is to postulate an intelligent designer—someone who "engineered in" all the purposiveness we see in nature. (*Telos* is the Greek word for goal, purpose, or end.)

Earlier thinkers often borrowed examples of such purposiveness, or "good design," from astronomy. From the nineteenth century on, however, the most popular examples have come from biology. Using biological organisms as our example, we can formulate the teleological argument as follows:

> Organisms have features that are purposive;
> Purposive features must be the result of design;
> Organisms don't design themselves,
>   and are not designed by humans;
> _____
> Therefore, there is a nonhuman designer, whom we call God.

Again, few contemporary philosophers accept the teleological argument. Its second premise, which once seemed "obvious" to most people, now seems highly questionable. Moreover, the postulation of a "Great Architect" of nature (with the attributes of omniscience and omnipotence) does not help to explain just how nature has solved its design problems. Indeed, nature—including all biological organisms— does not seem like the product of top-down design. One reason for thinking this is that nature displays as much conflict as harmony. For example, viruses, which could certainly be celebrated as examples of diabolically ingenious design, exploit the weaknesses of other biological organisms. But if those organisms themselves had been well-designed, one would expect them to be virus-proof.

Creation

Both cosmological and teleological arguments involve the common idea that the existence of the universe, with the order and purpose it displays, can be explained only by its having been created by God. As noted earlier, creation—in contrast with ordinary manufacture from existing raw materials—is suppposed to be creation *ex nihilo* ("from nothing"). Philosophers point out that we—that is, we humans—have no conception of what creation from nothing is. This does not mean that creation from nothing could not have happened; it does mean, however, that the concept of creation from nothing is not useful in the construction of explanations.

The Problem of Evil

The Basic Problem

"The problem of evil" labels a unique problem that arises in the context of theism. Essentially, it is the problem of explaining how evil can exist if God exists. We can formulate the problem most economically as an inconsistent triad. (An *inconsistent triad* is a set of three statements, the truth of any two of which implies the falsity of the third.) The inconsistent triad relevant here can be formulated as follows:

  (i)   God is all-powerful;

  (ii) God is all-good;

  (iii) Evil exists.

Evil is understood here to mean the intrinsically regrettable—anything that is in itself negative, anything that the world would be better off without. Physical pain and suffering are generally acknowledged to be examples of evil in this sense. It seems quite obvious, then, why many philosophers think (i), (ii), and (iii) form an inconsistent triad: (i) implies that God could prevent any instance of evil; (ii) implies that God would want to prevent any instance of evil; so if (i) and (ii) are true, (iii) should be false.

There are two other possibilities. Suppose (i) and (iii) are true—that is, suppose that, despite the existence of an all-powerful God, evil exists. It then looks as if (ii) is false—that is, it looks as if it is false that God wants to prevent evil. Finally, suppose (ii) and (iii) are true—that is, that evil exists despite God wanting to prevent it. It then looks as if God cannot prevent evil, which means that (i) is false.

The Existence of Evil

Some philosophers have indeed held that (iii) is false. Many complicated and subtle arguments have been advanced over the centuries to "explain away" the apparent existence of evil. Is it possible that something like pain should turn out not to be evil? What argument could possibly show that? It is sometimes argued either that pain serves a function, or that pain is necessary (and thus turns out not to be evil). How should this approach be evaluated?

First, even if pain serves a function (alerting organisms to negative states of their bodies), this does mean that the pain itself is not intrinsically regrettable. True, we might be inclined to tolerate something that is in itself evil if it does us some good, but an evil we tolerate in this manner is not transformed into something good. And although nature might not have been able to do so, God (being both omniscient and omnipotent) could presumably have devised a warning system that did not involve pain.

Second, even if pain is necessary, this does mean that pain is not an evil; all it means is that pain is a *necessary evil*. Most of us do think some pain is a necessary evil. In this spirit, I allow the dentist to cause me pain because I believe the pain is necessary for my long-term dental health (which in turn means, among other things, a future with less pain). Humans of good will try to eliminate pain where they can, though obviously much pain remains. Whether there is any pain God could not eliminate is a difficult question, and one not answered in the same way by all philosophers.

An Argument for Atheism

The problem of evil probably provides atheists with their strongest argument. The atheist argues as follows: God is by definition a being who must be both all-powerful and all-good. Since in our example (iii)—"Evil exists"—is obviously true, either (i) or (ii) must be false. It doesn't really matter which, since if either (i) or (ii) is false there is no being who is both all-powerful and all-good; therefore, God does not exist. The crucial assumption here (and one that many theists would not accept) is the incompatibility of the three statements: if (i), (ii), and (iii) turn out to be compatible, the atheist's argument fails.

The Theists' Consistency Claim

Most theists considering the problem of evil have not tried to deny the existence of evil. Rather, they have on the whole regarded this as a desperate and wildly unrealistic strategy. What they have claimed instead is that (i), (ii), and (iii) are consistent: they can all be true.

The Free-Will Defense

The most persuasive argument advanced by theists is called the *free-will defense*: an all-powerful and all-good God could not create the best of all possible worlds without granting some creatures free will; and, if some creatures have free will, they can use it in a way that generates evil. To put it in terms of a familiar Bible story, Paradise could have and would have continued if Adam had not chosen to eat the forbidden fruit. Whether or not all evil can be traced back to Adam's sin (or to the sins of other humans) is not a question that can be easily settled; indeed, there may be no neutral way of describing the data that would be acceptable to theists and nontheists alike.

The "Beyond Understanding" Defense

The theist is inclined to believe that the existence of evil must be compatible with the existence of an all-good and all-powerful God, even if humans cannot quite understand how this can be. Here, again, is a place where those with faith will see things very differently from those without.

The Immortality of the Soul

Religious beliefs and metaphysical views are likely to influence each other; thus, a person who is a physicalist in metaphysics, for example, cannot consistently believe that he has a nonphysical soul. Such a person will have the same problem with God and angels, since God and angels are spirits. For most people, however, the influence is in the other direction: because they believe in God, souls, and angels, they conclude that physicalism must be incorrect.

Philosophers, of course, cannot tell people what they should believe as a matter of faith. They limit themselves, rather, to two questions: (1) Is the concept of a soul (or of pure spirit in general) consistent?

(2) Independent of anything that rests upon faith or revelation, is there any evidence for the existence of souls or other spiritual beings?

Consistency

Although the idea of a personal soul is a very familiar one, and although many people take it for granted that they have souls, philosophers nevertheless worry about whether the concept of a soul is internally consistent. Perhaps the basic difficulty is that most of our thinking—even our thinking about persons—assumes that what we are thinking about has the form of a physical object. Persons, whether or not they are spirits *post mortem*, are in this life at least partly physical (bodily). Can our thinking, then, designed as it is to fit the physical, be transferred to the nonphysical?

Location and Motion

Persons have spatial locations. Do their souls also have spatial locations? This involves a question of consistency, for it raises the issue of whether we can coherently suppose something that is not a body is at a certain distance from various physical objects. But if we cannot say a given soul is at various distances from certain physical objects, then we cannot assign the soul any spatial location. But then we cannot—at least, not in the usual way—picture the soul as the companion of our body, nor can we consistently say that at death the soul leaves the body, even though something like this is often actually said (and believed) by religious people.

Again, although people picture souls (and usually also angels) as capable of movement, this only makes sense if souls (and angels) can have spatial locations (since movement is simply change of location). Perhaps modern physics will eventually provide a conceptual scheme more compatible with souls than is our current common-sense view of simply located macroscopic objects; it is too early to tell.

Thought and Experience

People who believe in souls presumably picture souls as capable of both thought and experience. Once again, the challenge is to work out an account of thinking and experiencing that does not essentially involve the physical. Ordinary experience is often closely tied to such bodily sensations as seeing and hearing; also, much of our thinking is triggered by (or is about, or is based on memories of) sensory stimulation. What are we left with when all this is taken away? (One interesting question concerns whether or not a soul, separated from the body, can be pictured as becoming *aware of* anything new.)

Complexity and Partlessness

Trying to grasp what it is like for a soul (or an angel) to have thoughts and experiences is made more difficult by the following consideration: Thoughts and experiences seem to have a certain intrinsic complexity. This is not the same as the complexity of the neurophysiological machinery ordinarily involved—and, according to the physicalist, necessarily involved—in our having thoughts and experiences; it is, rather, the internal complexity of the thoughts and experiences themselves, the complexity of their contents. The question is how we should picture the soul dealing with this complex content. Can the soul itself be pictured as complex?

One view of spirits—perhaps, the standard view—is that spirits do not have parts. But can something lacking parts possess nonsimple thoughts and have nonsimple experiences? Indeed, if a soul has a thought or experience, but is not identical with that thought or experience, it would appear that the soul must be complex. The fundamental difficulty here is that our thoughts about wholes and parts, developed as they have been in regard to physical objects, do not clearly apply to souls or spirits in general. (This is also a problem for our conception of God, who is also conceived of as without parts, as simple.)

Immortality

So far, we have considered certain perplexities that arise in connection with the concept of a soul itself. From a philosophical point of view, these are the most difficult issues. For if there can be souls—that is, if the concept of a soul is consistent—then there seems to be no reason why such souls cannot be immortal. The claim that souls are immortal is the claim that souls, though they came into existence at a given moment of time, will never go out of existence. This may seem surprising, since most if not all of the things we are familiar with eventually cease to exist. Most things are made of parts, so they can disintegrate, fall apart—literally fall to pieces. If souls, as spirits, really have no parts, then they cannot suffer the fate of ordinary physical objects.

Indeed, it is sometimes said that the only way a soul can cease to exist is via *annihilation*. Annihilation is the negative counterpart of creation, and, like creation, it can only be done by God. But it is something God could do. This just means that, although souls can be consistently regarded as immortal or everlasting, there is also no contradiction involved in the idea of a soul's ceasing to be.

Evidence

Is there evidence that would persuade a fair-minded and rational person that there are souls? This question is not one that has anything like a universally accepted answer. Part of the problem is that some people think that there is evidence of a supernatural realm, something fundamentally unlike the ordinary physical world. This evidence includes answered prayers, inexplicable feelings of mystery, paranormal phenomena, visions of various kinds, and the occurrence of miracles. If there is a supernatural realm, then that may be thought to entail the existence of—depending on the religious framework—God, angels, and souls.

Other people think that there are, additionally, purely philosophical arguments for souls. (These are just the arguments for Cartesian dualism.) However, few think that there are purely philosophical, faith-and-revelation-independent arguments for immortality.

Religious Experience

Definition

An experience is religious IFF it is an experience of the supernatural. This might include experiences of God, of angels, and of persons now dead, such as the saints, who are regarded as sent from God. In some traditions, the supernatural is experienced in a more free-floating, nonindividual form. Indeed, it should be emphasized that experiences of an enormous variety have been described as religious experiences. Some people would claim that an experience of oneness with the universe, although it does not involve the supernatural, should be counted as a religious experience.

Here is a case where a word that starts out describing one already very diverse set of cases (but having the supernatural as common denominator) comes to be used to describe other cases that are in some ways similar even though they do not involve the supernatural. Particularly vivid religious experiences that seem to put the experiencer in such direct contact with God that the boundaries of the self are temporarily dissolved are referred to as *mystical experiences*.

Significance of Religious Experiences

There is no doubt that many people have had quite extraordinary experiences, of which we have their perfectly sincere autobiographical accounts. (Almost all such accounts agree that human language is totally inadequate to describe these experiences.) The main philosophical question is whether or not such religious experiences provide evidence persuasive to a fair-minded and rational person that there is a supernatural realm. It might seem obvious that, if there are indeed experiences of the supernatural, then the supernatural exists; for, to underline the obvious, if it did not exist, it could not be experienced. And the general principle is correct. That there are experiences of elephants is an argument for elephants; for if elephants did not exist, they couldn't be experienced, either. But if I have what I interpret as, or take to be, an experience of an elephant in my bathtub, there might yet not be an elephant in my bathtub: I might, after all, be hallucinating.

We can all think, in less dramatic settings, of experiences being misinterpreted, misconstrued, misdescribed, misunderstood. This is not to say that an experience described as religious (or supernatural-contactive) is always misdescribed; it is simply to note that this is a possibility.

Explanation of Religious Experiences

It is sometimes also claimed that the only way of explaining the occurrence of religious experiences is by postulating some sort of supernatural causality. This claim is not easy to evaluate. In the first place, we often have no detailed explanation available of why people think what they think, feel what they feel, and in general have the inner life that they do. This is obvious in the case of great artists. We do not know exactly why or exactly how Shakespeare thought up all those incredible lines of poetry. ("Because he was a genius" seems like a flaccid pseudo-explanation.) But this does not—or, more accurately, should not—lead us to postulate a miracle in Shakespeare's case, or to suggest that God directly inspired him. We cannot rule out a purely natural explanation, either in the case of a great artist like Shakespeare or in the case of a religious—or allegedly religious—experience.

Religion, in one form or another, continues to play an important role in the lives of many people and, as we have seen, has inspired philosophical reflection along a number of lines. (We should remember that philosophy concentrates on a relatively small number of general concepts, and does not seek to take the place of more detailed studies of religious forms.) Most of the discussion of religion within philosophy has focused on the following topics: (1) how religious commitments (characteristically based on faith and revelation) relate to rationality; (2) whether religious language is cognitively meaningful; (3) how God should be conceived; (4) whether God's existence can be rationally demonstrated; (5) whether the existence of evil is a problem for theism; (6) whether it is possible that humans have immortal souls; and (7) what is meant by "religious experience."

In considering all of these topics, philosophers of religion must abstract themselves from any personal religious commitments they may have in order to examine religious language in a neutral and fair-minded way. In the area of religion, as in any other area of interest, the philosopher cannot assume that familiar language is cognitively meaningful.

Finally, the philosopher cannot assume that the claims made by religion are true; after all, something may be believed by many people and still turn out to be false. The philosopher must consider both whether there is evidence that supports the central claims of religion—in particular the claim that God exists—and whether there are any arguments that would convince rational people that the claims of religion are true. It must, of course, always be remembered that a claim may be true even though we have no evidence that supports it and no argument that proves it.

Recommended Reading

Once again, further reading might profitably begin with the *Encyclopedia of Philosophy*. Relevant articles appear under the following headings: "Religion"; "Religion, Naturalistic Reconstructions of"; "Religion, Philosophy of"; "Religion, Psychological Explanations of"; "Religion and Morality"; "Religion and Science"; and "Religious Language." See also "Cosmological Argument for the Existence of God", "Ontological Argument for the Existence of God", "Teleological Argument for the Existence of God", and "Religious Experience Argument for the Existence of God." There are also articles on *agnosticism*, *atheism*, and *theism*. In *The Handbook of Western Philosophy*, see "Philosophy and the Existence of God" and "The Philosophy of Religion."

The following is a good selection of relatively basic books either on philosophy of religion or the nature of religion itself: Mircea Eliade's *The Sacred and the Profane: The Nature of Religion*, translated by Willard R. Trask (1959); John E. Smith's *Philosophy of Religion* (1965); Ninian Smart's *The Religious Experience of Mankind* (1969); *Philosophy of Religion*, edited by Steven M. Cahn (1970); *The Philosophy of Religion*, edited by Basil Mitchell (1971); Paul Tillich's *What Is Religion?*, translated by James Luther Adams (1973); Ninian Smart's *The Science of Religion and the Sociology of Knowledge: Some Methodological Questions* (1973); Richard L. Purtill's *Thinking About Religion: A Philosophical Introduction to Religion* (1978); Ninian Smart's *The Philosophy of Religion* (1979); *Contemporary Philosophy of Religion*, edited by Steven M. Cahn and David Shatz (1982); David Stewart's *Exploring the Philosophy of Religion* (second edition, 1988); William J. Wainwright's *Philosophy of Religion* (1988); and John Hick's *Philosophy of Religion* (fourth edition, 1990). Most of the books listed above have sections on faith and rationality. A more specialized book on that topic that can be enjoyed by the beginning student is George I. Mavrodes's *Revelation in Religious Belief* (1988).

The following is a list of somewhat more advanced books that deal with the nature of God, proofs or disproofs of God's existence, and conceptual issues raised by religious language. (These topics are grouped together since they are in practice commonly treated together.) Etienne Gilson's *God and Philosophy* (1941); Frederick Ferre's *Language, Logic and God* (1961); Frank B. Dilley's *Metaphysics and Religious Language* (1964); *New Essays in Philosophical Theology*, edited by Anthony Flew and Alasdair MacIntyre (1964); Peter Geach's *God and the Soul* (1969); Anthony Kenny's *The Five Ways: St. Thomas Aquinas' Proofs of God's Existence* (1969); *Talk of God*, edited by G. N. A. Vesey (1969); Nelson Pike's *God and Timelessness* (1970); Anthony Flew's *The Presumption of Atheism* (1976); Anthony Kenny's *The God of the Philosophers* (1979); J. L. Mackie's *The Miracle of Theism: Arguments for and against the Existence of God* (1982); Anthony Kenny's *Reason and Religion: Essays in Philosophical Theology* (1987); and *The Concept of God*, edited by Thomas V. Morris (1987).

Michael Durrant's *Theology and Intelligibility* (1973) is worthy of special mention as one of the few books by a contemporary philosopher to discuss the Trinity.

Helpful books on the "problem of evil" include *God and Evil*, edited by Nelson Pike (1964); Peter Geach's *Providence and Evil* (1977); and *Facing Evil: Light at the Core of Darkness*, edited by Paul Woodruff and Harry Wilmer (1988).

Further reading in the area of religious and mystical experience (which also includes discussions of such categories as the holy and the sacred) might begin with Evelyn Underhill's *Mysticism: A Study in the Nature and Development of Man's Spiritual Consciousness* (1955); Rudolf Otto's *The Idea of the Holy*, translated by John W. Harvey (1958); R. C. Zaehner's *Mysticism, Sacred and Profane* (1961); Rudolf Otto's *Mysticism East and West: A Comparative Analysis of the Nature of Mysticism*, translated by Bertha L. Bracey and Richenda C. Payne (1970); and Frits Staal's *Exploring Mysticism* (1975). William James's classic *The Varieties of Religious Experience* (1902; many subsequent reprintings) remains one of the best surveys of religious experience.

Two short books on the special topics indicated by their titles are Terence Penelhum's *Survival and Disembodied Existence* (1970) and Richard Swinburne's *The Concept of Miracle* (1970). Finally, Alvin Plantinga's *The Nature of Necessity* (1974) should be singled out. In this book, Plantinga offers what he believes is a successful version of the ontological argument. There is also a very sophisticated discussion of "God, Evil, and the Metaphysics of Freedom."

CHAPTER 9

Aesthetics

Aesthetics deals with conceptual problems that arise in connection with either naturally beautiful objects, such as mountains and sunsets, or such works of art as paintings and symphonies. It is, accordingly, more inclusive than philosophy of art, which deals only with artifacts (human-made objects). The first question to be considered is whether mountains and sunsets and paintings and symphonies make up a homogeneous class with significant common properties. This question, in turn, cannot be answered adequately without addressing the question of whether works of art themselves constitute a unified class: in other words, do all artifacts that are works of art have important (or nontrivial) common properties?

Those who answer negatively hold that the concept of a work of art is a family-resemblance concept. According to this view, works of art in their enormous, irreducible variety show complex patterns of crisscrossing resemblance and difference. What gets into the category of art depends, at least in part, on historically variable decisions about how such similarities and differences should be evaluated. According to the most extreme view, parties with an interest—quite often, a frankly economic interest—in what gets counted as a work of art engage in a kind of negotiation of various items into and out of the category of art, with corresponding claims, counterclaims, and compromises. The hypothesis that museums, galleries, established critics, and the like effectively stipulate what is to be counted as a work of art is known as the institutional theory of art.

Most philosophers of art do not accept a purely historical/sociological account of what gets counted as a work of art, however. Although works of art make up a very diverse class, there may still be some interesting common features. We will consider the following suggestions:

(1) All works of art may require our looking at them with a special attitude: disinterested appreciation. Moreover, we like works of art even though we recognize that they typically serve no practical purpose.

(2) All works of art may have certain specific formal qualities. Aesthetic form is a difficult concept—a concept, in fact, that challenges our best efforts at verbal definition; nevertheless, for each type of art we recognize instances of aesthetic form.

(3) All works of art may give rise to certain special experiences known as aesthetic experiences.

(4) All works of art may produce a special kind of pleasure in those who enjoy them.

(5) All works of art may be sources of a special kind of knowledge.

These five suggestions are not incompatible; as a matter of fact, they could all be correct. They may indeed all belong to a single explanation of why art matters as much as it does.

Several other concepts have been advanced, historically, to explain the nature of art. Imitation, or mimesis, theories claim that we value works of art as particularly successful imitations of nature. Expression theories claim that we value works of art as particularly effective expressions of our deepest feelings. (Actually, each of these theories may capture some aspect of what art does.)

Finally, there is the question of the objectivity of taste. Obviously, not all people like the same works of art. Is there some objective standard, though, according to which one is supposed to like X better than Y? Can one be criticized for liking Y better than X? Not all philosophers of art answer these questions in the same way.

Aesthetics and the Philosophy of Art

Etymology

The term *aesthetics* comes from the Greek *aistheton*, meaning capable of being perceived by the senses. It was introduced as a modern philosophical term, however, only in 1750, by A. G. Baumgarten (1714–1762). As Baumgarten used the term, aesthetics is the science of the knowledge produced by the senses (so-called sensuous knowledge). It contrasts with logic, or the science of the knowledge produced by pure thought (so-called intellectual knowledge). Baumgarten held also that the goal of aesthetics is beauty, whereas the goal of logic is truth. It is from this idea that the characteristic modern use of *aesthetics* derives.

The word *art* originally meant skill, ability, or craft, corresponding to the Greek *techne* (from which we derive words like *technical* and *technique*). In the ancient world, a "work of art" was simply any object that required skill or craft in its production. Only gradually, beginning about the middle of the seventeenth century, did "work of art" come to mean "work of *fine*, or *high*, art." As a part of this same historical process, the "artist" as autonomous creator came to be distinguished from the "artisan," or "craftsperson," who exercised his skills only to satisfy his customers' demands.

Natural Objects and Artifacts

Such naturally occurring objects as rocks, crystals, and sea shells, as well as such large-scale features of nature as mountains, clouds, and waterfalls are experienced by many people as pleasing ("nice to look at") or even—particularly in the case of the larger phenomena—awe-inspiring or sublime. This kind of appreciation and enjoyment of nature is obviously different from the narrowly practical view that sees rocks as potential building material, sea shells as a possible source of food, and so on. Our *nonpractical* (or *contemplative*, or *disinterested*) interest in nature is very similar to the interest we take in those artifacts that are works of art. (Note that *disinterested* is commonly used in aesthetics as a technical term meaning nonpractical.)

Artifacts can be divided into three general classes: (1) practically useful, but not disinterestedly pleasing; (2) both practically useful and disinterestedly pleasing; and (3) not practically useful, but disinterestedly pleasing. Works of art will be found in the third class.

Natural Objects and Works of Art

Since many natural objects, large-scale features of nature, and works of art are alike in being disinterestedly pleasing, it would seem that a single category—"the aesthetic"—should cover them all. However, there are a number of arguments that cut the other way.

(1) Works of art can express ideas or feelings, but nature cannot.

(2) Works of art—like sentences, but unlike natural objects—can *mean* something. This point can perhaps be better put another way: works of art, like sentences but unlike natural objects, can embody *communicative intentions.* Reading a poem, we are presumably entitled to ask, "What is it trying to say?" We are certainly not entitled to ask such a question after looking at a waterfall or a cloud.

(3) Works of art can imitate nature (and be applauded for doing so), but nature cannot imitate nature.

(4) A single category of the aesthetic has been challenged by challenging the very idea of the disinterestedly pleasing. The history of art shows us, it has been argued, that paintings, for example, are almost always commissioned for such practical purposes as fostering religious devotion, enhancing the prestige of their owners, or as investments. All that this argument shows, however, is that works of art fall into the hybrid category of the practically useful *and* aesthetically pleasing—the very category into which all those natural objects that can be used *and* enjoyed also fit.

"Work of Art" as a
Family-Resemblance Concept

Diversity

Philosophers are often accused of looking for more unity than the objects about which they are thinking really display. Nowhere is this accusation more plausible than in the case of works of art. The argument that it is fundamentally misguided to look for a unified concept (defined in terms of relatively few shared properties) is based on the evident diversity of works of art. There are many different kinds or categories of works of art. Consider the following very short list of pairs: novels and symphonies, works of sculpture and piano sonatas, paintings and love lyrics, ballets and watercolors. Moreover, within any one category there is enormous diversity. Consider paintings, for example: Some paintings are designed to tell stories. Some paintings are designed to provide detailed visual information about a single object. Some paintings represent everyday realities. Some paintings present purely imaginary and totally fantastic worlds. Some paintings are interested in the real colors of objects. Some paintings use colors to trigger emotional reactions—many *different* emotional reactions. This list could be greatly extended.

It is not even true, the argument from diversity continues, that all paintings aim to be disinterestedly pleasing. Although some early thinkers—for example, all eighteenth-century writers on art—assumed that art should be pleasing, many of our contemporaries (artists and nonartists alike) reject that idea. A modern painter may wish his paintings to be disturbing, provocative, painful, disquieting, unsettling, and/or upsetting, rather than beautiful, pretty, or generally nice to look at. This all leads to the following characteristically contemporary paradox: "I like X's paintings because they are so upsetting," or "I like Y's novels because they are so disturbing."

Evaluation of the Argument from Diversity

Should we conclude that "work of art" is a family-resemblance concept grouping together historically related but fundamentally diverse items? Not all philosophers of art answer this question in the same way. Obviously, diversity is enormously important, especially when it is remembered that we are talking about all artifacts that might have earned the status "work of art," *whenever* and *wherever* produced. In the next five sections, we will look at attempts to find unity despite this obvious diversity; in other words, we will be looking at proposed common features of works of art.

Works of Art: Common Features

The Aesthetic Attitude

Disinterested Interest

Even if it is admitted that not all works of art are disinterestedly pleasing, it might still be claimed that they are all "disinterestedly interesting." The first thing to say here is that the usage *disinterestedly interesting* is not a contradiction in terms. We can distinguish practical interests—I need or want object *O* because I can use *O* to do something I need or want to do—from sheer interestingness. Since some people profess to find the idea of sheer interestingness mysterious, the following comparison may be helpful. Sheer interestingness is like idle curiosity: we often enjoy knowing that which we really don't need to know. For most of us, the gossip about the lives of movie stars that newspapers and magazines provide falls into this category.

The Aesthetic Attitude

In order to appreciate the sheer interestingness of anything, we have to approach it with the appropriate attitude—with, specifically, what is known as the *aesthetic attitude*. This is simply the attitude we have when we are interested in something without being dominated by practical interests. Probably, everyone occasionally assumes the aesthetic attitude, although it can also be deliberately cultivated.

It is probably also true that the aesthetic attitude—at least, in any sustained form—is a luxury available only to people who are in relatively secure possession of the necessities of life—that is, to those who can take at least brief holidays from attending to the satisfaction of their basic needs. An objection to this way of putting things is that the need for the disinterestedly interesting in some form or other is itself a basic human need. This is obviously a claim it would be difficult to test, however.

Perceptual Economy

It is apparently true that when we are caught up in some practical activity, we perceive just enough of the objects involved to accomplish the practical purpose. The matter of recognizing other people is a good example. We usually look at people just long enough to recognize them. Some husbands, though they can presumably recognize their wives, cannot recall the color of their wives' eyes. (There seems to be some gender difference here!) This kind of perceptual economy (though embarrassing in the case just cited) is generally a very good thing. When we take up the aesthetic attitude, either because an object elicits it or because we deliberately assume it, we are no longer dominated by a practical purpose that enforces perceptual economy. We look for a longer time (this may in practice amount to no more than a few extra seconds), and take in the whole range of displayed features.

Aesthetic Distance

The term *aesthetic distance* is used to indicate the suspension of preoccupation with ordinary cares and concerns that the aesthetic attitude involves. In adopting the aesthetic attitude, we "distance" ourselves from everyday practical attitudes. *Aesthetic distance* is also sometimes used to indicate certain properties in the works of art themselves that incline us to assume the aesthetic attitude. For example, plays are ordinarily performed on a stage, and begin with the raising of a curtain. The compression of long stretches of "real" time into a few hours of theatrical time also generates aesthetic distance.

Aestheticism

Artists can be defined as artisans who have the capacity to make artifacts that are disinterestedly interesting. It is, of course, appropriate to take the aesthetic attitude toward these objects. It is sometimes claimed that, having learned the aesthetic attitude for those practically useless artifacts known as works of art, we can then extend it to other things. This happens, for example, in the "aesthetic appropriation" of artifacts originally made for purely practical purposes. (Here, *practical* also includes objects made for religious purposes.) It happens also when we look at nature *as if* nature were a work of art.

It is generally agreed that there is a limit to the appropriate extension of the aesthetic attitude. *Aestheticism* is defined as the overextension of the aesthetic attitude, and an *aesthete* (generally, a term of contempt) as a person who takes up the aesthetic attitude in inappropriate situations. An extreme example would be a person who sits on the beach watching a drowning as if it were a ballet. "How interesting those arms are, waving about," he says to himself. "How interesting those screams sound." Such a person would be guilty of aestheticism, as would the engineer who builds a bridge that looks good but collapses under the weight of the first train to cross it (because he was more concerned with how the bridge looked than with its structural integrity).

Aesthetic Form

Structure and Pattern

All objects of which we are aware are structured or patterned. Even in the case of something that is described as *formless* (or *amorphous*), the fact is that it has such a complex structure that the eye or mind cannot immediately grasp it. We are interested in structure for a variety of reasons; practically speaking, for one, what we are able to do with objects depends on their structures. Science studies structures from a theoretical/cognitive point of view; it is true, however, that some structures are disinterestedly interesting. *Aesthetic form* is the general term associated with such structures.

The Nature of Aesthetic Form

There is no adequate verbal definition of aesthetic form. For one thing, form means different things in different arts. In music, form is a matter of how notes are put together; an analysis of musical form requires reference to such things as harmony, counterpoint, tempo, and so forth. In painting, form is a matter of how pigments are patterned over the surface of the canvas. In sculpture, finally, form is a matter of the shape given to a three-dimensional chunk of matter.

A much more difficult problem, however, arises in the analysis of aesthetic form. This can be explained as follows: Consider a set of abstract (nonrepresentational) paintings, some of which are very successful paintings and some of which are very unsuccessful. Each painting, whether successful or unsuccessful, is a patterning of pigments into certain shapes or forms. But only a successful painting will embody aesthetic form—that is, will have a form that is disinterestedly interesting, or—as it is sometimes put—enjoyed "for its own sake."

Connoisseurship

People who do not appreciate abstract paintings may see no difference between the successful and the unsuccessful specimens. However, for *connoisseurs*—persons with developed taste, extensive experience, and sharpened discriminatory powers—the differences between the good paintings and the bad will be evident. Nevertheless, the connoisseurs will not be able to prove that the paintings they favor are superior to the others. This does not mean, however, that there is really no difference between the paintings alleged to be disinterestedly interesting and the others.

Learning to recognize aesthetic form can be a long process that requires a great deal of careful, thoughtful, and comparative looking. A similar process of careful, thoughtful, comparative reading leads to connoisseurship of literary works of art.

Form/Content

Another way of approaching the concept of aesthetic form is by considering the standard form/content contrast. We can often, at least in a rough-and-ready way, distinguish the subject matter of a work of art—what the work is about—from the way the subject matter is treated. In the case of a representational painting, for example, we can distinguish what the painting depicts from how it is painted. Similarly, we can distinguish what a poem says from how the poem says it.

What the painting depicts, what the poem says, or—in general—the subject matter of an artwork is referred to as its *content*; everything else is *form*. There is considerable disagreement in aesthetics about whether the form/content distinction holds up. What is generally agreed upon is that two artworks with different forms cannot have exactly the same content, because form and content interact. However, we can still distinguish form and content, in a relative way, for many works of art. On the basis of this distinction, we can define two opposing exaggerations: philistinism and formalism.

Philistinism

A *philistine* is a person who does not appreciate the specific qualities of works of art—roughly speaking, the opposite of a connoisseur. One aspect of philistinism is an exaggerated interest in the subject matter or content of an artwork, accompanied by relative indifference to its purely formal, medium-specific qualities. A person who says "I like any picture so long as it is a picture of a cat" is guilty of this form of philistinism.

Formalism

Formalism is the thesis that the value of a work of art depends entirely on its formal qualities—that is, on its aesthetic form. According to the strict formalist, what makes Shakespeare's sonnets great works of art are those features relating to the poems' metrical composition—that is, such medium-specific effects as assonance and alliteration. The sonnets would be just as valuable, in this view, if they were about double-entry bookkeeping instead of about human beauty, desire, and love.

The formalist position is more plausible for some works of art than for others. But even in music—which is generally considered to be the purest, most abstract, or least "about" of the arts—there is ordinarily some reference to real world feelings. The formalist usefully emphasizes precisely those qualities the philistine ignores, but it would be wrong to claim (as do some extreme formalists) that these are the *only* qualities that count.

Aesthetic Experience

Ordinary Experience

Experiences are customarily divided on the basis of which of our senses is involved in their production: seeing produces *visual* experiences; hearing produces *aural* experiences; smelling produces *olfactory* experiences; taste produces *gustatory* experiences; and touch produces *tactile* experiences.

Three basic points about experience are signficant for this discussion. (1) Our overall experience at any given moment is ordinarily the fusion, or synthesis, of a number of kinds of sensory experience. (2) What we experience depends not only on what objects exist in our environment, but also on our own selective interest and attention. (3) What we experience depends on our intellectual abilities—on our capacity to interpret and classify.

Because objects enter and leave our environment in a basically chaotic and unplanned way, ordinary experience is fragmentary, with incomplete experiences being continually interrupted by new experiences. Large chunks of our life consist of disjointed, unsatisfying, and essentially inharmonious experiences, while even the occasional intensely pleasurable experiences are only bits and pieces of the general mix.

Experiencing Art

Works of art are designed to produce satisfying experiences. A painter is, in effect, designing a machine for producing visual experiences. Of course, the painter needs the cooperation of a spectator capable of assuming the aesthetic attitude and responding appropriately to what the painter has done. Two people looking at a single painting from almost the same vantage point will—assuming the same visual acuity—have almost the same visual experiences. However, one viewer may have and the other may fail to have an aesthetic experience; to put it another way, one sees the patterned pigment as aesthetic form, and the other does not.

The same thing is true of the other arts. Two people sitting in a concert hall will hear almost the same succession of sounds. However, for one person those sounds may organize themselves into fully appreciated musical structures, while for the other listener the same sounds may amount to not much more than vaguely pleasant—or even vaguely irritating—noise.

Isolating Art

Our perceptions of works of art take place in the ordinary world, of course, against a background of irrelevant noise. Why, then, do aesthetic experiences not become part of the general confusion of ordinary experience? In the first place, the world is sometimes so noisy that having aesthetic experiences is impossible. However, there are certain separate (although complementary) factors that help us have aesthetic experiences.

(1) Physical barriers against irrelevant noise are often built into places where works of art are experienced. The most obvious example is the acoustic insulation of a concert hall against outside noise.

(2) There are many conventional ways of isolating works of art from their perceptual surroundings. The most obvious example here is the frame around a picture, which helps to concentrate our visual attention and keeps it from seeping onto the adjacent wall.

(3) Anything that has the quality of sheer interestingness (that is, is disinterestedly interesting) wins our attention over things that are merely ordinarily interesting or not interesting at all. One exceptional class of experiences is *sexual* experiences. In their ability to magnetize, to fascinate us, sexual experiences have no rivals among other experiences except for those intense religious experiences known as mystical experiences. However, for better or worse, the real world does not very often place aesthetic and sexual experiences in direct competition.

Aesthetic Pleasure

Experience and Pleasure

We are pleased whenever one of our desires is satisfied, a project is accomplished, or a goal is reached. However, this "being pleased" (which is built into our awareness of success) should be distinguished from "feeling pleasure." Eating an ice cream cone, looking at a painting, and walking through a meadow on a beautiful day are examples of experiences that, for some people some of the time, have pleasure built into them. In other words, we should not think of pleasure as a separable consequence of these experiences. Although people sometimes say that they "want pleasure," and although the idea of pleasure-maximization is an integral part of some forms of utilitarianism, what people actually want are pleasures—particular pleasures that cannot be separated from the concrete experiences that embody them.

How many kinds of pleasures are there? The only plausible answer seems to be that there are as many different kinds of pleasures as there are different kinds of pleasant experiences. The pleasure of eating a chocolate ice cream cone is not the same as the pleasure of eating a strawberry ice cream cone. The pleasure of looking at a painting by Raphael is not the same (in terms of what is actually experienced) as the pleasure of looking at a painting by Veronese. Nor is the pleasure of looking at Raphael's portrait of Baldassare Castiglione the same as the pleasure of looking at his *Sistine Madonna*.

The Concept of Aesthetic Pleasure

The concept of aesthetic pleasure should probably be regarded as a family-resemblance concept. All of the diverse pleasures we take in experiencing works of art (and in nature experienced as if it were a work of art) compose the class of aesthetic pleasures. Some philosophers of art—specifically, those who believe (to some degree) in formalism—define aesthetic pleasure more narrowly, as pleasure taken in the experience of aesthetic form. It is doubtless correct to emphasize the pleasure of aesthetic form as most characteristic of our experience of works of art; but it should be remembered that such pleasure naturally combines with pleasures related to content or subject matter. A "purism" that attempts to segregate these pleasures is probably impossible and certainly unnecessary.

Aesthetic Knowledge

Learning from Art

Before the age of photography, much of our information about how things looked in places distant in time or space was derived from paintings and drawings. Similarly, poems, plays, and novels were and are a rich source of knowledge about the thoughts and feelings of the ages in which they were produced. They may also be the main source of psychological understanding outside of our direct encounters with other people (despite the existence of a science of psychology). Part of the pleasure we take in the experience of works of art is simply the pleasure of learning, of satisfying our curiosity. It is, however, generally regarded as a misunderstanding—indeed, as a form of philistinism—to think that art justifies its existence by being a source of knowledge. This is particularly the case if the knowledge is of a kind that we could, and often do, acquire otherwise than through the experience of art.

Art-Dependent Knowledge

The question arises whether there is a kind of knowledge that we can acquire only through experiencing works of art. There is at least some evidence that art provides us with certain knowledge about the world that we could not otherwise acquire. A great portrait, for example, gives us access to the inner life of its subject that we could not derive from casual scrutiny of the living person. The portrait works, as it were, as a kind of condensation of psychological insight in visible form. Painters teach us to see the world—to observe it accurately and disinterestedly—so that, even if it is now true that we can acquire certain subtle and precise forms of visual knowledge through direct observation, we may not have acquired this observational capacity if paintings had never existed.

Knowledge of Works of Art

Some of what we learn from works of art we could learn in other ways; some of what we learn from works of art we could not otherwise learn. There is yet another category of knowledge that deserves the name "aesthetic knowledge" in the strictest sense: knowledge of works of art themselves. Without Raphael's portrait of Baldassare Castiglione, for example, we might never have had an idea of what that Renaissance humanist looked like; in addition, our general visual knowledge of Renaissance "types" might have been diminished. But Raphael's *Portrait of Baldassare Castiglione* is itself an appreciable object, an addition to the world, of which—or so at least it is widely thought—it is worthwhile to have knowledge by acquaintance. Formalists may emphasize our coming to know the formal qualities of the painting, but it is the total set of properties the painting has, as an object in its own right, that we come to know on any account through our perceptual and aesthetic experience.

Getting to know a work of art is much like getting to know an interesting and likeable person: we are enriched as our acquaintance with the person or work of art deepens, enriched in a way that has nothing to do with practical interests. At best, our interest in people or works of art is—in terms used by John Dewey (1859–1952)—*consummatory* rather than *instrumental*—a matter of enjoyment, that is, rather than of utility.

What Art Does

Why Art Matters

The question of why art matters can be answered in more than one way, since not everyone agrees about what art does (or what art is supposed to do). We can, however, produce a fairly widely accepted answer by combining the five topics just discussed—the common features of art—into a single explanatory account.

The Aesthetic Attitude

Many people are able to distance themselves from ordinary cares and concerns and become *disinterestedly interested* either in certain features of their environment or in certain objects. Whether this is something that comes naturally to all humans or is something that some humans learn as members of particular cultures, there is no doubt that some people assume the *aesthetic attitude*. The aesthetic attitude—that is, the attitude of disinterested interest—is the appropriate attitude to take toward works of art, since works of art are precisely those artifacts which are disinterestedly interesting. Note that the category of works of art, so defined, will include both those artifacts expressly designed to be disinterestedly interesting and certain other artifacts, whatever their original purposes, that are now esteemed and appreciated for their own sakes.

Interestingness. To say that something is *interesting* is commonly regarded as an instance of damning with faint praise, since *interesting* is the adjective often used when people can think of no livelier or more specific compliment. We should, therefore, emphasize how important interestingness or being interesting really is. Perhaps this can be shown by considering its opposite, the boring. Nothing is worse than the boring; if everything were boring and nothing were interesting, life would not be worth living. One of the things that makes life worthwhile and gives it its meaning is the existence of the interesting. And works of art matter because they are interesting in the purest, least-conditional-on-particular-purposes way.

Aesthetic Form and Aesthetic Experience

We are interested in works of art for a variety of reasons. Some works of art can be bought and sold profitably. Some works of art can be displayed to impress people with our wealth, social standing, and/or taste. Some venerable works of art can be studied for the information they yield about past ages, while some contemporary works of art can be scrutinized for clues about what life means in our own time.

From the point of view of aesthetics, however, all of these considerations are secondary. What is primary (though not exclusively important) is the direct experience of the works of art themselves. Each work of art provokes a qualitatively distinctive experience. One of the things we experience when we are exposed to a work of art is its *aesthetic form*—the aesthetically relevant (perceptible/appreciable) aspects of its structure.

Aesthetic Pleasure and Aesthetic Knowledge

Our experience of artifacts that are disinterestedly interesting (or of naturally beautiful objects) is pleasurable; it is the kind of experience that we want to have for its own sake. Whereas many of life's pleasures are either short-lived or harmful in the long run (or both), aesthetic pleasures are of relatively long duration and entail no harmful consequences. Even if we did not learn anything from works of art, then, they would still be valuable. In fact, however, we do indeed learn about the world through our experience of works of art; furthermore, works of art are themselves the objects of an important kind of knowledge by acquaintance.

The Importance of Works of Art

Not all works of art are equally important. Some works of art, however, play an important role in human life, providing experiences that are both intrinsically pleasurable and cognitively significant for those people who can assume the aesthetic attitude. Through its aesthetic form, a work of art is designed to be experienced with disinterested interest, pleasure, and cognitive benefit. This is why art is important, and it applies to all works of art, however various. Additionally, though, philosophers of art have mentioned two other features that play important roles in our appreciation of certain works of art: imitation and expressiveness.

Imitation

The Greek term *mimēsis*, which has by now become a part of the English language, means imitation or representation. In his enormously influential *Poetics*, Aristotle defined tragedy as the *mimesis* of certain human actions and characters; since his era, it has been widely held that the main function of works of art is to imitate reality. An artist, in this same view, is conceived of as the person who has the skill to imitate—that is, make plausible "copies" of—reality. In extreme form, the best art should fool us into thinking it *is* reality. In this connection, one recalls the remark of the Roman writer Pliny about the painter Zeuxis, who "produced a picture of grapes so dexterously represented that birds began to fly down to eat from the painted vine." (The birds were, of course, incapable of assuming the aesthetic attitude.) People still praise paintings, and other works of art, for being "lifelike" or realistic.

The Importance of Imitation. No contemporary philosopher of art believes that imitation, or the creation of successful illusion, is either a necessary or a sufficient condition for the concept "work of art." An artifact—for example, an ordinary photograph—may be mimetic without being a work of art; another artifact—for example, an abstract painting—may be a work of art without being mimetic. Although it is wrong to define works of art in terms of mimesis or *representationality*, there is no need to deny all value to imitation. As Aristotle observed, people enjoy both imitating and witnessing successful imitations. Furthermore, artifacts that are mimetic may have appreciable aesthetic forms. (This is, in fact, true of all the great representational paintings of past ages.) And finally, of course, works of art that are representational will yield a kind of knowledge not available from nonrepresentational works.

Expressiveness

Works of art are sometimes defined in terms of special powers to express either feelings or ideas.

Expression of Feelings. We may feel sad, and—having no special gifts—be able to express our sadness only by uttering the banal sentence, "I feel sad." Indeed, some writers distinguish such mere assertion (or statement) from expression. In this view, "I feel sad" would count as an assertion of sadness, but not as an expression of sadness. In order to have qualified as an expression, it would have had to have crystallized the felt sadness in some unusually vivid, attention-grabbing way. Thus, poetry, according to this "expressionist" view, is valuable not because it invents new feelings, but because it invents novel ways of expressing certain feelings that we have all felt. For example, we feel pleasure (as well as a kind of clarity) in seeing what we feel presented with verbal precision and evocative power.

There is, of course, no requirement that expression be accomplished with words: paintings express feelings that we recognize but cannot verbalize, and the same thing is true of music.

Expression of Ideas. Most ideas can be straightforwardly stated. For example, the idea that human beings are in the grip of fate can be conveyed simply by saying, "Human beings are in the grip of fate." The novelist Thomas Hardy, among others, expressed the same idea through the creation of ingenious plots that show the slow but sure unfolding of fated events. Of course, it would be wrong to think of the idea expressed by a poem, a play, or a novel as an *extractable* (that is, separately statable) message. True, Hardy expresses the idea that we are in the grip of fate; however, his idea of fate and how it grips us is as complicated as the novels themselves.

Works of art as expressive of ideas can be said to mean something. And meaning, it is sometimes argued, is precisely that which strictly formalist theories of why art matters tend to neglect.

Evaluation of the Expression Theory. According to the expression theory of art, the whole point of art is to express feelings or ideas. Certainly many artists, literary and otherwise, assume that they are expressing feelings and/or ideas. This is surely something art does, and is one important reason we value art. It is nevertheless incorrect to make expression a defining characteristic of art. The extraordinarily expressive scream of a real person in a real emergency, for example, is not a work of art. In other words, being expressive is not a sufficient condition for being a work of art.

Are there any examples of works of art that are not expressive? In other words, is being expressive a necessary condition for being a work of art? In a very loose sense, a painter may be said to be always expressing his taste—his sense of which colors go together, his idea of what sort of painting it is worthwhile to make now, and so on. But if you were to ask the artist, "What feeling does your painting express?" or "What idea does your painting express?" the artist might claim that nothing—neither feeling nor idea—is expressed. (The painter may be right.) We can sum up by saying that expression, expressiveness, expressive power can be important, but it would be a mistake to see all art as expression. Here as elsewhere, only-one-thing-counts views are very likely to be incorrect.

The Objectivity of Taste

Variety

There seems to be a great deal of variety in what people like, enjoy, appreciate. Some people like classical music; others do not. Some people spend vast sums of money in order to attend the opera; other people couldn't be dragged there. Poetry is read with great enthusiasm by some; other people say, "I don't like poetry."

What is the appropriate theoretical response to this valuational variety? Few questions in aesthetics have provoked so many divergent answers. One response to the question is simply to deny what it assumes—to deny, that is, the variety itself. This is the position that apparent differences in taste or preference reflect differences in exposure to various works of art, differences in appreciative capacity, and similar "accidental" factors. There is at least some truth to this claim: after all, you can't like opera if you've never heard or seen one, and you can't read poetry with pleasure if you can't read.

Aesthetic Education

Why do schools—why *should* schools—in countries like our own mandate courses in art and music appreciation? One view sees the schools thereby imposing "elitist" or "establishment" tastes on the masses. Another much more charitable and optimistic view sees the schools multiplying options for and sources of aesthetic experience and pleasure. Unfortunately, aesthetic education often takes the form, "This is what you should like—this is what you are *supposed to* appreciate." But where art is concerned, there are no shoulds or supposed to's. No one has a moral—or any other kind of—obligation to like or enjoy anything.

Nevertheless, it may still be rational to try to increase our capacities to like and enjoy. The pleasure of getting drunk, which requires no particular expertise, may outweigh the pleasure of listening to a symphony; however, we may come, for very good reasons, to prefer the pleasure of the latter. It fits into a harmonious life, enhances our cognitive powers (simply because listening to it attentively requires processing complicated data), and carries with it the risk of neither short- nor long-term damage.

Facts and Mistakes

Many people claim that Shakespeare is the greatest playwright. Is there a *fact of the matter* about who the greatest playwright is? If you happen to think that someone else is the greatest playwright, are you making a factual mistake? The philosophical question being raised here is very similar to the question of cognitivism or realism in ethics—the question, that is, of whether or not there are moral facts. We generally expect, where there is alleged to be a fact of the matter, some set of instructions about where to look and what to look for to find out what the facts are. Perhaps, in the case of the judgment about Shakespeare, you could read all the plays by everybody who ever wrote plays that you could get your hands on, and then read all the plays that Shakespeare wrote. You would then "see" that Shakespeare is indeed the greatest playwright. But maybe not; maybe you would decide now that Racine is the greatest playwright.

Can anyone really demonstrate in a plausible way that you have looked in the wrong place or for the wrong things? Probably all that philosophers of art can safely say is that, if there are facts of the matter about aesthetic worth (particularly, about comparative worth), then people can be wrong. Alternatively, if a question can be answered wrongly (because it is not being answered correctly), then it is an objective question. And whether or not aesthetic questions are objective remains controversial.

Judgments and Feelings

Occasionally, people will say that, although they acknowledge that artist A is better than artist B, they like B better than A. If having good taste were simply a matter of being cognitively correct, people of this sort would have to be counted as having good taste, since they are obviously not making an intellectual mistake. However, this is not what good taste involves. Good taste involves actually preferring A to B if A is indeed better than B.

Suppose that we were able to classify artifacts, at least in some approximately correct way, on the basis of their capacity to provide pleasurable aesthetic experiences. There is probably no way to quantify here, simply because there is no way to bring the qualitatively distinctive pleasures of different artifact-stimulated experiences under any common measure. Nevertheless, we might still be able to "rank-order" artifacts in terms of certain features of the pleasurable experiences derivable from them. We might look at such features as intensity, complexity, cognitive interestingness, and long-lastingness. We could then count a person as having good taste whose preferences and enjoyments, for the most part, agreed with the rank-ordering. It remains controversial, however, whether or not a rank-ordering that has some "objective standing"—which does more, that is, than merely reflect either general cultural prejudices or the personal preferences of its sponsor—is possible.

Although the word aesthetics covers all the conceptual issues that arise in connection with both naturally beautiful objects and works of art, most recent attention has focused on the latter. An aesthetic theory, in the contemporary sense, should explain why certain artifacts have a special—indeed, a sui generis*—importance. This involves answering two questions: What makes an artifact a work of art? Why are works of art important? Not all philosophers of art set about answering these questions in the same way. But, as we have seen, any adequate (and plausible) theory of "the work of art" would have to take account, in some way or other, of the following five factors:*

(1) People are capable of being interested in objects that they don't need or want for ordinary practical purposes. In the shorthand of aesthetics, people are capable of assuming the aesthetic attitude.

(2) Works of art have certain formal characteristics that are specifically "designed in" to be disinterestedly interesting. For example, we find ourselves liking to look at a certain painting because of its aesthetic form, even though its subject matter is one to which we are relatively indifferent.

(3) When conditions are right, we are able to experience works of art in a particularly satisfying way. This experience is referred to as aesthetic experience.

(4) Aesthetic experience is pleasurable. Likewise, every experience we enjoy has its characteristic pleasure. The existence of works of art, therefore, makes available an enormous range of highly distinctive pleasures.

(5) Our experience of works of art is cognitively rewarding. This is one reason why art is distinguished from mere entertainment. (This is neither to say that entertainment is bad nor that art cannot be entertaining.) We learn about the world through art and also gain knowledge by acquaintance with the works of art themselves. (This we compared to coming to know new people that we find likable and interesting.)

Two other characteristics have been traditionally offered as characterizing some or all works of art. For one thing, it has been claimed that the essence of art is imitation, or mimesis, of nature. While it is false that this is the essence of art, many works of art are prized partly for their successful representation of reality; also, there is certainly no reason not to admire artists who are capable of achieving mimetic success.

It has also been claimed that the essence of works of art is to express feelings and/or ideas; and there is a sense, of course, in which the work of art is inevitably the expression both of the artist who made it and of the culture in which it was made. Nevertheless, it is wrong to hold, as expression theories do, that the main point of every work of art is to express something.

Given that works of art constitute an enormous class of very diverse items, no account of how art works or of what counts as artistic success that reduces everything to one single factor is likely to be correct.

Finally, not everyone likes the same works of art. If people differ in their taste, then, does it follow that some people have to be making a mistake? This is one of the most difficult questions in aesthetics, and, unfortunately, there is no general agreement among aesthetic theorists on how to go about answering it.

Recommended Reading

Again, *The Encyclopedia of Philosophy* is a good place to start. Most useful are the two long articles, each with its own lengthy bibliography, listed as "Aesthetics, History of" and "Aesthetics, Problems of." *The Handbook of Western Philosophy* also has a useful article under the heading "Aesthetics."

The literature on aesthetics is vast. There are general treatments as well as treatments of specific arts. There are also relevant writings by nonphilosophers, such as art historians and literary critics. Here, we include only contributions by philosophers to general aesthetics.

Among the more accessible books, the following are all worth looking at: Virgil C. Aldrich's *Philosophy of Art* (1963); Curt John Ducasse's *The Philosophy of Art* (1966); Richard Wollheim's *Art and its Objects: An Introduction to Aesthetics* (1968); A. Boyce Gibson's *Muse and Thinker* (1969); George Dickie's *Aesthetics: An Introduction* (1971); Ruth L. Saw's *Aesthetics: An Introduction* (1971); *Philosophy Looks at the Arts: Contemporary Readings in Aesthetics*, edited by Joseph Margolis (1972); *Aesthetics*, edited by Harold Osborne (1972); John Hosper's *Understanding the Arts* (1982); and *Puzzles about Art: An Aesthetics Casebook*, edited by Battin, Fisher, Moore, and Silvers (1989).

Among those books not intended for the beginning student (but neither totally beyond the range of anyone willing to make the effort), we recommend John Dewey's *Art as Experience* (originally, 1934; many reprintings); D. W. Prall's

Aesthetic Analysis (originally, 1936; many reprintings); Suzanne K. Langer's *Problems of Art* (1957); Monroe C. Beardsley's *Aesthetics* (1958); Ludwig Wittgenstein's *Lectures and Conversations on Aesthetics, Psychology and Religious Belief*, edited by Cyril Barrett (1966); Karsten Harrie's *The Meaning of Modern Art* (1968); *Aesthetics and Language*, edited by William Elton (1970); Alan Tormey's *The Concept of Expression: A Study in Philosophical Psychology and Aesthetics* (1971); Arnold Isenberg's *Aesthetics and the Theory of Criticism* (1973); George Dickie's *Art and the Aesthetic* (1974); Richard Wollheim's *On Art and the Mind* (1974); Nelson Goodman's *Languages of Art: An Approach to a Theory of Symbols* (second edition, 1976); Nicholas Wolterstorff's *Works and Worlds of Art* (1980); Arthur Danto's *The Transfiguration of the Commonplace* (1981); Roger Scruton's *The Aesthetic Understanding* (1983); George Dickie's *The Art Circle* (1984); Mary Mothersill's *Beauty Restored* (1984); Arthur Danto's *The Philosophical Disenfranchisement of Art* (1986); Peter J. McCormick's *Fictions, Philosophies, and the Problems of Poetics* (1988); Terry Eagleton's *The Ideology of the Aesthetic* (1990); and Kendall L. Walton's *Mimesis as Make-Believe: On the Foundations of the Representational Arts* (1990).

Students interested in comparing Western and non-Western philosophies of art should consult Richard Anderson's *Calliope's Sisters: A Comparative Study of Philosophies of Art* (1990).

In many fields of philosophy, the more interesting articles often appear in specialized journals. This is particularly true of aesthetics, where the most important publication is the *Journal of Aesthetics and Art Criticism*, published quarterly.

Glossary

ABOUTNESS. Fundamental property of mental states of having content, of representing something. Also known as *intentionality*.

ABSOLUTE. Term most commonly used to mean without qualification, not relative, not comparative. *The absolute* is used by some philosophers as the name of the ultimate reality, the whole.

ABSTRACT. Not having spatiotemporal location, as do ordinary material objects. Numbers, properties, and propositions are sometimes held to be abstract entities.

ABSTRACT PARTICULARS. Particular instances of such qualities as red and square, believed by some metaphysicians to be the ultimate building blocks of reality. Also called *tropes*.

ABSURD. Absolutely meaningless. Existentialism holds that life is absurd, and that man is a "useless passion."

ACCIDENT. Anything that is not necessarily the case. A property a thing happens to have but does not need to have is referred to as an *accidental property*. Sometimes also used as synonym of *property*.

ADAPTIVE PREFERENCE FORMATION. Changing one's preferences in response to opportunities for satisfying them. "If I can't have it, I don't want it." Sometimes referred to as the *sour-grapes fallacy*.

AD HOMINEM. Lat.: to the man. To attack a person on the basis of his or her character, credentials, etc., rather than addressing his argument, is to commit the *ad hominem fallacy*.

AESTHETICS. Branch of philosophy dealing with conceptual questions relating to works of art and the naturally beautiful. Sometimes spelled *esthetics*.

A FORTIORI. Lat.: with greater force. If argument *A* is a good reason for accepting something, a strengthened version of *A* is an *a fortiori* good reason for acceptance.

AKRASIA. Greek: weakness of will. An akrastic person knows what to do, wants to do it, but—under the influence of an inclination not to do it—doesn't manage to do it.

ALETHIC. Concerning truth.

ALGORITHM. Rule, such as the addition rule, that can be applied without judgment to a class of problems, yielding in each case the uniquely correct solution.

ALIENATION. Term used by Marx to describe the condition of the worker who owns neither the means of production nor his own work-product. Later used by existentialists to indicate a general estrangement from everyday reality.

ALTRUISM. Disinterested benevolence; state in which one is unselfishly interested in the welfare of others. Sometimes held to be the basis of morality.

AMBIGUITY. State of being ambiguous. A word or phrase is ambiguous if it has two or more distinct cognitive meanings. Stock examples: *bank*, *cardinal*.

AMORAL. Word that describes the condition of being completely outside or unaware of morality. (Note that most people who are immoral are not amoral.)

AMPHIBOLY. State of being amphibolous. A sentence is amphibolous if, because of its structure, it is open to being interpreted in two or more ways.

ANALOGY. Comparison. An analogy holds between *A* and *B* if *A* and *B*, though distinct, have interesting common features.

ANALYSIS. An analysis consists of an *analysandum*, the statement or concept to be analyzed, and an *analysans*, a set of statements providing the analysis.

ANALYTIC PHILOSOPHY. Perhaps the most prevalent school of philosophy in our time, it devotes itself to the analysis of concepts.

ANALYTIC STATEMENT. Statement that is true by virtue of the definitions of its component terms—for example, "All bachelors are unmarried."

ANARCHISM. Philosophical position that holds that all states and all laws are unnecessary evils.

ANIMISM. Doctrine that all of nature is alive.

ANOMIE. Condition of subjective lostness, uprootedness, and anxiety. Similar to *alienation* in the existentialist sense.

ANTECEDENT. *See* CONDITIONAL.

ANTHROPOCENTRISM. View that sees humans as the center of everything. Usually leveled as a charge by one philosopher against another.

ANTHROPOMORPHISM. View that something has human form. Usually, used in a theological context to indicate the view that God (or the gods) are similar to humans. Ancient Greek religions were both polytheistic (i.e., peopled by many gods) and anthropomorphic.

ANTIFOUNDATIONALISM. Name applied to all philosophical positions that deny that human knowledge rests on a small set of certain truths.

ANTINOMY. Pair of incompatible statements, each of which is supported by seemingly good arguments—each of which we have reason to believe is true.

ANTIREALISM. One of a number of views that denies the existence of a fully determinate reality that our true statements mirror. Any view that denies the principle of bivalence. (*See* BIVALENCE.) *Semantic antirealism* denies the utility of a truth-conditional account of statement meaning.

APODICTIC. Term used to mean provable, necessarily true, and/or absolutely certain.

APORETIC. Problem situation for which there is no (or, at least, no known) solution. From the Greek *aporia*, meaning dead end.

A POSTERIORI. Lat.: after experience. Most truths can only be known *a posteriori*.

A PRIORI. Lat.: prior to experience. Certain truths, such as "All triangles have three sides," can be known *a priori*.

ARCHE. Greek for source or first principle, from whence derive *archeology*, *architecture*, and—with the addition of a negative prefix—*anarchy*.

ARGUMENT. Set of statements containing one or more premises that provide reasons for accepting a conclusion.

ASSERTIBILITY. Property of statements whereby they are correctly, justifiably, or warrantedly made.

ASSERTION. One of the main "speech acts" by which we say that something is true. (Often used as synonym for statement.)

ASSOCIATIONISM. Psychological theory that holds that simple ideas (sense impressions) are connected in the mind on the basis of similarity, contrast, contiguity, causality, and so forth.

ASSUMPTION. Unargued, undiscussed starting point in a discussion or argument. What you are able to establish through discussion and/or argument will always depend on the assumptions with which you begin.

ASYMMETRICAL. Relations—for example, being taller than or being younger than—are asymmetrical if, given that they hold between *A* and *B*, they cannot hold between *B* and *A*.

ATOMIC FACT. Absolutely simple fact. Some thinkers hold that complex facts—for example, the fact that *X* is taller than *Y*—can be analyzed into atomic facts—for example, the fact that *X* is six feet tall and the fact that *Y* is five feet tall. *Atom* (Greek, indivisible) is now defined as something that cannot be divided into parts that are themselves atoms.

ATOMISM. View that the basic components of reality are atoms, or tiny bits of indivisible matter.

ATTRIBUTE. (n.) Quality, characteristic, feature, or property of anything. (v.) To *attribute* a property *P* to an object *O* is simply to say that *O* has *P*.

AUTONOMY. State of being autonomous. Something is said to be autonomous if it acts according to its own independent laws and principles. *Antonym*: heteronomy.

AXIOLOGY. General theory (or science) of value, including both moral and aesthetic values.

AXIOM. Assumed or self-evident basic principle from which some piece of reasoning or some subject matter begins.

AXIOMATIZATION. Body of knowledge organized as a set of derivations from (deductive consequences of) a small number of axioms and definitions. Euclidean geometry is the best-known example.

BASIC ACTION. Action of the human body that is not done by doing something else. In normal circumstances, raising my arm is a basic action.

BASICNESS. Quality of being fundamental.

BEGGING THE QUESTION. In a given context, assuming the very thing that you should be proving (or which you are pretending to prove). Also referred to as *arguing in a circle*.

BEHAVIORISM. In the philosophy of mind, the view that all mental or psychological terms can be defined in terms of observed behavior.

BELIEF. Propositional attitude of acceptance. "Belief that *p*" is intellectual commitment to *p*'s being true.

BICONDITIONAL. Technical term describing statement having the form "*p* if and only if [IFF] *q*." So called because it is equivalent to the conjunction of two conditionals: "if *p*, then *q*, and if *q*, then *p*." If *p* and *q* are synonymous statements, "*p* IFF *q*" will always be a necessary truth.

BIOETHICS. Branch of applied ethics dealing with all moral issues arising from the practice of medicine or from medical research.

BIVALENCE. Literally, the condition of having two values. Often used in the context, *principle of bivalence*, which holds that any properly formed statement is either true or false.

CARTESIAN DOUBT. Suspension of belief. Associated with Descartes' methodological doubt (or the attempt to doubt everything that is not absolutely certain).

CARTESIANISM. Label applied to the philosophy of René Descartes, usually with emphasis on Cartesian (that is, psychophysical) dualism.

CATEGORIAL. Concerning a category or concerning categories.

CATEGORICAL. Absolute, unconditional, nonrelative. According to some philosophers, moral obligations are categorical.

CATEGORICAL IMPERATIVE. Name given to the following principle advanced by Immanuel Kant: "So act so you can will the maxim [principle] of your action to be a universal law binding every other rational person."

CATEGORY. Class, genus, family, type, kind, etc. Term used to mark a basic compartment in a classification of reality.

CATEGORY MISTAKE. To commit a category mistake is to couple things of different categories that cannot be sensibly conjoined. *Examples*: red numbers, overweight virtues, inedible propositions.

CATHARSIS. Process of purgation or purification that, according to Aristotle, accompanied the witnessing of tragic dramas. Also spelled *katharsis*.

CAUSALITY. Relation between two events such that the first brings about the second. Also known as *causation*.

CAUSA SUI. Lat.: cause of itself. Some theologians and philosophers hold that God is *causa sui*.

CERTAINTY. Maximal cognitive security. Term applied to whatever, if anything, a person is fully justifed in being sure of.

CHARACTERISTIC. Term most commonly used as a synonym of property, feature, or trait.

CHEAP ONTOLOGY. Relatively recent term applied to any philosophical position holding a deflationary view of ontological commitment.

CHOICE. Decision reached to pick a given alternative from two or more options. Some philosophers hold that, if everything is causally determined, and therefore things can go only one way, there are no real alternatives, and humans accordingly do not make choices.

CLARITY. Property of being clear. Achieving clarity (elucidating) is generally taken to be one of philosophy's main goals.

CLEAR AND DISTINCT IDEAS. Cartesian phrase. Descartes claims that if our ideas about something are clear and distinct, we cannot be mistaken.

COGITO ERGO SUM. Latin phrase meaning: "I think; therefore, I am." Used by Descartes as the foundational certainty for all further thought.

COGNITIVE. Term most commonly used to mean concerning knowledge and/or truth. Attitudes, interests, and meanings can all be (or can fail to be) cognitive.

COGNITIVISM. View that such moral sentences as "Stealing is wrong!" are genuine statements.

COHERENCE. Term used in more than one way. Occasionally, the property of being logically consistent; more often, this property plus some stronger form of fitting together, such as mutual explanatory support.

COMMON SENSE. General name for what every sensible person thinks. Held by some philosophers to be necessarily correct, by others to be the repository of ancient error.

COMPARATIVE PHILOSOPHY. Comparative study of Western and non-Western philosophies. Modeled on comparative religion.

COMPATIBLE. Capable of coexistence, or co-truth (that is, of being true at the same time).

COMPLEMENT. The complement of a class is everything not in that class. For example, the complement of the class of trees contains all nontrees.

CONATION. Striving. Desires and wants are said to be conative, since having them is connected logically—though not straightforwardly—to the striving to satisfy or fulfill them.

CONCEIVABILITY. Capable of being conceived. It is generally held that anything is conceivable that does not involve a contradiction. (This means that more is conceivable than is imaginable.)

CONCEPT. Idea; notion. People grasp concepts, words express concepts, and objects instantiate concepts. In the latter connection, concepts are said to apply to the objects that instantiate them.

CONCEPTUAL ANALYSIS. Elucidation of concepts by exhibiting the precise conditions of their application.

CONCRETE. Term applied to that which has a definite spatiotemporal location, as do ordinary physical objects. *Antonym*: abstract.

CONDITIONAL. Technical term for statements having the form, "if *p*, then *q*." Conditionals are used to express a number of different relations between *p* (called the *antecedent*) and *q* (called the *consequent*).

CONFIRMATION. Relation that holds between evidence and that which the evidence supports. It is generally held that evidence only *partially confirms* any universal generalization of the form "All *S* are *P*."

CONJUNCTION. Technical term for statements having the form "*p* and *q*." A conjunction is true IFF both its conjuncts (components) are true.

CONNOTATION. Whatever is not part of a term's primary, or cognitive, meaning. This includes any positive or negative emotions (referred to as positive or negative emotive meaning) associated with the term.

CONSEQUENT. *See* CONDITIONAL.

CONSEQUENTIALISM. View that the moral permissibility, impermissibility, or obligatoriness of an action is to be determined on the basis of its expected consequences. *Utilitarianism* (q.v.) is the most familiar form of consequentialism.

CONSISTENCY. Absence of logical contradiction. Two statements are *consistent* if they are not logically contradictory. A set of statements is consistent if all its members are capable of being simultaneously true.

CONSTRUCTIVISM. View that claims that something ordinarily regarded as independent of human thought (for example, nature or mathematical reality) is really the product of human thinking, or at least not totally independent of that thinking.

CONTENT. Mental states have content insofar as they function as representations. A mental state such as feeling pain, since it is non-representational, is without content.

CONTEXT. Literally, other words with. In general, to emphasize context is to consider all circumstantial factors relevant to understanding and interpretation. The meaning of a word, remark, action, or gesture depends on its context.

CONTEXTUALISM. View that emphasizes the indispensability or importance of context in either the literal or the extended sense.

CONTINGENCY. Quality of being nonnecessary. Thus, anything not necessary is said to be *contingent*. An event that didn't have to happen is a contingent event; a property that a thing doesn't have to have is a contingent property; a being whose existence is not necessary is a contingent being.

CONTINGENT CONNECTION. Term describing the relationship of two properties that always, or at least often, occur together but are not conceptually linked.

CONTRADICTORY. Two statements, *p* and *q*, are *contradictories* if they must have opposite truth-values—for example, "All Swedes are Protestants" and "Some Swedes are not Protestants," or "No Swedes are Protestants" and "Some Swedes are Protestants."

CONTRAPOSITION. Transformation of a conditional "If *p*, then *q*," into "If not-*q*, then not-*p*." If the original statement is true, its *contrapositive* will also be true.

CONTRARY. Two statements, *p* and *q*, are *contraries* if both can be false but both cannot be true—for example, "All Swedes are Protestants" and "No Swedes are Protestants."

CONVENTIONALISM. View claiming that something is "just a matter of convention." One can be a conventionalist about morality, aesthetic value, or even truth.

CONVERSATIONAL IMPLICATURE. Anything that, though not following logically from what is said, would normally be taken to follow is said to follow as a matter of conversational implicature.

CORRELATIVE. Strictly speaking, the logically necessary complement of a relation—for example, buying in relation to selling, or being shorter than in relation to being taller than. Loosely, any succeeding relation associated with or implied by a first relation.

CORRIGIBLE. Subject to correction; correctible. Empirical generalizations are corrigible based on further experience.

CORROBORATION. Independent support for something.

COSMOLOGICAL ARGUMENT. Argument for the existence of God that tries to show that God's existence follows from features of the observed universe (cosmos), such as motion, cause and effect, and contingency.

CO-TRUTH. State of being simultaneously true.

COUNTERADAPTIVE PREFERENCE FORMATION. Irrational mode of preference change in which a person ceases to want what is actually possessed. Sometimes referred to as the "grass is always greener on the other side of the fence" fallacy.

COUNTEREXAMPLE. Example, or particular instance, that shows that some generalization or general principle is false. A white crow would be a counterexample relative to the generalization that all crows are black.

COUNTERFACTUAL CONDITIONAL. Conditional with a false antecedent. For example, "If Robert Kennedy had not been assassinated, he would one day have become President." How to determine truth-values of counterfactuals is a major problem in contemporary philosophy.

COUNTERINTUITIVE. Going against common sense or ordinary prephilosophical intuitions. Some philosophers regard counterintuitiveness as a sign of falsehood, while others dismiss it as wholly irrelevant to cognitive inquiry.

COVERING LAW MODEL. View that explanation of historical occurrences requires showing that they are instances of some general law.

CREATIO EX NIHILO. Lat.: creation from nothing. God is generally held to have created the world this way. We humans can understand various kinds of making, all of which involve transformations of raw material. *Ex nihilo* creation, however, is beyond our grasp. Perhaps if we could understand it, we could do it.

CRITERION. *pl.* criteria. Meaning-relevant factor that is neither a necessary nor a sufficient condition.

CYNICS. Followers of Diogenes of Sinope (*c*.400–325 B.C.). The Cynics believed in satisfying the biological minimum of desires in the simplest way, and looked on any additional efforts with contempt and ridicule.

CYRENAICS. Members of a school of philosophy flourishing in the fourth century B.C. They held that the only worthwhile thing is the enjoyment, here and now, of physical pleasure.

DATA. *sing.* datum. What is given at the outset of a problem; what is to be explained. Also referred to as *the given*.

DE DICTO. Lat.: of what is said. Used, for example, to express the view that all necessity is *de dicto*—that is, a property of sentences rather than of things themselves. Contrasted with *de re*.

DEDUCTIVE ARGUMENT. Argument whose conclusion must be true if all its premises are true. Contrasts with an inductive argument (q.v.), whose conclusion can be false even if all its premises are true.

DEFEASIBLE. Literally, capable of being defeated or overturned. Something (an obligation, right, or claim, for example) that is presumed to hold unless defeated by a superior consideration is defeasible. *Antonym*: absolute. *Synonym*: *prima facie*.

DEFINIENDUM and DEFINIENS. Two parts of a definition. The *definiendum* is that which is to be defined, the *definiens* is that which does the defining.

DEFINING PROPERTY. Property a thing must have to be what it is.

DELIBERATION. Process of thinking about what to do that often, but not invariably, takes place prior to action.

DENIAL. Negation. "It is *not* raining" and "It is *not the case* that it is raining" are two ways of expressing the denial, or negation, of "It is raining."

DENOTATION. Set of things to which a term correctly applies. Thus, the denotation of "apple" is all apples.

DEONTIC; DEONTOLOGICAL. Concerning duty or obligation. A deontological ethics makes morality a matter of absolute obligation independent of any considerations of consequences.

DE RE. Lat.: of the thing. To make the claim that some necessary truths are *de re*, for example, is to say that the truths are about things themselves, rather than about sentences. Contrasted with *de dicto*.

DETERMINISM. Usually, short for *complete causal determinism*—the view that what happens now is the only thing *causally possible*, given the laws of nature and the immediately prior state of the world.

DEUS SIVE NATURA. Lat.: God or Nature. Used by Baruch Spinoza to describe the single all-inclusive reality constituting the universe.

DIALECTICAL. Term often used to characterize any movement of thought that proceeds by recognizing and overcoming objections. Originally, closely connected with *dialogue*.

DIFFERENTIA. Technical term used to refer to those properties that differentiate (or distinguish) members of a subclass (sometimes called a *species*) from members of the larger class (sometimes called a *genus*). Aristotle's definition of a human as a rational animal is said to be a definition by genus and specific difference ("specific difference" = "differentia").

DILEMMA. Choice situation in which both of two alternatives are unacceptable. In argument situations, we may be led to "*p* or *q*" where neither *p* nor *q* is acceptable.

DISAMBIGUATION. Process whereby a potentially ambiguous term is in actual occurrence rendered unambiguous. Context and circumstance suffice to disambiguate most ambiguous terms.

DISCIPLINARY MATRIX. Term applied by T. S. Kuhn to the totality of shared group commitments characteristic of a particular scientific discipline.

DISCONFIRMATION. Fact of contrary evidence. It is ordinarily much easier to disconfirm than to confirm: one nonwhite swan, for example, effectively disconfirms "All swans are white."

DISCURSIVE. Of or concerning discourse.

DISJUNCTION. Technical term for any statement of the form "*p* or *q*." In logic, disjunctions are always interpreted as *inclusive* disjunctions, which is to say that they are counted as true if either or both of their disjuncts (components) are true, and are counted as false only if both of their disjuncts are false.

DISPOSITIONAL PROPERTIES. Properties such as solubility and fragility, that are defined in terms of what would happen in certain specified circumstances (whether or not those circumstances ever obtain). Many psychological properties are dispositional.

DISTRIBUTIVE JUSTICE. That part of justice, whether legal or moral, that concerns itself with the fair distribution of benefits and harms.

DOUBLE-ASPECT THEORY. Metaphysical view that sees mind and body as two aspects of a single underlying reality.

DOXASTIC JUSTIFICATION. In epistemology, demonstration that a belief is justified.

DUALISM. Metaphysical view that reality is composed of two fundamentally different kinds of stuff: the material (or physical) and the mental (or spiritual). Known also as *psychophysical dualism* and *Cartesian dualism.*

DUTY. Obligation. A duty is what a person ought to do, as a matter of morality or legality.

DYADIC. Two-place. Term used to classify relations. "Equals" and "loves" are both dyadic, whereas "lies between" is triadic (three-place).

ECLECTICISM. Word used to describe, usually with some degree of disapproval, any position that combines bits and pieces of a number of separate views.

ECONOMIC EXPLANATION. Explanation based on such economic factors as supply and demand, wages, prices, cost, marginal utility, and so forth.

EFFECT. Product of a cause. It is a necessary truth that every effect is caused, but not a necessary truth that every event is caused.

EGALITARIANISM. View that holds that humans should be equal, or that things should be changed so that humans will become equal. There are as many kinds of egalitarianism as there are ways in which people can be equal or unequal—for example, in income, wealth, opportunity, political rights, and so on.

EGO. Lat.: I; myself. Used in such terms as *egocentrism* and *egoism.* The *egocentric predicament* labels the epistemological problem of how "I" get beyond my experience to knowledge of an independent world.

EIDOS. Greek: form, particularly visible form. Plato's principal word for immaterial and unchanging ideas. There is, for example, the *eidos* of treeness imperfectly reflected in actual trees.

ELIMINATIVE MATERIALISM. Label for those metaphysical views that seek to explain away (or reduce, or eliminate) the nonphysical or immaterial. Especially, those denying the possibility of an autonomous level of psychological explanation.

ELUCIDATION. Process of making clear. Like *clarify*, based on a metaphor of light. Analytic philosophy sees conceptual elucidation as philosophy's main, if not only, job.

EMERGENT PROPERTY. Property that can be analyzed in terms of or reduced to a more fundamental property. For example, hardness is an emergent property relative to the more basic molecular properties that explain the hardness of hard objects.

EMOTIVISM. View that such moral sentences as "Stealing is wrong!" are nothing more than the expression of emotion or feeling.

EMPIRICISM. In epistemology, the view that experience— particularly, sensory experience—is the only or at least the main source of knowledge.

ENCULTURATION. Process of being made, through education and training, an integral and functioning part of a human community.

ENTAILMENT. Objective relation between propositions that has nothing to do with relations we notice or arguments we put forward. *A* entails *B* IFF *A* cannot be true without *B* also being true.

ENTHYMEME. Argument with an unstated premise—for example, "Socrates is a man; so, Socrates is mortal," which assumes, but does not state, "All men are mortal." (This is a harmless enthymeme, but not all are.)

ENTITY. Term similar to *thing* as the latter is used in its most inclusive sense. Entities are sometimes distinguished from events and processes, and always from nonentities.

EPICUREANISM. View advanced by Epicurus (*c*. 55–135) that a life of wisdom consists in the enjoyment of simple pleasures—particularly, the pleasures of friendship and conversation—untempted by competition, political ambition, or any form of worldly striving.

EPIPHENOMENALISM. Solution to the mind/body problem that holds that consciousness is an effect of the body but does not causally interact with the body.

EPISTEMOLOGY. Branch of philosophy that deals with the questions *What is knowledge?* and *How do humans acquire knowledge?* Also known as *theory of knowledge*.

EPOCHÉ. Greek: suspension. Used to indicate abstraction from all concerns about origin or real-world existence when one is attempting an accurate description of subjective appearances.

EQUIVOCATION. Property of having two meanings. To equivocate—a fault or fallacy—is to use words that are equivocal.

EROTETIC. Concerning questions. Erotetic logic is the logic of questions.

ESSE EST PERCIPI. Lat.: To be is to be perceived. Postulated of everything by those philosophers who hold that all reality is in the mind. It may be true of certain things, such as pains.

ESSENCE. Nature. The essence or nature of anything is what it has to be either to be itself or to be a thing of the kind it is. Essential properties are, accordingly, necessary properties.

ESSENTIALISM. View that things have *de re* essential properties—that is, necessary properties independent of our classifications or definitions.

ESTHETICS. *See* AESTHETICS.

ETHICAL RELATIVISM. View that moral beliefs are products of tribal enculturation (socialization), and that there is no rational basis for choice between the conflicting moral beliefs of different tribes.

ETHNOCENTRISM. Name for any view that attaches special importance, in theory or in practice, to members of one's own tribe or group. (From the Greek *ethnos*, tribe.)

EUDAIMONIA. Greek: happiness. Any ethical system that makes happiness the only or chief good is a *eudaimonistic* ethic.

EVENT. That which occurs; any change of property in an object.

EVIDENCE. That which lends support to some belief. Evidence for *p* consists of all the reasons for thinking that *p* is true. Evidence is often partial or incomplete.

EXISTENTIALISM. Movement of philosophers, particularly in France after World War II. Name derives from their claim that "existence precedes essence," which is a way of saying that humans have no nature, are absolutely free, and are blessed (or cursed) with "monstrous spontaneity of consciousness." Existentialists hold that absolute freedom generates free-floating anxiety and the need to create meaningfulness through arbitrary commitment.

EX NIHILO NIHIL FIT. Lat.: from nothing nothing comes. Sometimes regarded as a fundamental metaphysical truth.

EXPERIMENTALISM. View that emphasizes the role of experiment—or, more generally, experience—in the production of knowledge.

EXPLANATION. Provision of reasons that answer "Why?" questions. There are as many kinds of explanations as there are kinds of reasons or "Why?" questions.

EXPLICATION. Getting clear about what a text says.

EXTENSION. Denotation. The extension of a term is the set of things the term applies to. Contrasted with *intension.*

EXTRINSIC. Not intrinsic. Not part of the very nature of a thing, situation, concept, or the like.

FACULTY PSYCHOLOGY. Theory that the human mind can be broken down into a small number of separate powers, or faculties.

FALLACY. Strictly speaking, any pseudoargument; more loosely, any error in thinking.

FALLIBLE. Capable of being mistaken.

FAMILY-RESEMBLANCE CONCEPT. Concept applying to a collection of objects, not because the objects have a single common feature but because the objects have various partly overlapping resemblances. (Also called a *polytypic concept.*)

FATALISM. View that everything that happens happens necessarily, and that human effort can have no possible effect on preordained outcomes.

FIDEISM. View that all religious beliefs, including a belief in God's existence, can only be based on faith and never on argument or evidence.

FINITISM. View, most commonly applied to mathematics, that humans can neither understand nor have genuine knowledge of the infinite.

FIRST PHILOSOPHY. Old name for metaphysics.

FORMALISM. View that emphasizes formal qualities of a subject matter.

FOUNDATIONALISM. Name applied to all philosophical positions that hold that knowledge rests on a small set of certain truths.

FREEDOM; FREE WILL. In the most basic sense, humans may be said to have freedom or free will IFF their lives contain moments of genuine choice.

FUNCTIONALISM. View in the philosophy of mind that mental states are to be identified in terms of their causal functions, which, along with those of other mental states, eventuate in behavior.

GEIST. German: spirit; mind.

GENERAL. Concerning a larger class or more inclusive category. Strictly speaking, general only makes sense comparatively, since, for example, *dog* is more general than *collie* but less general than *mammal*.

GENETIC FALLACY. Attempt to deduce the present nature or value of something from facts about its origin. For example, even if religion began as primitive superstition, it does not follow that religion *is* primitive superstition.

GENUS. Lat.: kind; class. Genus and species (subclass) are relative terms, since something is a genus relative to a less inclusive class but a species relative to a more inclusive class.

GESTALT. German: structure; form. Gestalt psychology holds that we see the world in terms of organized wholes, rather than in unrelated bits and pieces.

GREATEST HAPPINESS PRINCIPLE. Phrase associated with utilitarianism in general and J. S. Mill in particular. Ideally, actions—both individual and political/legislative—should aim to produce the greatest amount of happiness, without concern for whose happiness it is.

HEDONISM. View that pleasure is the only, or at least the main, good. Different forms of hedonism reflect different views of what pleasure amounts to.

HERMENEUTIC CIRCLE. Alleged problem for interpretation based on the idea that one cannot understand a part of a text without understanding the whole text, but cannot understand the whole text without understanding its parts. Generalized, it is thought to apply to the relation between a single work of an author and the body of his work, and the relation between a cultural object and the whole culture constituting its context.

HERMENEUTICS. Science of interpreting texts. It is sometimes claimed that the human sciences, in contrast to the natural sciences, are essentially hermeneutic.

HEURISTIC. Rule of thumb; tentative hypothesis. Approximative procedure that, while not absolutely correct, still helps solve a problem or advances science.

HEXIS. Greek: habit. In Aristotle and many later thinkers, virtue is considered a kind of *hexis.*

HIERARCHY OF BEING. View that there is a single graded ordering of beings, arranged (starting from the bottom) as follows: nonliving things, plants, ordinary animals, rational animals (that is, humans), angels, God.

HISTORICISM. Label for a range of views having in common emphasis on the indispensability or importance of understanding theories, works of art, institutions, actions, statements, and the like within their historical periods. Sometimes, additionally, the claim that comparison across periods is impossible.

HOLISM. View that parts can be understood only within the wholes they belong to, and that wholes—at least, some wholes—are more than the sum of their parts.

HOLISTIC EXPLANATION. In a general sense, any explanation that emphasizes wholes rather than parts. More specifically, the explanation of parts in terms of their functional contributions to wholes.

HYLOMORPHISM. Doctrine, most commonly associated with Aristotle, that ordinary objects are a combination of matter (Greek: *hyle*) and form (Greek: *morphe*).

HYPOSTATIZATION. Term used interchangeably with *reification* for the treatment of abstractions or relations as if they were concrete entities.

HYPOTHESIS. Term applied to any tentative proposal, theory, or suggestion that has not yet been tested, or has not been fully established.

HYPOTHETICAL IMPERATIVE. Anything of the form, "If you want *X*, you must do *Y*." Our obligation to do *Y* is contingent on our wanting *X*. Contrasted with *categorical imperatives*, which bind unconditionally.

IDEALISM. In its most extreme form, doctrine that all reality is mental or in the mind. In less extreme forms, any doctrine that emphasizes the creative, world-making role of mind, or that denies the existence of a fully mind-independent reality.

IDENTITY. There are two concepts of identity: being identical by virtue of having the same properties though numerically distinct; and being identical by being the very same object or person through time.

IDENTITY OF INDISCERNIBLES. Principle according to which two things that are numerically distinct (that is, really two things) cannot have all their properties in common. Sometimes also called *Leibniz's law*.

IDEOLOGY. Term sometimes used, neutrally or purely descriptively, to refer to any system of interconnected ideas. Most often used pejoratively to refer to a system of false, or essentially biased, ideas.

IFF. Short for *if and only if*, meaning just in case or just when.

ILLOCUTIONARY. Done by uttering certain words. By saying "That's about to fall," I may, for example, be performing the illocutionary act of warning or threatening.

ILLUSION. Perceptual error or false belief.

IMPERATIVISM. View that moral sentences are disguised rules. For example, "Stealing is wrong!" is interpreted as "Don't steal!"

IMPLICATION. Objective relation between two statements, A and B, that has nothing to do with inferences actually made by humans. *A logically implies B* just in case A cannot be true without B being also true.

IMPRESSION. Term ordinarily used to indicate the immediate effect of sensory stimulation on consciousness.

INCLINATION. Tendency, propensity, or disposition.

INCOHERENCE. Internal inconsistency.

INCOMMENSURABILITY. Inability to be brought under some common measure. It is sometimes claimed that successive scientific theories are *incommensurable*.

INCORRIGIBLE. Not subject to correction based on further experience, information, or experiment. It is sometimes claimed that certain simple judgments of sense ("That's red") as well as certain necessary truths ("Squares have four sides") are incorrigible.

INDETERMINACY OF TRANSLATION. View that there is no such thing as *the* right translation from language to language—that is, that translation is undetermined by its linguistic data.

INDEXICAL. Determined by (or indexed to) the location of the speaker, time of utterance, and identity of the speaker. Words such as *here*, *now*, and *I* are examples.

INDIVIDUAL. Single person or thing. Although most commonly used of spatiotemporal particulars, abstractions such as redness or flatness as well as mathematical objects are also sometimes thought of as individuals.

INDIVIDUATION. Process whereby, guided by principles or criteria, we are able to identify a single individual of a given kind.

INDUBITABILITY. Property of not being open to doubt. Like its synonym *certainty*, it may be interpreted either psychologically or nonpsychologically.

INDUCTIVE ARGUMENT. Argument that, based on the observation or consideration of some members of a set, derives a conclusion about all members of that set.

INFERENCE. Actual process of drawing conclusions. If *A* implies *B*, someone can correctly infer *B* from *A*. Sometimes, inference is used to refer to the judgment that results from the process of drawing a conclusion.

INFINITE REGRESS. Alleged fault, either in a series of arguments having the form *A* follows from *B*, *B* follows from *C*, *C* from *D*, and so on, without end; or in a series of explanations having the form *A* because *B*, *B* because *C*, *C* because *D*, and so on, without end.

IN INTELLECTU. Lat.: existing in the intellect (or mind).

INNATE. Inborn. Philosophies can be arranged in terms of how much they claim is innate.

IN RES; IN REBUS. Lat.: existing in reality (or in things themselves). Used to indicate existence independent of mind.

INSTRUMENTALISM. View that scientific theories are not true pictures of reality but merely instruments useful for making calculations and predictions.

INTELLIGIBILITY. Property of being understandable, or graspable by the mind.

INTENSION. Set of defining properties relative to a given term. Those properties that each member of the term's *extension* must have.

INTENTIONALITY. Fundamental property of mental states of having content, representing, or being about something.

INTERACTIONISM. Solution to the mind/body problem that pictures mind and body in reciprocal interaction (or subject to causal influence in both directions).

INTERSUBJECTIVE. Capable of being detected, described, and evaluated by a plurality of people.

INTRINSIC. Not extrinsic. Part of the very nature of a thing, situation, concept, etc.

INTROSPECTION. Awareness by an individual of his or her own mental states. Whether introspection provides privileged access to a person's own consciousness (or should be even counted as a variety of observation) is controversial.

INTROSPECTIONISM. *See* METHODOLOGICAL BEHAVIORISM.

INTUITION. Form of immediate knowledge, of "just knowing" that something is so. Appealed to by some philosophers as the basis of our moral knowledge, it is rejected by many other philosophers as pseudoknowledge.

INTUITIONISM. In ethics, the view that knowledge of morality is based on intuition. *Mathematical* intuitionism is the view that mathematical knowledge is based on intuition.

INVALIDITY. Most strictly, deductive failure. Less strictly, bad nondeductive arguments and even false statements may be described as invalid.

IPSO FACTO. Lat.: by that very fact. A table is *ipso facto* a piece of furniture, a dog *ipso facto* a mammal.

IRRATIONAL. Not in conformity with the principles of reason and logic. Distinguished from *nonrational*, which means independent of reason and logic.

"IS" OF IDENTITY. Occurrence of the word *is* that—as in the sentence "The morning star is the evening star"—can be replaced with no change of meaning by the phrase *is identical with*.

"IS" OF PREDICATION. Occurrence of the word *is* that—as in the sentence "The ball is red"—is used to ascribe a property to an object.

ISOMORPHIC. Term used to describe two objects having the same form.

IS/OUGHT FALLACY. Alleged fallacy of inferring an "ought"-containing conclusion from premises that are purely descriptive. Sometimes also described as the *fallacy of deducing values from facts*.

JUSTICE. That desirable property of actions, laws, and institutions whereby they give to each person that to which he or she has a legitimate claim or right. Close synonym of *fairness*.

JUSTIFICATION. A person is said to be justified in believing or acting if, in actual circumstances, there is no ground for criticizing the person for coming to believe or for acting in a certain way. (We also speak, elliptically, of justified beliefs and justified actions.)

KANT'S COPERNICAN REVOLUTION. Radical thesis of Immanuel Kant (1724–1804) according to which the forms of our sensibility (sensory apparatus) and the categories of our understanding determine the nature of our experience. The view is in contrast to more traditional views, according to which the nature of our experience is determined by the objects in the world of which we have experience.

KIND. Synonym of *type*. How many kinds of things there are depends on the classificatory scheme being employed.

KNOWLEDGE BY ACQUAINTANCE. Knowledge of something based on direct sensory awareness. Contrasted with knowledge by description (second-hand knowledge).

LANGUAGE GAME. Term used by Wittgenstein to indicate a delimited area of language use that has its own point and follows its own logical grammar.

LAW OF EXCLUDED MIDDLE. Principle that p (a well-formed statement) is either true or false. Sometimes expressed as the principle that, where A is a well-formed predicate, an object either is or fails to be A.

LAW OF IDENTITY. Principle that if p, then p; everything is what it is, and not something else. The trivial truth that everything stands in the identity relation to itself.

LEARNING PARADOX. Alleged paradox—probably first raised by Plato—based on the idea that you can only learn what you do not know, but also cannot learn what you do not know, because you will not know what to learn.

LIAR PARADOX. Ancient paradox to the effect that the statement "I am lying" is true only if it is false, and false only if it is true. Sometimes used to show that some grammatically correct sentences are nonsensical.

LOCUTIONARY. Concerning the basic speech act of uttering a sentence with a definite meaning.

LOGICAL POSITIVISM. View particularly associated with philosophers known collectively as the Vienna Circle, which flourished in the 1920s and 30s. According to this view, all meaningful statements are either analytic (or logical) truths, or else empirically verifiable synthetic truths. Logical positivists claimed that many traditional statements of metaphysics are neither, and consequently are meaningless.

LOGICAL POSSIBILITY. Quality of not involving a contradiction. Honest politicians are obviously logically possible; square circles are obviously not logically possible. Postvention (changing the past) appears to be logically impossible, though some thinkers claim that God can postvent.

MATERIALISM. Form of metaphysical monism that holds that everything is material in character.

MECHANISM. Most commonly, the view that everything can be explained by the same principles that explain the functioning of machines or mechanical systems; the view (once popular) that nature is a giant machine.

MELIORISM. Lat.: *melior*, better. The view either that things are necessarily getting better or—in a weaker version—that it is possible for things to get better. In this latter (and more plausible) version, meliorism is often associated with the idea that human action can make a difference.

MENTALISM. Metaphysical position that holds that only minds and their contents exist. Sometimes used as a synonym for *idealism*.

MENTION. Reference to a word itself, rather than to what the word is customarily used to designate. For example, " 'Cat' has three letters." As in this example, quotation marks are used to mention a word (to form its name), but a mentioned word may also be italicized (*cat*) to the same effect.

META. Greek: after or beyond. In contemporary philosophical usage, it is most often used to indicate discourse about discourse. Thus, *metaethics* is discourse about ethical discourse; a *metalanguage* is a language used to talk about a language. (The language talked about by a metalanguage is frequently referred to as a *first-order language* or an *object language*.)

METAPHORICAL. Describing a word not usually applied in a given domain that is applied to bring out a similarity. Metaphorical use of language is distinguished from literal use. Thus, a color—which cannot, of course, be literally hot—may nevertheless be described as "hot" metaphorically.

METAPHYSICS. Branch of philosophy dealing with the question, *What is there?*

METHODOLOGICAL BEHAVIORISM. View in the philosophy of psychology that holds that only the study of behavior (and never introspection) can be used as the basis for a scientific psychology. Contrasted with *introspectionism.*

METHODOLOGICAL INDIVIDUALISM. View in the philosophy of the social sciences that holds that statements or theories about groups or institutions must ultimately be understood in terms of (or reduced to statements or theories about) individual human beings. Contrasted with *methodological holism,* the view that at least some statements or theories about social wholes cannot be reduced.

MIMESIS. Imitation of reality. Term most commonly used in connection with works of art.

MIND/BODY PROBLEM. Label used for a set of interrelated questions about whether there are both bodies and minds, and—particularly in the case of humans beings—how we should conceive of their relations.

MODALITY. Most commonly, the feature of statements indicating either that something is possible or that something is necessary. Modal logic is the logic of "modalized" statements. In this logic, *possible* and *necessary* are interdefinable: *possible* can be defined as not necessarily not, and *necessary* can be defined as not possibly not.

MODAL OPERATORS. The two most common modal operators are $\Box$, meaning *necessarily*, and $\Diamond$, meaning *possibly.*

MONADS. In the metaphysics of Leibniz, the basic units of reality. Monads are pictured as psychic centers, causally unrelated to each other but each mirroring the whole of reality.

MONISM. Metaphysical view holding that there is only one basic category (or only one fundamental kind of stuff).

MONOTHEISM. View that there is exactly one God.

MYTH. In modern usage, a false—though culturally significant—story.

MYTHICAL THINKING. Term used to refer to prerational thinking, involving magical or not causally explicable transformations and other violations of rational or commonsensical thought. It was once widely held that "primitive" people exist at this level.

NAIVE REALISM. View (generally rejected) that the world is exactly as it appears to be to our senses (or to "common sense").

NATURALISTIC FALLACY. Alleged fallacy that, in its most common form, involves the attempt to identify *good* with some natural (that is, ordinary or descriptive) property.

NATURAL THEOLOGY. Body of knowledge, if any, that the human mind can have concerning God that is based on reason rather than on revelation.

NECESSARY BEING. Being that cannot not exist—that is, whose nonexistence is impossible. God has traditionally been the main candidate for necessary being.

NECESSARY CONDITION. Condition that must be met by an item if it is to be included in a class or to fall under a concept. Being male, for example, is a necessary condition for membership in the class of bachelors.

NECESSARY TRUTH. Truth that cannot be false. Truths by definition, such as "All bachelors are unmarried," are necessary truths. Whether or not there are other sorts of necessary truths is controversial.

NEGATION. Denial. The negation of a statement is that statement which must have an opposite truth-value. For example, "It is *not* raining" in relation to "It is raining."

NEUTRAL MONISM. Metaphysical view that mind and matter are both aspects of a single "neutral" stuff that is neither mind nor matter.

NIHILISM. View that there are no values, or meanings, or truths. Confirmed nihilists should not even think it worthwhile to state their own position.

NOMIC. Concerning law. Ordinarily used in connection with laws of nature, as in the expression *nomic necessity*, meaning necessary given the laws of nature. Something that is logically possible may be nomically impossible.

NOMINAL DEFINITION. Definition that claims to be no more than the definition of a word, without claiming to throw light on the nature of what the word refers to.

NOMINALISM. View that only particulars are real, and that general terms apply to particulars on the basis of their mutual resemblance. Thus, there is no such thing as *redness*—only particular red things.

NONCOGNITIVISM. One of a number of views (but particularly emotivism [q.v.]) that deny that moral sentences are genuine statements, and that there are moral truths and falsehoods.

NONNATURAL PROPERTY. Property of a thing that differs fundamentally from ordinary descriptive predicates. *Goodness* has classically been the main candidate for this status.

NON SEQUITUR. Lat.: it does not follow. Critical observation to the effect that an alleged conclusion does not follow from offered premises.

NONSYMMETRICAL. Term describing such relations as the loving relation that, given they hold between *A* and *B*, may or may not hold between *B* and *A*.

NORMATIVE. Having the force of a norm. Ordinarily contrasted with *description*, a norm indicates not what is the case or is done, but rather what should be the case or should be done.

NOUMENAL. Term used by Immanuel Kant to indicate the supersensible world that lies beyond our experience. The noumenal world, or the world of things in themselves, contrasts with the phenomenal world—the world we can experience, and thus come to have scientific knowledge about.

NOUS. Greek: mind; spirit.

NULL SET. Mathematical expression referring to the set having no members. Also called the *empty class*.

NUMINOUS EXPERIENCE. Experience of the numinous—of the holy or sacred. Nearly synonymous with *religious experience*.

OBLIGATION. Duty; whatever ought to be done—particularly what someone, as a matter of law or morality, has a right to expect us to do.

OBSERVATION REPORT. In some formalizations of science, the basic, intersubjective statements of what is directly seen or otherwise perceived. They serve to confirm or disconfirm hypotheses and theories.

OCCASIONALISM. View about minds and bodies that holds that their mutual interaction is only apparent. Through God's coordinating action, a change in either mind or body is the *occasion*—but not the *cause*—of a change in the other.

OCCURRENT STATE. State of conscious awareness at a given moment. Pains and other feelings are examples of occurrent states. Contrasted with *dispositional states*, such as beliefs and desires.

OCKHAM'S RAZOR. Name given to the principle, "Do not multiply entities beyond necessity." Used more generally to refer to the requirement of intellectual economy. Also called the *principle of parsimony*.

ONTOLOGICAL COMMITMENT. Belief in the existence of something. As used in contemporary philosophy, one might ask whether acceptance of physics involves ontological commitment to electrons— or whether saying "God bless you" when someone sneezes involves ontological commitment to God.

ONTOLOGY. Science of being. Sometimes used interchangeably with *metaphysics*, the term is often limited to formal approaches to metaphysical questions.

OPAQUE CONTEXT. Context in which terms referring to the same thing cannot be substituted with preservation of truth. If I see you come into the room, and you are an escaped convict, then I see an escaped convict come into the room. (*See* does not establish an opaque context.) However, if I believe you just came into the room (even if you are an escaped convict), I do not thereby believe that an escaped convict has come into the room. (*Believe* does establish an opaque context.)

OPEN-QUESTION ARGUMENT. Argument most commonly used to refute the claim that *good* is identical with any other property. For example, if *good* were identical with *useful*, "It's useful, but is it good?" would not be—as in fact it is—an open question.

OPEN-TEXTURE CONCEPT. *See* FAMILY-RESEMBLANCE CONCEPT.

OPERATIONAL DEFINITION. Definition in terms of a series of operations. Length, for example, may be defined operationally in terms of procedures of measurement. The view that all respectable scientific definitions must be operational is known as *operationalism*.

OPINION. Word sometimes used as a synonym of *belief*. More often used in the same way as the Greek *doxa*, "mere opinion"—opinion that does not amount to knowledge.

ORDINARY LANGUAGE. Language outside philosophy itself. Ordinary-language philosophy sets itself the task of analyzing ordinary language, regarding this as more useful than constructing philosophical systems or introducing new concepts.

OSTENSIVE DEFINITION. Definition that works by pointing to or otherwise indicating a specimen, instance, or sample of the thing to be defined. Color words are commonly defined ostensively.

PANPSYCHISM. Form of metaphysical monism holding that everything that exists is mental in character.

PANTHEISM. View that everything is—or is a part of—God.

PARADIGM. Model; pattern; standard example. The *paradigm case argument* holds that, since the meaning of a term is learned from its paradigms, it must be nonsense to claim that there are no items in the term's extension.

PARADOX. Loosely, any surprising statement or conclusion. A paradox arises when two good arguments, having apparently true premises, lead to a pair of conclusions that contradict each other.

PARSIMONY. Intellectual economy. Of two views or theories, it is generally held that, other things being equal, preference should be given to the more parsimonious.

PARTICULARS. Individual things. Concrete, spatiotemporally located physical objects are the most obvious examples, but some philosophers hold that such *abstracta* as universals and numbers also count as particulars.

PER ACCIDENS. Lat.: by accident. Term used to indicate whatever is contingent or nonnecessary. A bachelor is necessarily unmarried, but—if he is short—he is short *per accidens*.

PERCEPT. That which is immediately given in perception. Percepts, unlike sensations, are already of objects, not just patches of color, and the like.

PERFORMATIVE. Term describing that aspect of an utterance that consists in what is done by what is said. Such first-person singular, present-tense utterances as "I promise" (to which can be sensibly added "hereby") are said to be performative.

PERLOCUTIONARY. In the theory of speech acts, a term applied to the speech act looked at in terms of its effects. The *locution* (utterance) "That's about to fall" may, in given circumstances, be the *illocutionary* act of warning and the *perlocutionary* act of frightening.

PER SE. Lat.: in and of itself; intrinsically. Thus, one might say that pleasure is good *per se*, and that pain is *per se* bad.

PERSON. Being (human or not) with whom humans can communicate in a relatively full way. God and angels are thought of as persons in this sense. Perhaps certain animals—dolphins are sometimes suggested—may also be persons. In legal theory, a *person* is a bearer of rights.

PERSONAL IDENTITY. Whatever it is that makes me me and you you, and which endures in the face of all the changes that persons undergo in the course of their lives.

PERSPECTIVISM. View that there are no truths outside particular perspectives (or ways of looking at things).

PETITIO PRINCIPII. Lat.: the fallacy of begging the question, or assuming as a premise the very thing to be demonstrated.

PHENOMENALISM. View that ordinary physical objects are to be analyzed in terms of patterns of sensations or perceptions.

PHYSICALISM. Form of metaphysical monism that holds that everything that exists is physical in nature—that is, of the sort studied by the physical sciences.

PLATONIC FORMS. Ideas thought of as having an eternal existence independently of both minds (which might apprehend them) and objects (which might instantiate them).

PLATONISM. Term used to refer, summarily, to the philosophy of Plato, but ordinarily with emphasis on Platonic realism—the view that there are Forms or Ideas, eternal and immutable, existing independently of human knowing, of which ordinary physical objects are but the imperfect copies and reminders.

PLURALISM. In metaphysics, the view that there are a number—and not just one or two—of basic kinds of stuff. In social philosophy, a principle of tolerance for a variety of life-styles, religions, and value systems.

POLEMICAL. Generated by argument or controversy. A polemical point is one that is directed against a specific opponent.

POLYTHEISM. View that there are many gods. Contrasted with *monotheism.*

POLYTYPIC CONCEPT. *See* FAMILY-RESEMBLANCE CONCEPT.

POSITIVISM. Used very broadly, vaguely, and with various qualifications, the common denominator of the various positivisms seems to be a commitment to the natural sciences as the best—if not the only—means of generating genuine knowledge.

POSSIBILITY. There are various kinds of possibilities. Of these, the most important are *nomic possibility*, or compatibility with the laws of nature, and *logical possibility*, or freedom from contradiction. There is also *technical possibility*, or what, given available technical resources, can be done.

POST HOC ERGO PROPTER HOC. Lat.: after this, therefore because of this. Fallacy in causal reasoning that confuses *happening before* with *causing*.

POTENTIAL. Capable of becoming. A potential X is anything, not now an X, that can become, and may have a tendency to become, an X. Acorns are, in this sense, potential oak trees.

PRACTICAL REASON. Part of human reasoning devoted to the discovery of optimal, or at least satisfactory, courses of action. Contrasted with *theoretical reason*, which aims to discover truths that need not have anything to do with action.

PRACTICE. Most commonly, a set of human actions organized to fulfil some purpose.

PRAGMATICS. Part of the theory of language dealing with the use of linguistic signs.

PRAGMATISM. Theory of truth holding that truth is to be understood in terms of utility. The utility of a true belief is understood to be similar to the utility of a good map.

PRAXIS. Although often used interchangeably with *practice*, this term was used by Karl Marx for the synthesis of theory and practice, and has retained some connection with this idea of *theorized practice* ever since.

PREDICATE. In philosophy, term used for either a property or a relation. A predicate, in this sense, is anything that can be predicated of—or said to be true of—something or some group of things.

PREDICTION. Statement about what will happen. Some predictions are mere guesses, totally unsupported; others are based on well-understood natural regularities—for example, astronomical predictions—and have a high probability of being correct.

PREESTABLISHED HARMONY. View of minds and bodies that holds that their mutual interaction is only apparent. Unlike occasionalism, however, which believes in a series of piecemeal adjustments of mind and body, preestablished-harmony theories picture God setting mind and body on parallel courses once and for all.

PREMISES. Those sentences of an argument that offer support, conclusive or probabalistic, for the argument's conclusion. Sometimes also called *assumptions*.

PRESUPPOSITION. Anything that has to be true in order for something else to be true.

PRIMA FACIE. Lat.: at first view. The phrase is sometimes used in this sense, but is more commonly used to indicate that something—an obligation, evidence, a right—has an assumed or presumptive force that will hold unless defeated by a superior consideration.

PRIMARY QUALITIES. Properties of things themselves, that things would have even if there were no minds.

PRIME MATTER. Matter in a state of pure potentiality; matter as it would be without form.

PRISONER'S DILEMMA. Phrase now commonly used in game theory or decision theory for cases in which two persons must choose between doing *A* or doing *B*, and in which it would be better for each if both do *A* than if both do *B*, but better for each if he or she alone does *B*.

PRIVATE LANGUAGE. Language that can be spoken only by one person, because it defines some of its terms by private ostensive definition or in some other way such that one person alone can learn them. Many philosophers have expressed doubts as to whether there can be such a language.

PRIVILEGED ACCESS. Condition of exclusivity and inerrancy relative to the states of a person's own mind. One part of the privilege consists in exclusivity (only I can know what is in my own mind); the other part consists in inerrancy (I can't be mistaken about my own mind). The existence and scope of both aspects of privileged access remain controversial.

PROBABILITY. Likelihood. There are degrees of probability ranging up to, but not including, certainty. Probability is sometimes intepreted as an objective property of events, based on their relative frequency in a series of events, and sometimes as a subjective (or personal) estimate of likelihood relative to the evidence a given person possesses.

PROCESS. Interrelated series of events. Process metaphysics holds that processes are more fundamental than substances.

PROOF. Reasoning that conclusively, or without any loophole for doubt, establishes a conclusion. Few arguments amount to proof, since arguments rest on premises that are seldom self-evident (or provable from self-evident premises).

PROPERTY. Most commonly, a synonym for *characteristic*, *trait*, or *feature*; whatever is *true of* an individual or a particular.

PROTAGOREAN RELATIVISM. View that things are as they are perceived to be by a given perceiver. Protagoras said: "Man is the measure of all things; of what is, that it is, and of what is not, that it is not."

PROTOCOL SENTENCE. In formalizations of science, used as a synonym for *observation report*.

PSYCHOPHYSICAL DUALISM. Metaphysical view that reality is composed of two fundamentally different ingredients, the mental and the physical. Also called *dualism* and *Cartesian dualism*.

Q.E.D. Abbreviation of Lat. *quod erat demonstratum*, meaning that which was to be shown or demonstrated. Used to mark the conclusion of an argument or proof.

QUA. Lat.: as. For example, Aristotle defined metaphysics as the study of being *qua* being.

QUALIA. Quality or qualities—particularly, the immediate, sensibly perceptible qualities of things, such as the redness of a cherry.

RATIONAL. Relating to reason. Aristotle defined humans as rational animals—animals with reason. Although it is in a sense obvious how we differ from nonrational animals, philosophers have not agreed on a precise characterization of rationality.

RATIONALISM. View in the theory of knowledge that the mind or intellect, rather than the senses, is the only or main source of knowledge.

REAL DEFINITION. Definition claiming to capture the nature or essence of what a given word designates. A real definition of colors, for example, would tell us what colors are, rather than what the word *color* means.

REAL DISPUTE. Dispute that is more than verbal—that is, any dispute that would survive full terminological clarification.

REALISM. In the most general and common sense, the view that there exists a world independent of mind to which our true statements correspond. In more specialized senses, one can be a realist about a particular sort of thing—for example, sets or classes, numbers, or values.

REDUCTIO AD ABSURDUM. Lat.: reduction to absurdity. Phrase used for the refutation of a position that works by showing that something absurd (or obviously impossible) follows from it.

REDUCTIONISM. Claim having the form *A*s are nothing but *B*s, that is objected to on the ground that something in the nature of the *A*s is ignored. Thus, whether or not the claim that humans are nothing but complex biophysical organisms is taken to involve reductionism will depend on whether anything true of humans is thought to be ignored in that characterization.

REFLECTIVE EQUILIBRIUM. State resulting from the mutual adjustment of competing principles or judgments.

REFUTATION. Disproof; reasoning that shows that a given view, position, or theory cannot be sustained.

REGULATIVE PRINCIPLE. Ordinarily used of statements such as "Every event has a cause" that are interpreted as norms guiding practice ("Always look for causes!") rather than as statements that are true or false.

REIFICATION. *See* HYPOSTATIZATION.

RELATION. Predicates divide into monadic (nonrelational) and polyadic (or relational). "Is fat" is a monadic predicate; "Is taller than" is a dyadic (or two-place) relational predicate; "Lies between" is a triadic (or three-place) relational predicate. Items related by relations are referred to as *relata*.

REPORTIVE DEFINITION. Purely descriptive definition that describes the way a word is actually used by members of a given linguistic community.

RETRIBUTIVE JUSTICE. Part of justice that relates to the distribution of punishment according to desert. Some thinkers justify punishment in purely retributive terms; others consider actual consequences of punishment, such as deterrence or rehabilitation.

RHETORIC. Art of effective speaking. Socrates, Plato, and many other ancients (though not Aristotle) regarded rhetoric as a "false" art, providing no more than the appearance of truth.

RIGHTS. Those things that are a person's due. There are legal rights, enforceable by law, and many believe that there are natural rights (or moral rights) that are both prior to and independent of particular legal systems.

SANCTION. Anything that motivates compliance, quite often in the context of laws. This explains why authority and punishment are both referred to by the word *sanction*.

SECONDARY QUALITIES. Qualities not in things themselves, but in the responses of a mind or subjectivity to things; also called *subjective qualities*. Some philosophers—famously, John Locke— regard colors as secondary qualities. Contrasted with *primary qualities*.

SELF-CONTRADICTION. Complex statement or set of statements that cannot as a whole be true because part of its being true entails the falsity of another part—for example, "It is raining and it is not raining."

SELF-EVIDENT. Obvious; not in need of proof. Philosophers disagree about which truths, if any, are self-evident.

SELF-INTEREST. Interest a person takes in his or her own welfare or well-being. Self-interest need not be selfish.

SELFISHNESS. Ordinarily used for that concern for oneself and one's own advantage or benefit that is judged as excessive or morally unacceptable.

SELF-REFERENTIAL. Term describing a statement such as "All generalizations are false." It gives rise to a *paradox of self-reference*, since if it is true, it is false.

SEMANTIC ASCENT. Going from one level to a meta-level. Taking "It is raining" to be on one level (direct talk about the world), we ascend semantically (to the level of talk about talk) when we say, "The sentence 'It is raining' is true."

SEMANTICS. Study of the relations between language and the world.

SEMIOTICS. Science of signs.

SENSE DATA. Term used to indicate what is given us immediately by our senses; what we are immediately aware of in sensing.

SENSIBLE. Term used to mean either concerning the senses and the data they provide, or reasonable.

SET. More mathematical term for *class* or *collection*.

SIGNIFICATION. Loosely, synonym for meaning, or even importance. More narrowly, the relation between a sign—natural or conventional, verbal or nonverbal—and what the sign signifies or points to.

SIMPLE LOCATION. Term used by A. N. Whitehead for what he regarded as the erroneous belief that reality is composed of isolated objects that can be assigned a single, delimited spatiotemporal location.

SIMPLICITER. Lat.: simply; period; *tout court*; without qualification or addition.

SIMPLICITY. Valuable property (in most views) of explanations and theories. Of two theories, other things being equal, the less complicated (or the one mentioning the fewest entities or kinds of entities) is considered better.

SKEPTICISM. Denial that humans possess knowledge. Global skepticism holds that humans know nothing. Various local skepticisms deny knowledge of particular subject matters, for example, morality or the supernatural.

SOCIAL CONTRACT THEORY. View that humans leave the state of nature by tacitly agreeing to a contract that sets up civil society with its laws, duties, and obligations. Generally regarded not as the description of an historical event, but rather as a hypothetical justification of the state.

SOCRATIC METHOD. Method of persistent questioning associated with Socrates, whereby one attempts to clarify the ground, meaning, and implications of an initial position.

SOLIPSISM. View, sometimes seriously maintained, that the person proposing the view is the only thing that exists. Ordinarily combined with the view that everything else is just bits and pieces of the one and only person's experience.

SOPHISM. False, misleading, or tricky argumentation. Also called *sophistry*.

SORTAL. Basic classifying term that answers the question, "What is it?" Terms such as *dog*, *chair*, and *telephone* are sortals, while *red*, *fat*, and *lazy* are not.

SOUNDNESS. Quality of a valid deductive argument that, additionally, has all true premises.

SPECIES. Subclass relative to a larger class or genus. Collies are a species of dogs, while dogs are a species of mammals and mammals are a species of animals.

SPEECH ACT. Term used to indicate what an utterance does, such as make a statement, ask a question, or issue a command.

STATE OF NATURE. Condition of humans outside organized or civil society wherein life (as the state of nature is usually pictured) is nasty, brutish, and short. Alternatively, a war of all against all.

STOICISM. View that the universe is a rational whole in which all things happen for the best, from which is derived the precept that the wise person is one who has learned to accept "stoically," or with good grace, whatever happens—even things that strike the unwise as negative.

STRAW-MAN ARGUMENT. Argument that attempts to generate support for one position by attacking another "position" that no one holds.

STRUCTURALISM. View that the meaning of a part (sign, symbol, linguistic item) is a function of its differential role within a larger structure or system. Thus, *chair* gets its distinctive meaning from its contrastive place in our whole inventory of furniture.

SUBCONTRARIES. Pair of statements that can both be true but cannot both be false. For example, "Some Swedes are Protestants" and "Some Swedes are not Protestants."

SUBSET. Part of a set or class.

SUBSISTENT. Having being or existence. Term sometimes used in contrast with *existent*, to cover whatever (if anything) has being outside of space and time.

SUB SPECIE AETERNITATIS. Lat.: as eternal. Some philosophers—most famously, Spinoza—held that the goal of metaphysics was to see or encompass everything at once *sub specie aeternitatis*.

SUBSTANCE. Most commonly, an individual thing that bears properties and is subject to change. Sometimes defined as that which is capable of independent existence.

SUBSTITUTIVITY. Property of being substitutable for. Ordinarily taken to mean *substitutable for salve vertitate* (with no change in truth-value).

SUBSTRATUM. Literally, that which lies below. Often used to refer to the bearer of properties or the subject of change.

SUFFICIENT CONDITION. Condition that, if satisfied by an item, guarantees that item's being a member of a class or falling under a concept.

SUFFICIENT REASON. A sufficient reason for X is anything that by itself would cause or explain the existence of X. The principle of sufficient reason associated with Leibniz holds that, for everything, there is a reason explaining why it is as it is and not otherwise.

SUMMUM BONUM. Lat.: greatest good. Theories of value have disagreed over what is the greatest good.

SUPERVENIENCE. Condition of being supervenient. A property is supervenient if it depends on other properties and cannot vary unless they do. Color properties are supervenient, for example, because they depend on more basic physical properties.

SUPPOSITION. Assumption—usually for the sake of argument, discussion, or further investigation.

SUSPENSION OF JUDGMENT. State of neither believing a certain proposition nor disbelieving it (that is, believing its negation). The appropriate attitude where there is no reason or evidence favoring belief in the proposition over its negation or its negation over it.

SYLLOGISM. Traditional argument pattern composed of a major premise, minor premise, and conclusion. For example, all dogs are mammals; all mammals are warm-blooded; therefore, all dogs are warm-blooded.

SYMMETRICAL. Word describing a relation such that, given that it holds between a first item and a second item, it must hold between the second item and the first. The *equality relation* is the most important symmetrical relation.

SYNTACTICS. Part of the theory of language dealing with the relations of linguistic signs to each other.

SYNTHETIC A PRIORI. Phrase describing those truths (if any) about the real world that can nevertheless be known by reason independently of experience.

SYNTHETIC STATEMENT. Statement not necessarily true or necessarily false by virtue of its meaning. Although "Every effect is caused" is analytic (nonsynthetic), "Every event is caused" is synthetic (nonanalytic).

SYSTEM. Interconnected set of claims or statements.

TABULA RASA. Lat.: blank slate. Metaphor used by such empiricists as John Locke to characterize the mind at birth, before it is written on by experience.

TAUTOLOGY. Statement necessarily true by virtue of its logical form—for example, "It is raining or it is not raining." Tautologies are generally regarded as devoid of information.

TELEOLOGICAL EXPLANATION. Explanation that explains in terms of goal-directed functioning.

TELOS. End; goal; purpose.

TEMPORALITY. Property of existing in time. Process metaphysics emphasizes temporality.

TERM. Word or phrase.

TESTABILITY. Capable of being tested. Some philosophers of science regard testability as a necessary feature of any genuine empirical statement or theory.

THEOREM. In a formal system—for example, a formalization of Euclidean geometry—a statement that can be derived from the axioms of the system.

THEORY-LADENNESS. Property of terms, observations, and reports of observations of being unintelligible outside the framework of a particular theory.

TOKEN/TYPE DISTINCTION. Distinction between particular physical occurrences (whether spoken or written) of words, called *tokens,* and the different words that are physically instanced, called *types.* There are more word tokens in this sentence than word types, because some word types are used—or *tokened*—more than once.

TOPIC NEUTRALITY. Property of being applicable to all subject matters or topics. The laws of logic are topic neutral, since they apply to whatever is being thought about or discussed.

TRANSCENDENTAL. Lying outside or beyond ordinary experience or knowledge.

TRANSITIVE. Word describing a relation such that, given that it holds between a first item and a second item, and also between that second item and a third item, it must hold between the first item and the third item. The *equality relation* is the most important transitive relation.

TRIVIAL TRUTH. Phrase ordinarily applied dismissively to truths-by-defintion or to platitudes.

TRUTH-CONDITIONAL SEMANTICS. Semantics, or meaning theory, that holds that the meaning of a statement can be exhaustively and nontrivially explained via its truth conditions.

TRUTH-VALUE. In standard logic, either of the truth-values, true and false. There are also three-valued logics using true, false, and undetermined.

UNDERDETERMINATION. Condition in which facts or data do not determine a single and unique outcome. Most commonly applied to the relation between evidence and theory, and between linguistic data and translation.

UNIFORMITY OF NATURE. View, sometimes regarded as crucial for science, that the physical world obeys the same laws in all places and at all times.

UNIVERSALIA ANTE RES. Lat.: universals prior to things. Term used to describe the ontological status accorded universals by Platonic realism, or the position that universals exist independent of mind and of instantiation.

UNIVERSALIA IN REBUS. Lat.: universals in things. Term used to describe the ontological status accorded universals by thinkers such as Aristotle, who hold that universals exist independent of mind but not of the particulars they characterize.

UNIVERSALIA POST RES. Lat.: universals after things. Term used to describe the ontological status accorded universals by nominalism, or the position that universals exist only as general terms.

UNIVERSALIZABILITY. Quality of a rule or principle that applies to all persons. Being universalizable, in this sense, is often regarded as a necessary condition for being a genuine moral rule or principle.

UNIVERSALS. Abstract ideas, such as *redness*, *triangularity*, and *justice*. The ontological status of universals is controversial.

UNIVOCAL. Having one meaning. A term is said to be univocal if it means the same in all its uses.

USE. Where a word is not itself under discussion and makes its normal contribution to sentence meaning, it is said to be *used*. Contrasted with *mention*, where a word is itself being spoken of.

UTILITARIANISM. Theory that holds that the moral permissibility, impermissibility, or obligatoriness of actions depends on their consequences evaluated in terms of the pleasure/happiness or pain/unhappiness that the actions produce. There are two forms of utilitarianism: *act*, which considers consequences act by act; and *rule*, which considers the general consequences of adopting and adhering to certain rules.

UTILITY CALCULUS. In consequentialist decision-making, the attempt to predict and measure, comparatively, the costs and benefits of a given line of action. Also described as the calculus of expected utilities and disutilities.

UTOPIA. Literally, nowhere. Term used to refer to an imaginary ideal world. *Utopian* is ordinarily used to mean unrealistic.

VAGUENESS. A term has the property of vagueness (or is vague) IFF, besides clear-cut cases of its applicability and clear-cut cases of its inapplicability, there are borderline or "hard-to-say" cases. *Bald*, *old*, and *rich* are examples of vague terms.

VALIDITY. Most strictly, deductive success. Less strictly, good nondeductive arguments and even true statements may be described as valid.

VALUE. Positive quality of anything whereby it is desirable, useful, interesting, good, important—only a few of the terms available for the expression of positive values. Whether values are part of the intrinsic nature of things or simply a matter of how humans respond to things is controversial.

VALUE THEORY. Systematic inquiry into the origins, nature, or interconnections of values of any sort. Also known as *axiology*.

VERBAL DISPUTE. Philosophical dispute or disagreement that can be settled by careful and explicit definition of terms. Contrasted with *real dispute*.

VERIDICAL. Literally, true. An experience is veridical IFF it is of what it appears to be of. *Antonym*: nonveridical.

VERIFIABILITY. Property of being open to verification. Logical positivists hold that all nonanalytic statements not open to verification are cognitively meaningless.

VERIFICATION. Set of procedures, relative to a particular statement, used to determine its truth-value.

VIRTUAL. Word most often used (or misused) as a synonym for *almost*. Strictly speaking, a virtual *X* is something that has the power of *X* without being *X*.

VIRTUE. Positive characteristic, or excellence, of a thing or person. A virtue is sometimes more narrowly defined as a good habit.

VITALISM. View that there is a fundamental (or metaphysical) difference between living and nonliving things. Vitalists once held that organic chemicals cannot be synthesized outside a living organism. Of course, they have been proved wrong.

VOLUNTARISM. View that emphasizes the importance of volition or willing. For example, a voluntarist would hold that acts contrary to the will of God are wrong; a nonvoluntarist would hold that acts that are wrong (that is, independent of God's will) are contrary to God's will.

WARRANTED ASSERTIBILITY. A statement is *warrantedly assertible* IFF we have reasons for thinking it true that are good enough to exempt our asserting it from reasonable criticism.

WELTANSCHAUUNG. Ger.: world-view. An overall way of understanding reality, sometimes explicitly formulated, sometimes implicit.

WILL TO BELIEVE. Phrase coined by William James to emphasize the element of decision or commitment in adopting a belief.

WISDOM. In its original sense, the goal of philosophy. A theoretically wise person has the correct view about the nature of things; a practically wise person knows how to live.

ZEITGEIST. Ger.: spirit of the time.

ZENO'S PARADOXES. Zeno of Elea (*c.* 490 B.C.) tried to show that motion is impossible by inventing several paradoxes. Typical is the *stadium paradox*, which claims that no one can cross a stadium because one has to cross the first half, then half of the remaining half, half of *that* half, and so on, *ad infinitum* (to infinity).

Index

299